Uncommon Ground

Also by Patrick Galbraith

In Search of One Last Song

Uncommon Ground

Rethinking our relationship with the
countryside

PATRICK GALBRAITH

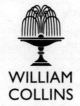

**WILLIAM
COLLINS**

William Collins
An imprint of HarperCollins*Publishers*
1 London Bridge Street
London SE1 9GF

WilliamCollinsBooks.com

HarperCollins*Publishers*
Macken House
39/40 Mayor Street Upper
Dublin 1
D01 C9W8, Ireland

First published in Great Britain in 2025 by William Collins

1

Set in Adobe Garamond Pro by Jouve (UK), Milton Keynes

Printed and bound in the UK using 100% renewable electricity at
Great Britain by CPI Group (UK) Ltd

This book contains FSC™ certified paper and other controlled
sources to ensure responsible forest management.

For more information visit: www.harpercollins.co.uk/green

For EMB, CMB Sr.,
and particularly for John Smelt

CONTENTS

Contents

Introduction

Hard-earned Ground

I can't remember how I first met Paul and Dave Upton but it must be over a decade since they first took me out at dawn, onto the mud, to where the Ouse meets the Trent and the Humber. As boys, in the 1950s, the two brothers wanted to join the cod fleet but their mother wouldn't allow it, on account of all the Hull trawlermen who had drowned at sea.

When Paul and Dave left school they got jobs in the shipyard and like lots of working men on the east coast, they spent all the spare time they had, out on the mud, in the halflight, shooting geese for the pot.

One February morning, a couple of years back, just before dawn, Paul and I were hunkered down on the mud beneath a rowan tree. Somewhere out in the estuary, a redshank cried, ducks whistled high in the blackness, and to the west you could hear the low rumble of the Humber Bridge.

As we sat there, sharing a flask of tea, Paul told me that the mud we were sitting on is contested ground. Down the decades, men like Paul and Dave have fought to preserve what they see as their right to go wildfowling. There are people in the Humber Wildfowlers Club, Paul said, who don't have much else. Membership isn't expensive and for them, 'the pinks' returning in autumn, after spending the summer on their breeding grounds in Svalbard, is an almost spiritual thing.

When the Wildfowlers' Association of Great Britain and Ireland was founded, by a railway worker called Stanley Duncan, in a since washed-away hut in 1908, his concerns were drainage and the rich. Duncan recognised that areas like the Humber Estuary were being claimed for agriculture, which resulted in less habitat for birds, and he was also troubled by the prospect of wealthy sporting tourists buying up and renting land that had long been shot over by local people. Paul and Dave's latest worry, over a century on, is that the marsh will have to be sacrificed when the river rises. After all, mitigating flooding in Hull must take precedence over the preservation of the dark mud and reedbeds.

After retracing our steps through the reeds, we drove to a bakery to buy breakfast, then we sat at a bus stop outside an old Methodist chapel to eat our pies. As we ate, Paul told me that if I had time, he'd show me Stanley Duncan's grave. When the old wildfowler died there hadn't been money for a headstone but years later the Uptons worked out, using parish records, where it was he was buried, and local wildfowlers had a whip-round on account of what Stanley had done for them.

There was a cold northerly blowing through the firs and we stood for a while, next to the grave, with the traffic on the road behind us, running into Hull, backing up at a set of temporary lights. At the top of the headstone there was a carved goose and the words 'Not for one but for all' had been inscribed beneath it. That was, Paul explained, the way Stanley saw the land.

Every year, in autumn, when the geese return from the north, Paul and his brother collect feathers from the mud and leave them at the grave. 'I'm not religious', Paul said with a shrug, 'but sometimes I'll scatter a bit of gunpowder too.'

Paul might not be a man of any sort of traditional faith but it's clear that he has a profound, almost pagan, connection with the land. The marsh for him is a sacred place and the goose is his totem. That morning on the Humber confirmed to me that for some people, to lose access isn't a trivial thing, it's truly existential. It was also a reminder of how extensive and varied the battle for access is in Britain.

Currently, the fight for land access makes the news regularly but it is almost always about camping on Dartmoor or some MP calling, usually without having much of an understanding of the subject, for a new Right to Roam Act. Often, the most interesting access battles going on are completely overlooked.

All the same, there is a narrative that access to the countryside in England and Wales is as bad as it's ever been and it's often said that landowners and politicians are intentionally trying to exclude us. Once upon a time, the story goes, we were all free men who farmed the fields together and lived sustainably. Whereas currently, it's claimed most weeks, we are only able to access 8 per cent of the countryside. This is simply untrue.

In England and Wales, we have 225,000 kilometres of right of way, which can't be shut, built on, or ploughed up by any of us, no matter how mighty. The American novelist, Nathaniel Hawthorne, in his *Series of English Sketches*, was amazed by the status of footpaths. American farmers, he wrote, would have just sown them with corn but in England 'these little footsteps of the centuries are protected, "by the full and mighty power of the law"'. Our network of permanent rights of way is so extensive that if you joined them all up and walked from one end to the other, it would be the equivalent of walking round the globe six times.

It's often said, or shouted (frequently through a megaphone), that the land was stolen from the people but just the scantiest bit of research makes it clear that for as long as land has been a source of sustenance, wealth, identity and status, we have fought over it and have sought to exclude others from it. 'The commons', for instance, weren't an egalitarian free-for-all. People were quite literally beaten for grazing animals on common land without having the right to be there.

The more I explored the question of access and listened to the dominant discourse around it, four things emerged very clearly. First, that for many people, like Paul and Dave, it matters immensely. Second, that access in England and Wales is far greater than some would have you believe. The third point is that access can have profoundly negative consequences for nature, and lastly that in spite of the access we have, many of us remain chronically disconnected from the land. Perhaps counterintuitively, that disconnect is not because of a lack of access but often in spite of it.

To create a complete and meaningful picture of access in Britain you need to speak to people who are often forgotten. The most involved, yet least listened to. Over the course of three years, I met with men who live in the woods, gamekeepers, poachers, historians, Britain's most-hated landowners, poets, county lines drug runners, senior Defra officials, and grassroots activists. I went to Gypsy horse fairs, slept on kitchen floors, visited South London boxing gyms, poached with Travellers, picked magic mushrooms, and went out fox hunting.

As ever, it became apparent that we spend too much time listening to those who shout the loudest. On the road, I met conservationists who are on the verge of losing the species they've devoted their lives to, from the capercaillie to the black grouse, in part because of mountain bikers and dog walkers. I met people who weep not because of a lack of access but because of what it's doing to the creatures they love. There is a nature crisis, there is a crisis in terms of ecological understanding, and there is a crisis in terms of a lack of empathy between the public and farmers, but what is much harder to identify is an access crisis.

Campers regularly trash beauty spots and threaten those who try to stop them, people have no idea that the species they're disturbing are endangered, but at the same time opportunities to actually do meaningful things on the land, like coppice, fish, forage, and even manage deer are limited. Opportunities to have the sort of connection that Paul and Dave have with the geese and the marsh, are hard to come by.

Education and opportunities to engage need to be at the heart of restoring our relationship with nature. It isn't about throwing everything open or taking bolt cutters to every padlock. There are even places where there is a very real case for limiting access severely. There should never be another dog off the lead on the beach in spring and there are some landowners who ought to do more to protect the wildlife on their land from the public. It would be an act of immense arrogance to see species become extinct in Britain, in part due to us being unable to limit our human desire to wander through every habitat.

In a country where the population is at an all-time high and where birds like the curlew and lapwing are on the brink of local extinction, we need to be intelligent about creating a countryside that works for all forms of life. In 1500, we had a population of 2.5 million. It is now almost 30 times that. Clearly, what might have worked then, might not work now.

Currently the loudest voices are drowning out nuanced conversation and limiting understanding. To get to a better place, a place where the land unites and inspires people, rather than divides us, we need to work with each other and we need to start by understanding the extent of the access we have and its many consequences. It's not that we can't have more but it's about what 'more' should look like.

1
History

The history of land access, a true and remarkable saga

Beneath the cherry blossom, at the end of the street, a man in a gas mask is standing in the rain. He has big rubber boots on, a large coat draped over his shoulders, and a pair of Y-fronts pulled high up over his sinewy belly. When I get closer, I hear two paramedics asking him why he's been hanging women's underwear in the trees but he shakes his head and looks away as though it's important business that they wouldn't understand. The girls at the coffee shop on the corner tell me that for months, the man has been doing naked yoga in the park, and now the police are on their way. Apparently, nobody seemed to mind much until he started picking tulips from the garden in the square. 'I think', says the Peruvian barista, 'that he is maybe not well. He used to be well but now I think he is not.' When I pass again, on my way back through the park, before setting off to drive north, a patrol car has turned up. 'And the maddest thing', I hear one of the young policemen telling another, 'is that the Porsche he's been living in . . . fully taxed, got its MOT, the lot.'

By the time I arrive at Hayfield, a little village in Derbyshire, for the 91st anniversary celebration of the mass trespass on

Kinder Scout, the whole thing has already been going on for some time. On the green, outside the village hall, Dave Toft, the chairman of the Hayfield Kinder Trespass Group, is standing up at the front, telling the crowd about a moment of realisation he recently had while flying back to Manchester. All he could see, he tells us, while holding his arms out as though conjuring a miracle, were green fields. It was something he'd never noticed before but doesn't that dispel the myth, he asks the crowd, doesn't that just dispel the myth that we, as a country, are running out of space? 'There are huge swathes of land', he goes on, 'from riverside sites to fields that we don't have access to.' Toft, who grew up in Salford, first made it to the top of Kinder Scout at 12 years old and he's climbed it at least once a year since. After graduating from Cambridge he became a teacher and he speaks as though he's telling us things that will forever make us see the world differently. There must be 150 people in the crowd, mostly retirees and families with little children but there are communists too, dressed up for the occasion in braces and woollen trousers. 'The land literally underpins everything, doesn't it?', Toft continues. 'It's where we live our lives. It's where we grow our food and build our houses. But most of it is not built on. We only have access to eight per cent of it but only two per cent of it is built on.' I look round at those sitting beneath the gazebos. Some are eating pizza, others are drinking beer out of plastic cups; the young communists are rolling cigarettes, and everyone is politely nodding along.

In 1932, Benny Rothman, who was the son of Jewish Romanian immigrants in Manchester, led a now-infamous march up the side of Kinder Scout. The fabled event is seen as being a defining moment in the fight for land access in England. Rothman, who was just 20 years old at the time, was the chairman of the British Workers' Sports Federation (BWSF), which was initially established by Labour Party activists, trade unionists, and The National Clarion Cycling Club before being subsumed by the Communist Party in about 1928. The trespass on Kinder Scout was inspired by a confrontation, three weeks previously, at the BWSF Easter camp when members tried to get to the top of Bleaklow, some 20 miles north of Hayfield. The trespassers were forced to turn back after a violent run-in with a group of grouse keepers. Over the next three weeks a larger trespass was planned, which would see Rothman's young Mancunians converging with other groups on Kinder Plateau. As a diversion, the BWSF announced a rally in Hayfield. The event drew in a third of the police in Derbyshire as the authorities feared there would be a noisy communist faction. With the police focused on the town, the crowd massed a few miles away at Bowden Bridge Quarry where Rothman addressed them before they set off.

At William Clough, halfway up Kinder Scout, a fight broke out with the Duke of Devonshire's grouse keepers but unlike three weeks previously, the ramblers broke through and stormed on up the hill. That afternoon when they walked back into Hayfield, six of the organisers, including Benny Rothman, were arrested and five were imprisoned. The event inspired an outpouring of support and is now seen as being the most important land access protest in the twentieth century. Two months later, when Rothman was up in court, he told the judge that 'we ramblers, after a hard week's work, in smoky towns and cities, go out rambling for relaxation and fresh air. And we find the finest rambling country is closed to us . . . our request, or demand, for access to all peaks and uncultivated moorland is nothing unreasonable.'

Ewan MacColl, the Salford-born musician and Labour activist, was a member of the Young Communist League and was there that day on Kinder Scout. MacColl was tasked with managing the publicity around the event and supposedly, just the night before they set off, he wrote the now-famous 'Manchester Rambler', which recalls a conversation with a gamekeeper:

He said 'All this land is my master's'
At that I stood shaking my head
No man has the right to own mountains
Any more than the deep ocean bed.

While MacColl was writing 'The Manchester Rambler', MI5 were opening a file on him. He was, it was said, 'a communist with very extreme views'.

Looking down at his notes, Toft introduces the panel: Owen Hayman from the Outdoor Swimmer's Society, Cath Flitcroft from the British Mountaineering Council, and James MacColl from the Ramblers Association. As they take their seats on the stage at the front, I walk to the bar. While I'm waiting, a lady in a red fleece prods the woman next to her in the ribs. 'See her', she hisses. 'See who', the woman replies. They both turn round. 'Her, see.' It takes the first lady some time to explain to her friend who it is she's pointing at. 'Her there.' We are all mostly, except for the communists, wearing slightly different variations of nylon and fleece. 'Her there in the hat. She's from the *New York Times.*' The woman she identifies is surrounded by dictaphones and notebooks and has a red-haired photographer standing at her shoulder. 'Never', the second lady says, incredulously. 'She's come all the way here to write about this?' The lady peers at the journalist hard as though she might have missed some important detail. I order a pint when I get to the front of the queue and then I walk back and sit on the wall.

James MacColl, the Head of Policy, Advocacy, and Campaigns at The Ramblers Association, is up first and he tells us, in a reassuring way, that we must see it for what it is. The Conservative Government has been saying that access matters to them but it's become clear, he thinks, that they are actually 'against access to the outdoors. They are hostile to access, and we need to do something about it.' MacColl doesn't claim to have the answers – instead he says he's looking for them. What we need, he suggests, is to work out how to make land access a priority for the next government. He receives a little cheer and Toft thanks him earnestly for his contribution before introducing Cath Flitcroft, Head of Access at the British Mountaineering Council.

Flitcroft talks about it being a ripe moment for a new vision, and a new approach to public access. She says it all as though she's said it a thousand times. She tells us that part of the problem is that the fight for access doesn't have a home within government. 'It runs across Defra, the Levelling Up department, and Health.' But bureaucracy aside, this moment of opportunity, she concludes, must not be allowed to pass. What we want, she tells the crowd, 'is the ability to move across land and water as part of a continuous journey, so you're not actually aware of who owns the land'. The crowd applauds and an old man standing with the communists whistles loudly with his finger and thumb in his mouth. Toft stands at the microphone and pushes his hands into his jeans. 'It's interesting', he says when the applause dies down, gesturing towards Kinder Scout, a couple of miles to the east, 'it's interesting that what's emerging today is that the legal way of trying to extend access is being shown to work alongside the tradition of direct action.' He says it as though he's trying to reassure himself that the whole event is *radical* and is actually honouring Benny Rothman and the movement's genesis, rather than just being lots of middle-class people in walking boots drinking craft beer.

Before we move on to the next speaker, Toft points towards the back of the crowd and says that there are a couple of new people present. 'People from a group called Right to Roam.' They wave and Toft takes a moment to pick over their name. 'You know, as in "rights"', he tells the crowd and then number two, 'to roam'. They wave and we all turn to look at them. 'Anyway', Toft says, 'they've got some very interesting literature with them.'

Owen Hayman, of The Outdoor Swimming Society, a ginger-haired man from Sheffield, who looks to be in his late thirties, is on the microphone next. Where the first two speakers didn't have much in the way of answers, Hayman tells us that the secret to winning more access, is making people realise that it's a fight that affects them. 'It's not just swimming. It's hula hooping, it's yoga. We need to bring all those people in, to make them realise they are part of a big access struggle.' Think of an Amazon factory worker, he tells us, who might want to swim at four in the morning at sunrise because it fits in with their schedule. 'But then they realise how few places they are actually allowed to swim and every one of them becomes an activist.'

Toft leads everyone in a round of applause before inviting members of the crowd to ask questions. 'Short questions.' This is not, he emphasises, an opportunity for people to give speeches of their own. As soon as Toft sits, a man in his sixties takes his place and heads off on a passionate multi-point journey about how unwelcoming Britain is. His main point, he tells us, five minutes in, is that the police are 'criminalising Gypsies' for just living their lives. 'We're destroying their culture', he says, turning to look at the crowd accusingly. The National Trust, he goes on, are building car parks on land where the Gypsies used to stop. 'We are letting them do it.' A little terrier starts barking and the man glances over at it and appears to lose his thread for a moment. 'If we're gonna do this', he concludes, 'we have to do it seriously.'*

Next up is an old communist called Bill, who says he's come with the *Morning Star* group. 'They're going to close', he begins, 'a number of visitor centres.' Bill suggests that what we need to do is quite obvious. 'Why don't we occupy the one in Bakewell?' Two ladies sitting at the front start clapping. The point, Bill continues, would be to occupy one and then to tell

---

* It is believed that Gypsies came to Europe in the sixth century and that they arrived in Britain in the early sixteenth century.

the press about who actually won the National Parks for the nation and how they were won. Bill concludes by suggesting that next year, rather than heading up Kinder, we find somewhere that we aren't allowed to go and actually have a proper trespass. 'It's important to celebrate what Benny Rothman did but let's do what he did. Find an area where the ruling class says you can't go and we say we will go.'

Rothman is seen as the grandfather of the land access movement in Britain but quite what was achieved at Kinder Scout in 1932 and who has the right to claim any associated glory is disputed. The Ramblers call it 'a landmark trespass' but Peter Frost writing in *The Morning Star* in 2021 claims that the Ramblers dress the event up as being something they were involved in when really they 'wanted nothing to do with the young communists', and actually opposed any 'militant' action at all.

Those who celebrate Kinder Scout believe that the effects were tremendous and that the trespass and the mood it created led to the creation of National Parks as well as leading to the Access to the Countryside Act being passed in 1949, but others feel this is an exaggeration. It no doubt raised the profile of the struggle but quite what led to what is fuzzy.

After Bill has finished, Toft decides it's the right moment for him to read a poem that he wrote some years ago to honour Benny Rothman. He tells us that, in part, he wrote 'Climbing Kinder for the 1932 mass trespass', because he wanted to capture the beauty of Kinder Scout and he was thinking about the impossibility of learning to love the natural world if there are huge parts of it we aren't able to access. The curlew, the poem goes, has a voice 'like a drop of Kinder water', and 'the walkers came', it goes on, 'to claim for those who followed, the right to hear that song [. . .] to pause a moment from the draining waste of hard industrial existence'. He concludes the poem by pointing once again towards Kinder Scout in the distance. 'Remember there are those who would have kept this from us and those who even now if they could, would keep us from the silver stream and open moor and windswept wood.' At access protests the spectre of landowners who dream of kicking us all out again always looms large.

I go to the bar for another beer and on the way back, heading in the direction of the men dressed in Spanish Civil War outfits, with tight shorts on and with legs that look as though they've never seen the Salamancan sun, I pass the journalist from *The New York Times Magazine*. I stop to introduce myself and she looks up from her notebook. Brooke Jarvis, born in Tennessee but now living in Seattle, is a little aloof but it becomes clear, after she rejects my suggestion that she really ought to speak to the communists and the men in the Spanish Civil War outfits, that we aren't pursuing the same story. She wants to speak to the organisers. We talk about access in America and how different it is. The concept of private property, she explains, means everything there and ownership is seen as an absolute right. It's sort of strange, I tell her, because we always think of America as a place of wilderness and being on the road, and Ken Kesey and his bus, a place where people are free. She has over the years, she tells me, been yelled at countless times.

She wants to know what sort of book I'm writing and I explain that I want to speak to everybody. I want to speak to farmers, people from the Right to Roam campaign, pilgrims, Travellers, landowners, naturists, and conservationists. I tell her I want to create a complete picture of the fight for land access, why it matters to people, and what the consequences of more land access would actually be. She scribbles in her notebook. 'I guess we keep being told', I continue, 'that we can only access a tiny percentage of the land and that we're massively restricted.' She looks up, stops writing, and asks if I don't think that's a fair representation? 'I'm not entirely sure it is', I reply.

The photographer for the piece, Muir Vidler, a Scottish guy with long red hair, appears at Brooke's shoulder and tells her there's an old man, 'who was with Benny'. I turn to see that he's standing just to the left of the bar, thin and hunched. Brooke nods and then asks me what I think private land owner-ship means in the UK. I suppose, I reply, gathering my thoughts as I go, it's about identity. 'You can kind of buy status through buying land. When people make money in England, they often buy land, or they did, anyway. It makes them feel like they're someone.'

I wander over to talk to Don Lee. Lee, when he was a young man, was a firebrand in the Peak and Northern Footpaths Society. His mantra was that you need three things when you go for a walk: 'your boots, a map, and a pair of wire cutters'. Lee wasn't at the first protest but he helped to plan the 50th anniversary of the Kinder Scout. The event wasn't universally popular. The Manchester Ramblers Federation declined to give the celebration its full support and people in Hayfield, whose relatives had been employed as gamekeepers were vocal in their opposition. The chair of the parish council objected to anybody wanting to remember such a 'violent' and 'misconceived' occasion.

Don leans towards me and tells me with great pride about the walk that Sunday. 'I was a whipper-in, they called them in those days – you know, like the beagles – and Benny was organising.' The walk, he explains, 'was against the National Trust', who had 'recently taken on the moorland round here and the first thing they wanted to do was close it'. He squints at me as though reckoning with my naivety when I ask him about the National Trust being an organisation that promotes access. 'The National Trust', he replies, 'were all just a bloody bunch of landed people.' Up at the front, the band starts playing Leon Rosselson's 'The World Turned Upside Down' and I ask Don if he thinks land access has improved. He tells me that it's a lot better than it was when he was young. This is a really inter-esting observation, in that it runs counter to the narrative that in the good old days you could wander wherever you liked until landowners started restricting access one field at a time. It is important to note that in 2002, the then-Duke of Devonshire, Andrew Cavendish, 70 years after the event, apologised and said that it gives him 'great pleasure' to welcome people onto the very land that his family's gamekeepers had fought the trespassers on.

In the village hall, they are showing Charlotte Bill's film, *Right to Roam*: *the story of the fight for land access from 1932 to 2022*. I buy a packet of crisps, slip in at the back, and try to eat them as quietly as I can. The film starts with a song about roots, trees, family trees, and stolen land, then cuts to a video of Guy Shrubsole standing on a private hill on the Sussex Downs in 2021. 'The first figure I want to give you', he tells the crowd, 'is one per cent.' One per cent of the population, he goes on, 'owns half of all England'. A little boo goes up. 'The next figure', he continues, 'is eight per cent. We have a right to roam over just eight per cent of England [. . .] That's why I decided to set up the Right to Roam campaign.' The final figure, he offers up, is 50 million, which is a rough estimate of the number of pheasants released in England. Maybe, he concludes, we make more room 'for us peasants' and 'a little bit less room for the pheasants'. A lone, overweight policeman looks on.

The twenty minutes of film that follows is a gentle compilation of footage from land access protests down the years interspersed with vox pops. Lisa from Bristol thinks that having access to less than 10 per cent of the land is 'disgusting'. There is a man called Joe who tells us he's long enjoyed the countryside but he didn't get fired up until he read Guy Shrubsole's *Who Owns England* and Nick Hayes' *Book of Trespass*, and also, Joe adds, 'the way it's linked back to colonialism and the way land has been passed down through these estates and the way no one's ever challenged them'. Joe adds with some uncertainty that what he thinks the campaign is about, presumably answering

16

a prompt that's been cut, is fighting for a Scottish-style right to roam. 'It seems to work well there.' Some say, Joe adds, playing with a piece of grass, that people don't behave well in the countryside but that, he thinks, 'is a complete myth'.

The film cuts to archive material of the trespass on Kinder Scout, including recordings, held in the Working Class Movement library in Salford, of the voices of the organisers. 'It was the beginning of Spring, April 24th', the gentle voice of Benny Rothman recalls. 'And when we got there, there was a tremendous number of ramblers there. Far more than we ever imagined.' When they were three-quarters of the way up, Benny remembers that the gamekeepers, who had been watching on, descended from higher ground shouting, 'Get back, get back.' Benny's friend Wolfie, who later went off to fight in the International Brigade in the Spanish Civil War, was hit over the head. But not being 'the sort of chap who would accept that, he just slammed the keeper and took the stick off them and they all carried on'. They'd come, Benny concludes, to make a point and they would face up to the consequences.

The film winds up with Guy Shrubsole speaking into a megaphone: 'The land is ours, so let's take it back.' The credits roll over signs reading 'Hidden dangers', 'Private woods keep out', and 'No trespassing. Violators will be shot'. A lady sitting along from me, with wild white hair, drags her chair over. 'What kind of mindset', she asks me, 'what kind of mindset, what kind of man, would put up a sign like that?'

Outside, people are heading off but the band is still playing and Brooke Jarvis is writing up notes. I walk down to the side, where the young communists are gathered next to a table of Spanish Civil War memorabilia. 'Some of it's genuine', an old guy in uniform tells me: 'the belt's genuine. Hat's genuine.' His shorts, he confirms when I ask, are not genuine. There's a student standing next to me, who has a copy of Mao's Little Red Book sticking out of his shirt pocket and we talk for a bit about public spaces in Manchester being privatised, then he tells me about an article he wrote, on Kinder Scout, in the latest edition of the *Socialist Worker*. He produces a copy and we're looking it over together when the chorus of Ewan MacColl's 'Manchester Rambler' begins. 'Sorry, comrade', he says, breaking away and starting to sing, his right hand raised in the cold spring air.

*

On a foggy Thursday in December, I pull up on the double yellows outside a tired-looking semi-detached Victorian villa behind the University of Bristol library. I lock the car, push open the rusty black gate, and ring the buzzer. There are posters stuck up in the dirty windows: 'Hands off our pensions', 'Support the UCU strike', and 'Pay down 25 per cent since 2009'. While I'm reading them, the heavy footsteps of Dr Leonard Baker sound on the stairs.

As I follow him up to his colleague's office, which he's borrowing for the day, he explains that he normally works from home near Shepton Mallet. His family have been 'dirt farmers' there for hundreds of years and it's where he writes best. He points at a chair and invites me to sit but he stays standing a moment while he looks at his phone. Reading a message on the screen, he tells me that the postman is due, at any moment, with his new cricket shoes.

Leonard spends much of his time studying enclosure. 'I suppose I look at', he says, gathering pace as he goes, 'the way that agricultural improvement was perceived, performed and punished by rural communities.' His doctorate, 'Spaces, Places, Custom and Protest in Rural Somerset and Dorset, 1780–1867', explores various ways that popular narratives about rural society don't always apply.

When he finally sits down, Leonard starts telling me, in order to explain the sort of thing he's interested in, about a West Country constable in the spring of 1811, who was woken in the night by 'rough music', and came downstairs to find that the villagers, who were protesting against enclosure, had torn up a hedge and 'were scolding it like a cuckold'. There were apparently so many of them that the constable felt threatened and he decided that the best thing to do was to supply them with beer and play the fiddle while they marched out of the village, holding the hedge above their heads. He later received a fine of five pounds.

The trespass on Kinder Scout, in the long and bloody story of the fight for land access, is one relatively recent chapter. For as long as land has been a source of wealth and status, people have fought over it and have sought to exclude others from it. Much of the current land access campaign is built on flimsy foundations. That well-worn 8 per cent figure is the most obvious sham but the idea that the land was stolen from the people is also dubious. The claim makes for a powerful rallying cry but it's a thread that leads to such obscure places that it becomes absurd. 'When was this field stolen, who did the stealing and who should we give it back to?' The sentiment, Leonard admits, is both a great motivation for protest and a fascinating line of historical enquiry, but it's a lot more complicated than most people realise. Leonard was invited to speak to the London chapter of the Right to Roam campaign when they were trespassing in Sussex. But he couldn't make it. He did think, though, he explains, that he would have had to tell them that his findings are at odds with their narrative.

It's true that for a long time, land wasn't owned in any sort of way that people in contemporary Britain would recognise. When Augustine arrived in Kent in 597 AD, to re-establish Christianity, nobody was considered to own the earth beneath our feet. The land was 'folkland' and it was held by kinship groups and was generally passed down within that group. It's worth noting that in Anglo-Saxon England at least 10 per cent of the population were slaves, with some historians suggesting the figure was as high as 30 per cent. In the early Anglo-Saxon period, slaves were often descended from the Britons, who had been conquered first by the Romans and then by the Saxons. Clearly, these people did not, in any sense, own the land they worked. The emergence of 'bookland', under King Ethelbert, was a way to endow the church. Ethelbert gave Augustine land in Canterbury by charter or 'bok', on which to build an abbey. The land also gave Augustine a means of raising taxes.

This set a precedent that was applied in the case of new and expanding monasteries, and eventually various powerful individuals were granted 'bookland' estates. In a sense, when this happened, land was privatised but it would be difficult to claim that this was the moment that the land was stolen from the people. It hadn't actually been theirs and it would clearly be a reach to suggest that this was when picnickers and wild campers got screwed, but the emergence of 'bookland' is an important moment when you're chasing this big land-theft hare that the access campaign has set running.

The idea that freemen, up until when Harold Godwinson was defeated at Hastings, could do as they liked on the land, has been popular with various radical groups. In the seventeenth century, for example, it was evoked by the Diggers in their fight against enclosure. But Leonard Baker isn't alone in his scepticism about the idea of a utopia before the oppression of the Norman yoke. Dr Tim Flight, in an essay published in 2017, in the journal *Anglo-Saxon England*, suggests – based on evidence in *The Memorials of Saint Dunstan* (Dunstan being the Archbishop of Canterbury until his death in 988 AD) – that 'hunting was a socially-inscribed pursuit, legally restricted to the ruling classes long before 1066'. That said, even if the Norman aristocracy just continued what the Anglo-Saxon *thegns* had already been enjoying, there were changes in terms of how people interacted with the landscape. Same grind, different landowner, but with caveats. Peasants were restricted from fencing off their crops as it would reduce hunting ground; they were banned from taking wood and scrub for fuel, and if you were caught poaching you would likely be hanged.

In the *Peterborough Chronicle*, under the entry for 1087, the year that King William died, there is a poem thought to have been written by a member of the king's household. The American professor of literature, Seth Lehrer, calls it 'an elegy for an age, as much as for a king'. The anonymous poet writes that King William 'established many deer preserves and he set up many laws concerning them such that whoever killed a hart or a hind should be blinded'. The king, the poet goes on, 'loved the wild deer as if he were their father'.

Over a century after King William's death, in 1217, the Charter of the Forest, sought to re-establish some of the rights that the free had lost. The charter permitted the cutting of turf and firewood for fuel, the digging of marl to spread on the fields, and the grazing of livestock.

A couple months after I went up to Hayfield, Brooke Jarvis's piece was published and I managed to find a copy of the *New York Times* at St Pancras Station.* It was charming and wide-eyed in that way that American journalists writing about English culture often are. Early on in the piece she writes that Kinder Scout 'many centuries ago' used to be 'king's land' and 'the access was free'. It's so vague as to be pretty meaningless, what does she mean by 'free' and 'king's land' has never existed as a designation. Kinder Scout was in the royal forest of High Peak and therefore between 1217 and 1600 when it was disafforested and the land was sold, free men could graze their pigs on it but there would have also been people in chains in Peak Castle for hunting boar and deer. It's not that she's totally wrong but her breezy oversimplification illustrates the complexities of

---

* Https://www.nytimes.com/2023/07/26/magazine/right-to-roam-england.html

historic land access and serves as a warning against reductive narratives.

Two years prior to the Charter of the Forest, the concept of 'common land' had been enshrined in law as part of the Magna Carta, in order to provide a living for those who had no ground of their own. At one point, nearly half of Britain was common land but today, due to enclosure, that figure has fallen to just 3 per cent.

In total, between 1604, just after King James VI was crowned, until the outbreak of the First World War in 1914, 5,200 enclosure bills were enacted. These bills changed the relationship that people had with the land but it's important too to recognise what common land wasn't. At land access protests, you often see banners reading 'Give us back our commons', and countless variations on that theme. But access was often tightly restricted and Leonard says it's a mistake to suggest the commons were some sort of 'egalitarian' space. Leonard points to a record of a farmhand in Dorset, in 1834, who after allowing his horse to graze on the common, was struck across the head twelve times by James Young who believed that the farmhand, being a mere farmhand, didn't hold 'common of pasture'. In court, Young argued that in striking the boy, as well as asking a passing 'jew' for a knife, presumably to harm the boy further, he was in the right as he needed to 'defend the commons'. Less dramatically, in Lancashire on 'common fields', farmers had 'the right to tread on part of their neighbour's strip during cultivation'. But they seemingly weren't permitted to wander freely.

There were areas that were a free-for-all, known as 'common waste', to which the 'landless poor' did have access. This was generally land that nobody else wanted. In the sixteenth century this constituted some 4 per cent of farmland and was usually of very marginal agricultural value. 'Give us back our waste' or 'we want the 4 per cent' would be a more historically accurate campaign slogan to rally behind but it doesn't, admittedly, feel all that empowering.*

It is quite possible that the existence of areas such as the 220-acre expanse of Clapham Common, in southwest London, complete with ice cream stalls, public toilets and ponds for sailing model boats, causes a degree of confusion. Such places are sometimes referenced by those spearheading the access campaign but Clapham Common, as with a number of other similar sites in London, was officially turned into parkland by an Act of Parliament in the nineteenth century. It was because it became parkland that people started to be able to use it in the way they do, not because it is common land. It is important to add that in 1925 the Law of Property Act gave the public the right of access 'for air and exercise' to all urban commons in England and Wales. People were granted the right to use commons in urban spaces as parks. They were not using them as commons in their original conception.

Up until about the mid-nineteenth century, the campaign for greater access was generally about livelihoods. Campaigns against the creation of royal forests and enclosure were not about wild camping, wild swimming, or having picnics. Folkland was not a place to walk one's Anglo-Saxon 'hund'. To suggest that modern campaigners for recreational activities are in league with pre-Norman peasantry or early medieval serfs is ridiculous. An anachronistic picnic on your local common in 1550, with an off-the-lead labradoodle sniffing around the villagers' pigs, would have probably resulted in a horsewhipping. There are places, like Dartmoor, where common land is still an important part of farm businesses. They are not owned by the commoners, the commoners pay rent to the landlord, and what you can do on

---

* For more on this, read: Gregory Clark and Anthony Clark. 'Common Rights to Land in England, 1475–1839.' *The Journal of Economic History*, vol. 61, no. 4, 2001, pp. 1009–36.

them is limited. You can't legally, for example, hold a fête without the landowner's permission. The commons were and are a place of work for a specific group of people.

One afternoon, while trying to understand the commons, I unearthed a vellum map of an estate in Lincolnshire which was given to a family who had provided support to the Crown during the Civil War. In the top right corner, a common is visible and I dug into various regional archives in an attempt to discover when it was enclosed. The trail became hard to follow but I came across a letter, dated 1805, which was sent to a London lawyer by the new landlord (who had recently inherited). The landowner was making the case for the parishioners of Spanby, in the Fens, having the same access to the manorial common as parishioners in two adjacent parishes. The value of the letter is that it shows the extent to which access to the commons was both very restricted and immensely complex. It also provides real intimacy with the psychology of an early nineteenth-century landowner, somebody who wasn't trying to restrict tenants' rights but instead was trying to gain them rights that he believed they had lost.

Leonard doesn't believe, as was suggested at the time, by some, that commoners were incapable of maintaining the land and continuing on as they had. Their lives were often very modest but not impossible, and it is important to set enclosure in its economic context. In the medieval period, landowners sought to capitalise on the booming wool trade by turning over their ground to sheep and then in the early modern period, when the wool price fell, landowners set their sights on grain. In Scotland, the provision to transport cattle into England without duties was included in the Act of Union, which created an incentive for landowners to convert small holdings into pasture and to run larger folds across the hill on what had previously been common grazing. In the southwest of Scotland this was met with fiery opposition and in the Stewartry of Kirkcudbright in 1723, men who had been evicted in order to create cattle parks 'rose in a mob and with pitchforks, gavelocks, and spades, leveled the park-dykes'. Almost a century on, during the Napoleonic Wars, from the autumn of 1806 to the spring of 1814, England was under blockade and as a result of being unable to trade with the continent, the domestic corn price rose – it made no financial sense for landowners to have commoners grazing livestock where wheat could be grown.

It is notable that the land access campaign in Britain is hugely hung up on enclosure, whereas 'farm engrossment' hardly gets a look-in. I can't recall ever hearing the word 'engrossment' at a campaign meeting but 'enclosure' is almost always mentioned. Engrossing is simply the process of landholdings being subsumed into others. It is a mistake to imagine that all landowners were rich aristocrats – in some parishes in the eighteenth century for instance you had upwards of twenty small landowners who might seek to strengthen their position. It wasn't the gentry grabbing land – it was a case of yeomen buying out other, lesser yeomen. This changed land ownership patterns and resulted in fewer people being employed on the land but it doesn't have quite the same weight as the idea of a rural pauper having their vegetable patch stolen by some lofty peer.

Leonard looks at his phone, confirms that his cricket shoes have still not arrived down in Shepton Mallet, then tells me that as land started to be seen as having more value, property laws were strengthened. In 1820 the Malicious Trespass Act was introduced, which provided the basis for convicting those caught causing 'malicious injury' to any 'building, hedge, fence, tree, wood, or underwood'. But, Leonard says, leaning back in his chair, what was and wasn't malicious was decided by the magistrate and the whole thing was pretty arbitrary. In researching his doctorate Leonard discovered the case of William Barnes, who in 1822 was imprisoned for a month for taking a drunken shortcut through an orchard and a decade later, Thomas Mitchell was handed the same sentence when he 'wilfully trespassed in the corner of a field'. Mitchell protested that it was simply his 'usual journey home'. According to Leonard, by 1853 16 per cent of all imprisonment in England was due to malicious trespass of one form or another but while ordinary rural people were enduring bleak conditions in jail for walking among apple trees, change was steadily coming. Middle-class intellectuals were starting to argue that access in industrialised England mattered. Not to collect firewood or to graze your pig but simply to escape from toil and the smog.

In 1851, at the age of 18, Octavia Hill, who went on to become a pioneering social campaigner, dedicated to securing access to open spaces for the urban masses, wrote to her friend Mary Harris. In the letter she notes how much of a positive impact an outing to Epping Forest had on some labourers she'd spent time with. But the very land she watched them playing cricket on was under threat.

Throughout the 1850s and 60s Lord Mornington, the nephew of the Duke of Wellington, and the then Lord Cowley, Lord Mornington's nephew, were seeking to enclose parts of the forest in order to build a cattle market and new housing. Their efforts were met with opposition from the sort of people Hill wrote about as well as from Hill herself and other affluent progressives like the artist William Morris. Morris, of course, created a whole aesthetic out of a world that never really was, a place of dryads and elves. Throughout history the campaign for land access hasn't been part of a single continuous movement and it's intellectually feeble to pretend otherwise. One theme that does recur, however, is the involvement of what we might call, although admittedly somewhat anachronistically, the middle classes. From, as Leonard explained, people like Robert Kett, of Kett's Rebellion in 1549, through to cobblers and shopkeepers who fought enclosure, and had their own idealised conceptions of England, through to Octavia Hill. The contemporary Right to Roam campaign, with its barristers, Morris dancing, and chunky book advances, is much more similar to the likes of Hill and William Morris, than Wolfie and Benny Rothman. Interestingly, like Morris and like the Diggers, the current campaign draws extensively on mythology, whereas Rothman was concerned with the practical pleas of the working classes.

In 1871, the situation in Epping came to a head when 30,000 Londoners gathered to listen to speeches. Those organising the event called for calm but that evening, fences put up by Lord Cowley were torn down and in the days that followed, the Gladstone government got behind the battle to keep Epping accessible. In the aftermath, just three years after Cowley was routed, the Master of the Rolls ruled that all enclosure to happen in the forest since 1853 was illegal. The preservation of Epping Forest is remembered as being an early success for the Commons Preservation Society, of which Octavia Hill was a founding member. The group, which also saved Hampstead Heath, is now known as the Open Spaces Society.

While Londoners were fighting for their right to escape the city, driven grouse shooting was taking off across Britain. Up until the 1870s, walked-up shooting took place across swathes of the British countryside but as firearms technology improved, bigger bags became possible and the number of gamekeepers employed rose dramatically. Where landowners and their guests had previously only gone out a couple of times a season to shoot relatively low numbers of grouse, big shooting parties at places like Kinder Scout became standard fare and people picking berries or wandering packhorse trails were no longer welcome.

Some months after I went to see Leonard, I spoke to Dr Rowan Jaines, a geographer at the University of Sheffield, who said to me that the problem I'd come up against is one she knows well. 'A free bucolic land, that everybody has access to and that is all bountiful, never existed.' Rowan thinks that however we look at it, there has never been a history of people without violence and struggle and there has never been a landscape that hasn't been contested as well as generative. The perpetual ebb and flow of rights is a far more useful way to understand access to the land, rather than the idea that it has been stolen from us.

*

When Emily Oldfield and I push through the front door of her flat, five flights up, above the High Street in Todmorden, Ramsey Janini, who has thick dark hair and a tea towel over his shoulder, looks round nervously. He is standing over a small cooker, holding a large pan upside down with a plate clasped beneath it and yellow rice is spilling out onto the floor. Ramsey and Emily are together, but most of the time she lives across town in a house built into a hill beside a cobbled packhorse trail.

Ramsey, whose father is Palestinian, tells me he's spent all afternoon making *maqluba*. Literally meaning 'upside down', *maqluba* is a layered dish of meat, rice, aubergines, tomatoes, and onions, with lots of turmeric, chilli and cinnamon. Cooked on a stove top before being upended onto a plate, it often marks a celebration or, Emily tells me, it's made when a guest comes. Outside it is dark and streaks of rain run across the skylight in the low ceiling.

All day, Emily has been waiting for copies of her new poetry collection to arrive. She called up the editor in Salzburg, a matter-of-fact Austrian called Wolfgang, and he told her all he knew was that they were in a warehouse somewhere outside London and they would no doubt be with her shortly.

The following morning, we're going to walk across Winter Hill in Lancashire, where 126 years previously, thousands of people marched in protest against being shut out by Colonel Ainsworth, a landowner, who wanted to maximise the grouse shooting on his moor. It is thought to be the biggest land access demonstration to ever take place in Britain but it went, as far as Emily has been able to work out, almost unmentioned in the national papers and even now, it is often overlooked. Emily knows Winter Hill well. She recently set 12 months aside to walk across it, every couple of weeks, with various local writers and artists and she recorded their conversations about what the hill means to them and how it inspires their work.

Emily thinks that for most of those who marched on Winter Hill in 1896, it was about escape. Their lives were hard and getting out onto the tops was a chance to rise above the smog. Looking back, they probably wouldn't have even been able to see Bolton below them because it would have been so thickly shrouded. To Emily, though, it's about connecting rather than escaping. 'I think the past lives on in the packhorse trails and corpse roads. I think there's a kind of depth. It goes so far beneath the surface. Walking connects me to the past.' Emily tells me that if she was no longer able to walk in the places she always has, she wouldn't think of it as a loss of some sort of right. It would be more like a severance.

Calder, Emily says, as she sits down next to me, is a collection about walking. It's about going out on foot into the edgeland between Lancashire and Yorkshire to explore 'presence and absence' and to think about what the landscape really means: the rivers and the moors, the shoe factories and the packhorse trails, to her and to everybody who has ever called Calderdale home.

Ramsey passes me a plate of *maqluba*, and apologises for not making it quite as he's been told you should, then he lies on the floor, resting on his elbow with his belly protruding over his trousers. 'Do you want a chair, love?' Emily asks but he shakes his head. As she eats, Emily tells me that the road down in the valley bottom is pretty recent. It was so marshy down there, she explains, that it would have been impassable and 'the proper thoroughfares' would have been the packhorse trails that run through the hills.

Emily has been a wanderer for as long as she can remember and her father and grandfather were wanderers before her. Her family were sheep farmers originally but when the people were cleared from the hills, they came down into the valley in search of work. Like most men in Bacup, where she grew up, a town five miles west of Todmorden, her grandfather and then her father worked in a shoe factory. As a girl, Emily walked a lot with her grandad. He was almost illiterate but he was apparently a clever man. He grew up collecting birds' eggs and he could identify almost every species they came across. At her grandad's funeral, the local bank manager, a man called Gordon, turned up and wept. Her grandad and Gordon had struck up what she thinks was a pretty unlikely friendship. They were the first people to film a kingfisher nesting on the River Irwell. Gordon had all the cameras and a car and her grandad knew every clump of reeds and every ditch.

Emily's dad spent eight years in the shoe factory before he decided he wanted more from life. He had always hated school and authority but typically, when he was older, he decided that school was exactly where he wanted to be and he took night classes, so he could eventually become a teacher. When Emily was a child, they would walk together through the fields to the primary school where she was a pupil and where he had become the headmaster, and he would tell her all about the land around them and its history. 'There was some right crazy farmers', Emily says, over the top of her wine glass, 'there was one farmer used to chase us with a gun.' All his life, Emily's dad has escaped into the hills, and since retiring from teaching, some years ago, after a breakdown, he now spends his time writing about Lancashire, about the overlooked and forgotten. But much to his annoyance, his books have led to people visiting the places he writes about. Emily's interests are what they are because of her dad and her grandad and their interests, in turn, came from the land.

Ramsey wants to have a cigarette and I follow him down the stairs. The rain has worsened and we shelter in a doorway with a sign above it that reads 'Todmorden Industrial & Co-operative Society'. It was the headquarters in the nineteenth century of a group, formed by factory workers, who protested against the high price of flour and it is now a health food shop. As he smokes, Ramsey talks about his own sense of home. His family were displaced from Palestine in the forties and the building they lived in is an Israeli-run arts centre now. It's an interesting thing, he tells me, when you ask Palestinians where home is, because they will often tell you about a place they've never been to, somewhere they were forced out of long ago.

Back in the flat, Ramsey helps me unfold their sofa bed and Emily finds me a copy of *Grit* from the shelves in the corner of the room next to an umbrella plant. It was her first collection but all the copies are gone now and it's the only one left. We say goodnight and I lie there reading. There is a poem about being in hospital, a poem about going home, a poem about bloody feet in worn-out trainers, one about the mud at the bottom of the River Irwell, and there's one about a badger. In the night the rain worsens and geese fly up and down the canal, calling in the blackness.

In the morning, we leave the flat and drive south. Heading over the top, at Cloughfoot, a pair of ravens drift high in the wind, and the last of the winter snow lies in the shadow of a low stone wall.

In Bacup, I stop for a moment to look at the art deco bingo hall, which was later a cinema, and is now closed. Emily tells me it's beautiful inside, with its grand staircases and painted plaster. She tells me too that not many people had heard of

Bacup until the murder of Sophie Lancaster and the brutal beating of her boyfriend in 2007. The couple were walking through Stubbylee Park in the early hours when a group of local teenagers attacked them. The incident became synonymous with 'broken Britain' and Lancaster, who had pink hair and a metal bar in her bottom lip, was known as the girl who was killed because she looked different. But her boyfriend, who lay in a coma for a week after the attack, said the press had got it wrong. It wasn't, he thought, because they were 'goths' or anything like that, it was that the boys who attacked them were 'forgotten people'. They had been left behind, with nothing much to do, in a town rinsed by the industrial revolution.

Acts of violence have always occurred but I don't think we can overlook the impact on young people in rural, post-industrial towns, feeling disconnected and cut off. Relationships that once gave them a sense of identity and purpose have been lost: fishing towns with empty harbours, market towns where the livestock in surrounding valleys goes elsewhere, and shut-up pubs that would once have been full of farm workers. Hollowed out places, without context and connectedness, which have lost much of their culture and identity, are unhappy places and Britain is full of them.

We turn left near Rivington Services and head up a steep single-track lane. There are passing places all the way up but 'No Parking' signs have been fixed to the trees by the local state. The residents and emergency services need access, the signs reason, 'due to the pandemic'. We drive up and down the road twice and then decide that the only thing we can do is leave our cars pulled over to the side at the top.

A couple of hundred yards up the track, there is a gate across a path and a weathered sandstone slab, with a chiselled inscription running across it, has been sunk into the grass: '*On Sunday 6th September 1896 10,000 Boltonians marched by this spot to reclaim an ancient right of way over Winter Hill. The path is now dedicated as a public right of way for the enjoyment of all.'* We stand next to it for a moment and Emily tells me that obviously her grandad wouldn't have been born at the time but when he was a young man, four or five decades later, the march was still a very big part of local lore. Even if people hadn't been there, they spoke about it as though they had. Emily recounts the details, like a child who's learned a list of capital cities – 'It set off from Halliwell Road in Horwich and then joined Coalpit Lane. The crowd swelled and swelled as the march went on and when they got to the gate, Colonel Ainsworth, the landowner and heir to a cotton-bleaching fortune, was there with the police.' Emily tells me that a fight broke out and despite Ainsworth telling the protestors he'd have writs issued against them, they threw one of the policemen over a gate, ducked Ainsworth's land agent's son in the stream by our feet, and then marched over the hill.

Emily was in her mid-teens before she found out about the trespass. Despite the numbers being far larger than the estimated 400 who marched on Kinder Scout with Rothman in 1932, the Winter Hill protest never achieved the same profile. It's difficult really to know why but Emily thinks that Kinder Scout gained more notice among the middle classes. The enduring popularity of Ewan MacColl's 'The Manchester Rambler' has no doubt had an effect too. Emily also thinks that the authorities were keen to suppress the momentum that the march on Winter Hill appeared to be gathering – the whole thing was initiated by the Social Democratic Foundation, who had placed a small advertisement in the *Bolton Evening News*, and she suspects that the socialists, under the leadership of a man called Solomon Partington, were considered to be dangerous. After the success of the 10,000-strong march in early September, another protest was scheduled for the following Sunday and a song was commissioned: 'Will yo' come o' Sunday morning,

For a walk o'er Winter Hill. Ten thousand went last Sunday, But there's room for thousands still!' There were 500 song sheets printed but in spite of trying, Emily has never managed to find one. It rained hard that Sunday and she wonders if the sheets were destroyed.

Emily, as well as writing poetry, and teaching at Manchester Met, is currently working on a book about northern food culture and packhorse trails. She isn't sure really when her interest in old roads and forgotten routes began but she thinks it was probably when she came across a road called the Long Causeway. 'It connects Burnley and Hebden Bridge and then goes on to Halifax and sometimes on old maps it's just called "Causey". It's properly ancient.' As well as walking the Long Causeway, Emily started reading up on its history and learned all about the preaching crosses on the road that signify places of spiritual gathering. She soon realised that almost all the paths she's ever known, the railways, the canals, and the roads through the valley bottoms, are relatively modern and that for thousands of years before they were constructed, packhorse trails would have been the paths that her family and people like them would have used every day. She often thinks, she tells me, about all those people whose footsteps she's walking in: the farmers, post boys, and murderers. Further up the hill there is a memorial to George Henderson, a Scottish merchant who was shot through the head in 1838.

As we walk, the temperature starts to rise and the morning becomes muggy and close. Up ahead of us, a lapwing cock rises and tumbles across the moor. In the late eighteenth century, Baptism and Methodism became popular throughout Lancashire; as a consequence, Emily says, of industrial work being so grinding. 'It was basically a death sentence and methodism preached universal salvation so even if your life was miserable and short, you'd still go to heaven.' It was, she supposes, a great source of hope. Emily thinks it's sort of sad really but she supposes it brought people peace and they would often walk for miles and miles over the hills to listen to 'open-air preachers'. In a way she thinks that the walk itself, the actual journey to hear that misery wasn't going to be eternal had a sort of spiritual quality. It wasn't just about the words. It was about the journey to get there too.

In front of us, running along a Rylock fence, large gritstone slabs, each of them a slightly different size, are sunk into the heather. Ramsey has walked all over the world but he thinks there's something unique about paths like the one beneath our feet. 'The slabs round here just have this sense of heft and resilience. They kind of meet you and they have a sense of importance.' He talks slowly and in a considered, thoughtful way, as though every word counts. Emily, who is walking behind me, tells me that when she was very ill her relationship with the landscape changed. 'I was like proper ridiculously skinny. My writing's really tactile about the land because when you're so thin everything's amplified.' When the wind blew and snow came down and she was out, she felt suddenly as though her concerns were small. 'I felt like the land could just swallow me up and it was kind of reassuring.' Publishers, Emily keeps finding, want her to dress her writing up as a sort of post-anorexia thing, a kind of journey to recovery. 'People invite me to literary events and they want me to go in a certain vein but I don't want to do that.'

For a long time, Emily didn't eat meat but walking and 'kind of talking to everybody along the way' made her change her mind. 'When you're a student you're kind of in this bubble and it affirms what you believe.' But out on the hill she started to realise that small-scale farming was an essential part of the landscape. 'It's hard to explain', she tells me as we turn right onto the road over the top, 'but I just had all these encounters with all aspects of life in an unrehearsed way. I don't like to make any assumptions. I just wander and I talk. I talk to farmers. I talk to people in the pubs. Life in these small hill-farming communities is hard.'

Ahead of us, a radio mast, held on each side by steel wires, rises up in the fog. 'It's so weird' Emily says, looking up at it. 'You see all those cables and there's that mound down there. It's a Bronze Age hill fort.' I ask Emily about her poetry and whether the things she writes about are always specific things she's seen when she's wandering, or whether they are the drawing together of lots of things. 'Like that badger in that poem in *Calder*?' She tells me that actually the badger lived very near her grandad's house and he'd always go out to feed it in the fields at night. 'I was there one night and he said let's go and look at the badger. He'd feed it out his hand. And you know that moment with a wild animal when you look into its eyes and it looks into yours and you're not quite sure what's going through its mind and you want to convey that you don't mean any harm but there's no medium of language.' We walk on and she says that not long after she went with her grandad to see the badger, he got moved into a hospice, and then at the end, he couldn't talk but Emily remembers that 'his eyes were still looking at me and there was a moment, just like the badger. It was the same.'

Where the track comes to a stop there is a small plastic plaque, to commemorate where the trespass ended. Some of the protestors just wandered back to town and others went on to the Black Dog pub in Belmont, a village at the foot of the hill. Over the months that followed the first trespass, there were further demonstrations and prominent socialists including Keir Hardie and Eleanor Marx visited the town, which was becoming a centre of dissent. Then, in mid-September, Colonel Ainsworth sent his land agent's son to deliver writs to those who were considered to be the leaders of the protest. That afternoon, the number of marchers on Winter Hill was much reduced and over the days that followed, 32 further writs were issued.

In an attempt to split the campaign, Ainsworth instructed his solicitors to ask those 32 if they were socialists. If they answered 'no' and confirmed they wouldn't trespass on Winter Hill again, the writs were withdrawn. Eventually, just the original ten faced charges and the trial began on Tuesday 9 March, 1897. The radical barrister, Richard Pankhurst, who represented the defendants, claimed that access to Winter Hill had long been part of the lives of Boltonians. There had been a stile, Pankhurst told the judge, for a long time at the start of the disputed path. Witnesses also told the court that there was a long tradition of going up onto the hill to inns like Black O Jack's and William Fletcher's Cottage, near where the radio mast now stands to buy gingerbread, which came with free beer (in order to get round licensing laws). It was also noted that the poor had gone out to live on the hill when they were unable to pay the rent on their cottages. Other witnesses spoke of a long history of people walking over the tops to get to the mills in Bolton and Horwich, and of a tradition of old ladies picking 'whimberries' in autumn, hence 'Whimberry Hill', the historic name for the eastern end of 'Winter Hill'. But Ainsworth had instructed his gamekeepers to build butts for driven grouse shooting on the side of the track and witnesses for the prosecution, witnesses who were largely his tenants, confirmed that wandering and berry picking couldn't go on. The judge found in Ainsworth's favour and costs were awarded against the defendants along with injunctions to keep people out. Over the following weeks, Ainsworth hung flags on the walls of his bleaching factories to celebrate his victory.

At the Black Dog pub, Emily and Ramsey and I sit beneath a sign advertising psychic readings the following Wednesday, and Ramsey tells me it's a funny thing because he's never known a country where you can walk quite so freely as you can in Britain. Being an Arab in America, as he was for quite some time, meant staying on the path and England, he thinks, is a country that looks as though it's just been created for walking.

The relationship that Emily has to Rossendale gives her poetry both richness and heft. It's born out of a sense of belonging and connectedness. Emily loves the land and those who shape it and are shaped by it in turn. Her work is a testament to what getting out onto the land can do for people. They might not write but being able to engage with the beauty and bleakness of a place and to understand something of its history gives people a sense of identity. The opportunity to do that is something that everybody should have, the opportunity to connect and feel part of rural culture.

People were kept off Winter Hill and that was a great injustice, but they no longer are. You can head up there anytime you like. Our challenge now is not to fight Colonel Ainsworth but it's to think hard about how we overcome a culture where people don't get into the hills to pick berries. Our challenge is to give people a little of the love that Emily has. In a sense, the idea of fighting the man is appealing because the enemy is a very obvious one – it's 'us versus the elites', the narrative runs but what if the enemy, in truth, is more insidious? The enemy is a lack of understanding, a lack of experience, and a lack of opportunities to engage. And that enemy is strengthened by spreading misinformation about the countryside being a closed shop. Why bother leaving the city at all if, as some would have us believe, we're locked out and there's nowhere to go?

*

On a rainy Friday night, a couple of months after I visited Emily in Todmorden, I caught the bus to The National Gallery in Trafalgar Square. Except for two men behind me who were having a loud conversation about whether or not 'this is still a Christian country', the queue was mostly made up of foreign tourists. In the middle of the square an enclosure was being disassembled where three weeks previously, a big party had been held to celebrate the end of Ramadan. 'Well, it might not be, in practice', one of the men said to the other, 'but it's still a Christian country officially.'

The man checking bags waved me through and I walked up the stairs to a long room where the Hogarths and Gainsboroughs hang. *Mr and Mrs Andrews*, painted in 1750 when Gainsborough was in his twenties, has been written about extensively. It is a double portrait of two sitters, in town finery, set against the backdrop of a sort of agrarian idyll. There are corn stooks, some sheep in the distance, cattle off to the left behind a white gate, and there is wooded moorland on the horizon.

The two sitters look a little odd in the painting, as though they are ill at ease and the other notable oddity is that they are the only people at all. It is an imagined idyll, the gentry's gaze: sheep without shepherds, corn stooks without field hands, and cattle without stockmen. The fruits of labour are present but not the labourers.

On the wall to the left, there were more Gainsboroughs: more landowners and more dogs. There was a portrait too of Gainsborough and his family. It was painted when Gainsborough was in London but it depicts the Suffolk countryside. There is nobody, in Gainsborough's mind's eye, collecting firewood, gathering acorns, or tending pigs. It is a lifeless dreamscape.

Much of Gainsborough's countryside was a fantasy. He generally depicts it as a garden for the rich with a very occasional labourer as a folly. But it's no more real than the countryside as conjured up by some land access campaigners holding megaphones at rallies. It wasn't just a place where the gentry sat beneath old oaks in pretty clothes and nor is it a place that the Normans took by force from you and me and that has been a no-go zone ever since.

The commons are complicated and rights throughout history

have been fuzzy but, in order to get the most of the access we actually have and if we're going to be able to have useful conversations about what more we might want, we need to try much harder. There's something bleak and duplicitous in claiming you're shining a light on uncomfortable truths about the history of land ownership and land access in Britain while merrily ignoring things that are pretty cut-and-dried.

A year or so after going to see Leonard Baker I caught up with him again. The previous summer, he'd had the opportunity, he told me, to speak at a 'knowledge exchange' in London with a group of land access activists. Alongside Professor Carl Griffin from Sussex, Leonard had spoken last and he found himself pouring a bucket of 'ice-cold water' over the audience after a day of listening to fanciful misrepresentations of enclosure.

There is an argument to say, 'so what?'. These guys are repeating a story built on half truths in the hope of bringing about the change they want to see in the countryside. But misrepresentation, in lots of cases, can be counterproductive. There is a risk of bringing people on board who then desert your cause when they realise it's about memory and feeling rather than fact.

There are people demanding what we've already got. As Don Lee suggested at Hayfield, things have got a lot better than they were a century ago. The Countryside and Rights of Way Act provided open access to 4 million acres. This where the great myth of that 8 per cent figure comes from. The Act granted people access to 8 per cent of the countryside but clearly that isn't the whole extent of access. That figure doesn't, for instance, include beaches and it doesn't include any woodland or permissive access. We are, many of us, chronically disconnected from nature, which is an immense and destructive problem but it didn't all start with the land being taken from us, once upon a time, many centuries ago.

2

The Current Movement

Protest and papier-mâché

Except for the night buses and a man standing next to his car, down on the Embankment, after apparently crashing into a set of traffic lights, central London at 4 a.m. on a Saturday morning in mid-January is almost empty. In Fulham, Christmas trees line the pavement, somebody in Hammersmith still has a neon flashing Rudolph stuck to their railings, and the guy at the petrol station won't let me in to get coffee. 'No coffee, boss. Security risk at night time.' On the M25, I listen to the World Service, on the M4 I finish a podcast about a Dutch librarian who drilled a hole in his head in the hope it would make him high forever, and by the time I get to Stonehenge, on the A303, the sun has come up.

The previous Friday, Sir Julian Flaux, Chancellor of the High Court, ruled there was no right to camp on Dartmoor and with nothing much else going on across the country, journalists had been covering the story all week. Dartmoor had previously been the only area in England where, due to local byelaws, it was understood that people could pitch a tent wherever they liked without the landowner's permission. Lawyers acting for Alexander Darwall, the hedge fund manager and Dartmoor landowner who had brought the case, successfully argued that the Dartmoor Commons Act of 1985 enshrined a custom of 'open access' on the moor which included walking or riding a horse but not 'wild camping'.

Flaux accepted the argument. There was, as he understood it, 'no local custom of camping which has the force of the law'. He also accepted Darwall's claims that wild campers harm wildlife and cause problems for farmers. Flaux concluded that if people did have the right to camp, it would technically mean the landowner would suffer 'a loss of control or a usurpation of their own rights over their land'.

Inevitably, the whole thing was seen as being about much more than tents and cooking beans on a Trangia Stove. What people were kicking back against was the idea that a man – with a seemingly extraordinary understanding of Asian equity markets – can buy a slice of England and keep the stars to himself. The Right to Roam campaign announced that they would 'be going to war'.

In the days that followed Flaux's ruling, a hazy agreement had been struck between Dartmoor's landowners and the Dartmoor National Park Authority which permitted wild camping in designated areas. Some saw the agreement as positive but it wasn't universally well received. Those leading the Right to Roam campaign claimed that it was 'a ransom note'. They wanted, they made it clear, to camp where they liked whenever they liked, and they believed that the proposed system would have given people like Darwall the ability to remove the right to camp further down the line, potentially by injunction. Campaigners also objected to the idea that they might have to pay. It wasn't totally clear how the system would actually function and whether individuals would be charged or whether the National Park Authority would pay through its publicly-funded budget but the anger was galvanising and an army, some of them in boots and donkey jackets but most of them sunny-faced, middle-aged people in lycra, descended on Dartmoor.

Up at the front, a young woman in a hi-vis vest and a purple hat with a banner that reads 'The stars are for everyone' is addressing the crowd. Two men on my right, both of them pushing forty, one of them in a big grey beret, are talking noisily about revolution and I can only hear bits of what the woman is saying. 'We never have revolution here', one of them says to the other. 'That's the trouble, man. Think of the French, the Spanish, the Russians. We like being oppressed.' They stop for a moment and then continue. 'That's just it, brother, we like queuing.' There are banners that read 'Whose land? Our land' and 'Once we were all wild campers', and somebody has seemingly printed off a run of posters with Alexander Darwall's face on them.

The woman up at the front raises her arms. 'And we want to camp', she shouts, 'without the express permission of the landowner.' A cowbell sounds and we all spill out through the car park, past Walter Parson's Funeral Directors, burying Devonians for 180 years.

Over the next couple of hours I meet locals in their twenties who tell me about camping on Dartmoor when they were little at Halloween; I meet a wild swimmer who reckons that the thing about Darwall is that he's 'very *nouveau*. He's behaving, I suppose, like he thinks landowners ought to.' And I walk for a while with a young guy called Dan who has long hair and a wooden staff. Dan is hoping to lead the 'direct action' wing of the campaign. The situation, as he sees it, is that landowners only really needed workers during the industrial revolution but now that 'automation has come they don't need to keep people like us on side'. The most creative placard I see all day has a picture of Darwall on it as Shrek: nobody, it has been scribbled beneath, is welcome in his swamp. It's extraordinary how many people have a story about him. I hear an account of Darwall chasing a lady off the hill at dusk on his quad bike. His interest in the land, one man tells me, is actually to do with the money that can be made from pheasant shooting. Then again, according to another man, who has 'been doing some digging online', Darwall actually bought the land because of mineral rights – 'That's the way these people think.' But a middle-aged lady in an anorak explains to me he didn't actually buy it at all, he inherited Blatchford from his father. Journalists find him almost impossible to track down, but Alexander Darwall is everywhere and he's whoever you want him to be, not so much a man as an idea.

In Cornwood, at midday, the crowd masses together, and I sit on the wall outside the pub next to a girl playing 'The Diggers' Song' on the ukulele. All down the road, cars are beeping their horns, and one of the leaders of the protest, standing on the steps of the village cross, calls for quiet. 'And if I could ask. If everyone could put your hand on someone's shoulder just to feel our deep connection to each other.' Some of the crowd move towards each other, and just as many move further apart. A man standing beside me, who has a Devon flag draped over his shoulders, places his hand on my arm and closes his eyes. Behind us a horn starts beeping and there is a small commotion. I look round to see a farmer in a pickup towing a trailer. He has a cigarette in his mouth and he's staring down at the road. 'Don't you take my picture', the woman sitting next to him says to a man with a camera round his neck. 'Why would I want to do that?', the man replies. 'You shouldn't be here anyhow', the woman continues sourly. Through the trailer slats, I can see a tup. It holds its legs stiffly at each corner to stop itself falling when the truck eventually pulls away.

A cheer goes up as Guy Shrubsole is handed the megaphone.

'Can everybody hear me?' – cowbells ring and people applaud. 'I'm going to say a little bit about the story of Old Crockern and then I'm going to give you some next steps.' There is something ageless about Guy. He could be 28 or he could be 45. 'Because of what the landowners have done, we're here', Guy says into the megaphone. 'We're here to summon up the spirit of Old Crockern and to defend Dartmoor and its wild camping rights.'

Guy tells us about a wealthy Mancunian industrialist – adding 'or a London hedge fund manager', which, after a moment of awkward hesitance, receives some booing – who came down to Dartmoor long ago. 'The industrialist thought it a shame that so much land was going to waste and sought to improve it.' Behind us the cars start beeping again and Guy raises his voice to keep the crowd with him. 'One day, a poor man, an old farmer, met this newfangled landowner.' With a look of merriment, Guy then drops into a broad Devon voice. The farmer, he goes on, told the rich incomer he'd had a dream in which Old Crockern had vowed that if the landowner so much as 'scratched his back, he'd tear out his pocket'. The dream transpired to be a prophecy and the industrialist returned north, some years later, a ruined man.

Guy pauses and among the crowd people start drumming. 'Today', he continues, over the noise, 'we will summon this gurt spirit of Dartmoor. We've all seen what Dartmoor's large landowners have forced upon us this week, taking away our right to camp on the moor and replacing it with a system of permissive access.' A man beside me wipes tomato soup from his moustache, shouts 'disgusting' at the sky, then carefully puts the lid back on his Thermos. 'This is a ransom note', Guy continues, 'whereby the public will end up paying landowners for access. We cannot and will not accept this erosion of public rights.' He finishes up by calling for us all to write to our local MP, to urge them to commit to a new Right to Roam Act, then he raises his hand above his head. 'Let's go and summon the spirit of Dartmoor.'

Twenty minutes on, I get to the back entrance to Blatchford Manor, where two men are shouting at a group of security guards. 'He pays you well does he?' . . . 'Hope Darwall treats you well.'

While those men were putting things right at the end of Alexander Darwall's drive, Snowy Parker, a 76-year-old game-keeper, was on guard in a pheasant pen in the valley below. 'Frightened the shit out of me', he admits, when I visit him five months later. In the 43 years he's been involved in the shoot at Blatchford, Snowy has never seen anything like it but 'the funny thing was', he continues, while cutting up a rack of venison ribs laid out on a red plastic block in front of him, it seemed like 'there wasn't a bad person among them'. At the end of the day he drove up there in his mule* and they had all, apparently, been absolutely fine.

In spite of his age, Snowy is boyish. His shoulders, beneath his green V-neck jumper are wide and sloping, his hair is thick and white, and when he speaks, he turns to face me square on. What 'them lot' don't understand, he tells me as he walks over to the chiller to put the ribs in a box for his dogs to eat later on, is that he'd have no interest in banning them from the moor 'and nor would Darwall'. For the most part, Snowy thinks those who came to Cornwood that day love the moor for the same reasons he does, because of the beauty of the ancient woodland and the rivers and the wide open hill. It's 'the scrotes' that worry him. With 'them lot', he thinks you only have to take your eye off the ball and next thing you know you're up there, the following morning, tidying up with a tractor bucket.

On the wall, above an old tub of air-rifle pellets, there is a

---

* A small ATV.

laminated poster about Dartmoor's endangered lapwings. Snowy explains that they started putting them up because people were destroying traps intended to catch crows that were eating lapwing eggs. 'Only place on Dartmoor where lapwings survive is Hanger Down', he says proudly. 'Because it's keepered hard. Anywhere else, there's fuck all.' Too much shooting has seemingly ruined Snowy's hearing and he stands there shouting about the lapwings as though I'm two fields away on a windy February morning. Then every couple of sentences he pauses, and says in a quieter voice, as though he is speaking to himself rather than to me, 'Just a minute now, we'll go inside and I'll make you a cup of tea.'

As he wipes his hands down and puts his knives away, he tells me, fondly, that he was only a boy when he started working on a shoot in Nuneaton in the 1950s. The gamekeeper, Reg Vernon, was apparently 105 years old when he died and according to Snowy he was still very much in charge right up until the end. As we walk from the larder to Snowy's cottage, across the yard, the dogs run happy circles in their kennels. 'He used to hit me with a galvanised bucket, did Reg, if I didn't do what I was told and I was only trying to help him.'

Snowy's wife, when we let ourselves in, is sitting in a pink cardigan at the head of the table, looking at a puzzle book with an elephant on the back. She looks up at me, smiling, and nods then turns to Snowy. 'Who is he?' She says it twice but Snowy doesn't answer and she turns back to her puzzle book for a bit before looking up again to tell Snowy to stop shouting. He seems not to hear her and he continues on about the slag heaps back in Nuneaton and all the poppies that grew there, and the English partridges that hung on 'for years and years' but that he thinks are probably gone now.

While the kettle boils, Snowy tells me that in spite of the protestors seeming like good people, he thinks that the whole camping situation has raised the profile of the shoot in a way that means he can't go on. Just a couple of days prior to my visit, he found a load of people in one of his pens. In the end, the police turned up and 'hoicked' them out. It wasn't, he admits, that clear what they were going to do but he suspects they were planning to smash up the pen. Mrs Parker, this time without looking up from her puzzle book, reminds Snowy to get on with making the tea and asks him again, who this boy is. I explain that I'm writing a book on land access and I tell her I want to know about the farmers and gamekeepers and conservationists who get caught up in the middle of it. 'Oh, Alexander who owns Blatchford', she replies, saying his name in a maternal way before she nods thoughtfully and goes back to her puzzle.

Snowy pours me my tea then perches on the sideboard to drink his. As he sips, he explains that just next to his cottage there's a big house owned by a man who has 10,000 acres. He has, however, unlike Alexander Darwall, seemingly just kept his head down, but the difference Snowy thinks is that his part of the moor is pretty bleak and nobody seems to want to camp there. It's not as though he's got a bit of ancient old woodland like Piles Copse. 'Beautiful is Piles Copse', Snowy continues, blowing on his tea in irritation as though it being too hot is holding him up in some way. 'In a fold by the river, is Piles Copse, just beautiful.'

The thing with the whole wild camping situation, according to Snowy, is that it's all got a bit blown out of proportion. As much as anything he thinks Alexander Darwall was just fed up with the National Parks Authority being 'cunts to him' and telling him what to do. As Snowy sees it, Darwall's done a lot for the area. He's quite literally spent tens of millions and done up buildings that were in a dire state of repair. Do I, he asks, know that Darwall had actually said people could camp in the end but they were worried that it would be on his terms?

In the end, being 76, Snowy reckoned that it just wasn't

going to get any better. 'I said to myself, Snowball, this is it.' And he knocked it on the head. He didn't want to be in the midst of an access battle, and his plan now is to spend the rest of days in his caravan, driving round Europe. It's amusing to hear that Snowy, as well as being the keeper, was the shoot tenant – he rented land from Darwall and monetised the shoot himself. Whereas now, by all accounts, Alexander Darwall is looking to run something much more modest. 'Difference for Alexander', Snowy explains, 'is that he don't need to make money from the shoot.'

The great irony of all the placards I saw, in Cornwood, claiming that Alexander Darwall makes a fortune out of pheasant shooting is that in reality, he was seemingly making a comparatively small amount, almost certainly no more than about £20,000 a year from renting land to Snowy, who has made just about enough for him and his wife to do a bit of caravanning on before they are too old. The economics of shooting are not easily understood but it's seldom a road to riches. And it's often the tenant who makes the money, rather than the landowner.

While Snowy is telling me about his caravanning plans, a truck pulls into the yard. 'This here', he says, in the quietest voice I've heard him use yet, 'now this here is young Simon. Really the best gamekeeper you'll ever meet.' Snowy caught him when he was only seven years old hunting pheasant poults in a patch of game cover with a stick. 'I run down, grab him by the ear and he wets his self.' As he ran off, Snowy told him to be at his house on Saturday at eight o'clock. The boy turned up, he put him in the beating line, and 30 years on Simon has taken over as headkeeper.

Mrs Parker heads outside to ask Simon in. While we wait Snowy tells me that back when he first started on Dartmoor, it was just endless with kids from the village. They'd all be at pheasants and when the pheasants went they'd be at the rivers trying to catch the salmon. They don't, apparently, Snowy says with some sadness, really bother anymore. The door opens and a tall man in green waterproofs and short dark hair appears behind Mrs Parker with a young lad standing next to him.

'This here', Snowy says, pointing to me, 'this here is trying to put together a book about this Right to Roam.' Then without asking anybody if they actually want any, he announces he's going to make everybody coffee. 'I was just telling him', Snowy continues, as Simon takes his boots off, 'about the two thousand people in the village and we were expecting aggro but there weren't a bad one among them.' Simon leans back in his chair, yawns, then nods thoughtfully.

Outside the setting sun is turning the edges of the grey clouds gold and light rain is starting to fall against the kitchen window. 'That lockdown though', Simon says to Snowy when he passes him a mug, 'unbelievable what came out.' Simon tells me in quiet disbelief that it was as though Dartmoor was a totally different place and he doesn't think people understand really the impact they actually have. Snowy cuts him off and starts shouting about the lapwings. 'They wanted to give him an award for those lapwings. Only lapwings on the moor.' Snowy hands me a mug and then gets another for the boy who takes it from him nervously.

Simon looks me up and down and then says that sometimes he almost has to laugh. He'll find people having a picnic right in the middle of his lapwing plot and they've got no idea they're disturbing anything at all. Some of them, he admits, are really respectful and want to learn but others just seem to want a fight. There is a guy, he goes on, a longhaired guy from Totnes, who carries a wooden staff, 'guy called Daniel' who set up a direct action group after the march and then went on to tear a load of fencing down. Snowy laughs and laughs as though it's the best joke he's ever heard. 'He thought it was Darwall put it up', Simon continues, 'but it was Natural England. It was to stop the sheep getting in the ancient woodland.'

Snowy shakes his head then tells us that it was before our time really but it was during foot and mouth that he first realised the impact that the public has on nature. The whole thing, he recalls, was terrible but because there was no movement, everything changed. 'I saw adders. I saw birds in places I've never seen them, and the insect life in the grass was just totally different.'

We sit in silence for a few moments with Snowy shaking his head and then Simon says that in truth he doesn't agree with everything Darwall's doing but he's the sort of man that won't be beat. You can't, in Simon's view, keep the public out. It just doesn't work. He tells me that over the past year or so, the closure of a car park is all they've talked about in the local pub. 'I told him he'll be a legend overnight if he reopens it.' All the same you can't, Simon thinks, if you want to restore curlew and lapwings, just have people everywhere. Snowy cuts him off again and tells me – pointing at him – that conservation is where Simon's future lies. 'If they ban shooting', Simon will be a conservationist. 'Only lapwings on Dartmoor he's got. They wanted to give him an award.'

Snowy takes our mugs back from us, makes us all more coffee, then turns to the boy. 'Toby, what do you think of it all?' Toby, Snowy explains, is the son of a local farmer but he went to gamekeeping college and he'd like to work on a shoot. The boy glances at me, then looks away. 'Well I think', he says eventually, looking down at the table, 'I think that most of Right to Roam is just a bunch of rich Londoners trying to tell us what to do.' He pauses as though I might not believe him and then adds that if I ask any young farmer they'd tell me the same.

We drink our coffee then Snowy grabs his coat and says he needs to show me the farmhouse Alexander Darwall has done up. 'Features in the *Domesday Book*. £2.5 million he spent on it, I heard.' He wants to show me the farmhouse, then he wants to show me the gate, the gate Alexander Darwall closed 'that kicked this whole thing off'. It's the very gate, Snowy explains, that all the protestors marched through back in January. As we leave, Mrs Parker appears in the kitchen in a towel on her way to the bathroom, telling us not to be long. She's worried, Snowy says, as we climb up into his truck that we'll be up on the moor all night but those days, he says as we pull out onto the lane, are over now.

While I'm driving back to London, in the early evening, I ring a number that I found online for Alexander Darwall's office. A young French guy picks up and listens patiently. It doesn't, he tells me, really have much to do with Devon Equity Management. 'No', I admit, 'not directly, anyway.'

*

Back in January, up on Stall Moor, when the drumming stopped, and when the crowd had eventually quietened down after chanting 'Darwall . . . arsehole', Martin Shaw, the writer and mythologist spoke. 'What is going on here', he said, standing below us with his thumb stick and pork pie hat, 'is more than an issue of politics. It's more than an issue of class. This is about how our fundamental relationship to nature has been compromised and this staggering display, that is happening here, will be part of history.' He asked us to repeat after him: 'We dedicate this walk to the land.' After our collective offering he concluded by saying that 'the kind of activism we're involved in is all about delight. It's about wonder. It's about goodness.'

Up above us, on the skyline, a cry went up and we turned to see a troupe of thirty dancers, their eyes covered in a streak of black paint like bandits, and in the middle of them, there was Crockern, a 7-foot-tall puppet many months in the making. A little child, next to me, with long blonde hair, broke away from his mother, and ran towards the creature holding out a piece of paper with 'Ware the Crock-ern' scrawled across it in felt tip pen.

Martin Shaw is interesting. It's said by those who've spoken to him recently that he has mixed feelings about the Right to Roam movement. He is right, though, that our relationship with nature has been compromised but that compromise has happened because of a myriad of things.

To find wonder and enchantment in lapwings, as Snowy clearly does, has become all too rare and part of the reason that nature is doing so badly in Britain is because we don't value it. We need, very urgently, to fix that. But in many ways, the argument that Right to Roam makes, that if access was greater, we would all become enlightened nature-lovers simply doesn't hold much water. Four years ago, I slept out on a capercaillie lek in Speyside where I awoke to the sound of the cock birds, up in the pine trees, making a woody popping sound before they all dropped down onto the forest floor. The man who showed me those extraordinary birds spends a huge amount of time talking to local mountain bikers and walkers about the need to stop disturbing the capercaillie. In Scotland, you have the right to walk where you like and to pitch a tent on the hill but the Scots haven't become a nation of wild nature lovers. Curlew, black grouse, and lapwings aren't thriving north of Hadrian's wall and capercaillie are rapidly heading for extinction. What we need to do is to give people the opportunity to be enchanted by the countryside. We need to give people the opportunity to learn about wildlife and important habitats but that is about much more than just being able to camp and wander where you like. Enchantment and learning has to be facilitated and encouraged, which incidentally is something Martin Shaw works hard to provide. In fact, the courses he runs on Dartmoor, where people spend time sleeping out in isolation, are only possible because he liaises with local landowners.

It was also interesting to hear him talk about the 'kind of activism' we were 'involved' in, up on Dartmoor, as being a sort of gooey campaign characterised by 'delight' and 'goodness'.

From the off, the Right to Roam movement has felt needlessly toxic. Not only are the numbers misleading but printing pictures of somebody's face to put on banners, descending on their land, terrifying the 76-year-old gamekeeper, and verbally abusing their employees doesn't really sound like a campaign sewn together with a happy thread of 'goodness'. Nor, as one activist told me they'd been doing, does sending Darwall 'hate mail' seem to come from a place of much goodness.

As Snowy saw for himself, most of the people on Dartmoor that day were the sort of merry outdoorsy folk you might meet at a bothy in the Highlands but there were people there too who would hate Snowy and what they think he stands for and many of those leading the land access campaign cheerfully misrepresent his work. Over a year after I went to see Snowy, a piece ran in the *New Statesman*, written by Guy Shrubsole, noting that sadly there are now no lapwings on Dartmoor. It pointed to those running shoots as being part of the reason for the moor's poor biodiversity. Snowy and Simon, as gamekeepers, clearly try to do everything they can for the last of the lapwings and a Dartmoor landowner, who wished to remain anonymous, said to me the day after the piece landed that they have lapwings breeding on their 'ground on the edge of the moor: that's a fact'. According to the landowner, their gamekeeper controls predators at nesting time in order to give the birds a chance of flourishing. The landowner said it had brought them 'sheer joy' to see the chicks hatch in spring, and they added that they feel dog walkers and the public are the biggest threats. They urged me not to make the whereabouts of the birds known, because they worry (apparently in light of Guy Shrubsole interfering with a lapwing conservation project in Sussex) that activists might do the same thing on their ground.

There is an important point to be made that for all that the Right to Roam campaign claims they are fighting power, they also wield a great deal of it themselves. Being able to place a piece in a widely-read and generally well-respected magazine that tells a pointed half-story about conservation, while fitting up the wrong guys, is quite a play. In contrast, Alexander Darwall reportedly tried to get a piece into *The Spectator* but they wouldn't run it.

*

Following the march on Dartmoor, meetings, fundraisers, and trespasses sprang up across the country. In late February, my friend Mark organised a party to raise money for the Right to Roam campaign at a café in South London. Mark is a sort of floating activist on the radical left and it was diverse in the sense that there were people there from almost every Oxbridge college. There were films, there was music, and there was dancing. One girl, who hadn't made it down to Dartmoor but who at that point was very involved in the campaign, told me in a quiet corner that she wished they'd drop all that 'white hippy shit' like the spirit of Old Crockern and the drumming. She just felt, she explained, that the best way to affect change is not to fulfil society's every preconception about your campaign.

Other than that, the party went well. Paul Powelsland, a radical barrister from Right to Roam, who had just spent a week up a tree, turned up towards the end and told me outside, where the smokers were standing on the pavement, that Darwall might have won the battle but he wouldn't 'win the war'. The tide, Paul seemed to think, was turning.

Three days later, Mark and his girlfriend came over for dinner and we talked about the party. Mark thought it had been a success but he was, he admitted, unimpressed by 'that Paul guy'. He was, Mark reckoned, a bit middle class. It felt a little unfair but it does speak to an interesting chasm. I suspect that what my friend wanted was a one-legged Salford boy to come down by bicycle, while whistling Ewen Maccoll's 'Manchester Rambler', after a tricky week at the loom. But the Right to Roam crowd aren't a group of factory hands dreaming of escaping to the hills. It is a largely middle-class and very white organisation. That said, I later learned that Paul Powlesland was one of just a few people in his year at school to go to university. Paul isn't, my source at Right to Roam confirmed, from the sort of family who become barristers.

I shrugged and told Mark that I guess they sent whoever was free and whats more I like Paul. He's got a lot of energy and his work on cleaning up rivers and raising awareness about their degradation has been impressive. Mark wasn't able to make it down to the protest and he was disappointed to hear that it all went off relatively peacefully. 'Drive them off the land', he replied, in a West Country accent, when I told him that no, it didn't – as he put it – 'get aggie'. Topping up Mark's girlfriend's glass, I said to her I sometimes wonder if Right to Roam is going to get criticised for overlooking the rural working classes, those for whom the land is a place of work rather than simply being a place of recreation. She asked me if I was talking about work or labour but it wasn't really a distinction that I understood in the context and she went on to tell me we can't just preserve a rural peasant class. For a moment I wondered, quite genuinely, if I should ask her which particular rural jobs she was thinking of but I did not.*

*

In mid-May, the veteran Green Party MP, Caroline Lucas, opened a debate in Parliament on public access to nature. The

---

* In the Marxist tradition there is a popular discussion about the distinction between work and labour. Labour tends to be thought of as exploitative. Writing a book that takes three years for an advance of £5,000 might, for example, be considered to be 'labour'. A hedgelayer who makes £400 a day might be considered to be doing 'work'. Engels, as a fox hunting man, knew hedges well. What Marx knew of hedges we don't know.

Deputy Speaker of the House, Eleanor Laing, prefaced proceedings with a reminder that the wild camping ban on Dartmoor had been appealed by the Dartmoor National Park Authority, was consequently 'sub-judice', and could therefore not be referenced.*

Before Members started highlighting, at some length, worthy endeavours they'd championed in their local area, Lucas provided context on the current situation. She explained that in the year 2000, the CROW act had given people the right to roam over mountain, heath, moor, and downland, a designation that covers 8 per cent of the countryside. The issue, though, she went on, is that not only is this meagre but there are patches – often called 'access islands' that can only be reached by using land that landowners voluntarily allow people on. Her concern, she explained, is that at any point their goodwill might dry up.

Lucas told the house that last year she tabled a Bill which would have extended the right to roam to include woods, rivers, grassland, and green-belt land. This new designation would have amounted to some 30 per cent of England. The public, she suggested, are on her side and she thinks the time is now right to actually go further and to follow Scotland's lead, where access is generally permitted across the country with some exclusions, such as school playing fields, rather than access being an exception as it is, according to Lucas, in England and Wales. It was hard not to perceive a slight feeling that the veteran Green Party MP didn't want to be left behind, feebly calling for 30 per cent when the real radicals wanted the lot.

Lucas gave way and for what felt like hours we heard details, from various Members, of tree planting, fond memories of family

* The *sub judice* rule prevents MPs or Lords from referring to a current or impending court case. Although the House is entitled under parliamentary privilege to discuss any subject, *sub judice* applies to avoid the House from debating a subject and possibly influencing the legal outcome of a case.

camping trips, and some thoughts on Constable. What we didn't hear about in any detail at all were what the implications of access might be for farmers and conservationists – no mention of the threat posed to those capercaillie by mountain bikers, no mention of jet skis terrorising wintering birds on the coast, and no mention of the thousands of sheep killed each year by dogs that aren't on the lead.

At about 1 p.m., a man in tight shorts came and sat down next to me. He explained, with his lips to my ear, that it was his day off. Did I, he wondered, 'know about Labour and the magic mushrooms?' I shook my head. 'What it is', he explained loudly, his lips still brushing my lobe, 'is that senior members of the Labour Party all take magic mushrooms together'. I turned to look at him and he winked conspiratorially.

At half-past one Alex Sobel, the Shadow Minister for Nature Recovery and the Domestic Environment, made the contribution that everybody had been anticipating. A Labour government, he assured Lucas, would give the public 'a right to experience, the right to enjoy, and the right to explore our countryside'. Marion Shoard, the environmentalist, author, and land access campaigner, who was sitting to my left shook her head. Lucas, getting to her feet, looked across at Sobel who was smiling dumbly. 'Could the Honourable Member answer a question about the kind of Right to Roam Labour is supporting: is it a universal right, based on the Scottish model, or is it a more specialised one, based on exclusion?' Lucas seemed to have Sobel on the run but on being pushed he assured her that Labour would 'replace the default of exclusion with a default of access' and would 'ensure the restoration and protection of the natural environment'. He didn't at any point address how more access and more protection would actually work. In fact, his speech was completely devoid of any detail at all and to an even greater degree than Lucas, he seemed to simply be hitching his happy wagon to a zeitgeist campaign.

A couple of days later, I learn that Daniel Zeichner, the Shadow Secretary of State for Defra, spent the afternoon, after the debate, calling up farming groups and countryside groups to tell them that Labour had no intention of bringing forward a Right to Roam. Sobel had been on the loose.

*

In the summer of 2023, I became a very regular attendee of London Right to Roam meetings. I was there in the earliest of days, when we met under Grimston's Oak in Epping Forest. I even practised a Morris dance in a London park that we were going to perform after storming the Royal Geographical Society but were regrettably all overcome with self-consciousness at the door, and I was there when we met in a burned-out townhouse in Spitalfields to plot revolution.

That evening we listened as a young guy suggested that this must really just be the beginning and what we should be fighting for is the abolition of the right to own land at all. We listened too as the leader of the group suggested golf should be banned, and we all nodded along earnestly when it was claimed that the public has no real impact on biodiversity. A bit of extra trampling, in a countryside ruined by farmers and landowners, we all agreed, wasn't going to make a difference.

The most interesting moment of that particular meeting in Spitalfields was when we looked at an open letter to Extinction Rebellion that criticised XR for not listening to 'communities on the land'. I was reminded, when we read it, of that sheep farmer who got stuck in Cornwood that day because of all those protestors who had been bussed in from across the country, and I was reminded of old Snowy. Not of course somebody to be listened to, in spite of living on Dartmoor for decades, but somebody to be blamed for the moor's environmental degradation.

The meeting concluded with a reminder that in two weeks'

time, Jon Moses and Paul Powlesland would be hosting a work-shop on everything a trespasser needs to know: planning, the risks, and what to do when it all goes wrong.

On a warm early June night, forty of us gather at Pelican House in Bethnal Green. Jon Moses, of Central Campaign, has come up from Wales and Paul Powlesland has stopped by on his way home from his Chambers. 'Paul', Jon tells us, 'is a barrister, which is why he's dressed like a cunt.' Jon gives us a bit of an update on where everything's at. The vision, he explains, 'in short', is to try to get England to introduce a Scottish model of access whereby access is the default and any exclusions are decided sensibly on a democratic basis. Jon is keen to empha-sise that where Right to Roam differs from other access campaigns is that they want the right to access land to be the first step but ultimately they want that access to give the public a way to be involved in protecting and restoring the country-side. The current model, he continues, whereby wealthy landowners are designated as custodians, is broken and access is the first step towards fixing that. His message is pretty different to the revolutionary stuff that has come to characterise London Right to Roam meetings.

Jon explains that it's vital that the movement is a non-violent, non-disruptive one. While he understands, he tells the room, the appeal of 'gnarly tactics', we need to show the world that there is nothing to fear about the public being able to wander freely. He concludes by reminding the room that it's 'a long road between politicians making promises and things actually happening', but that the campaign does seem to be bearing fruit.

Over the following couple of years, Jon Moses and I are in touch frequently. Jon is likeable and thoughtful and I can't help but feel sorry for him – there are points when I wonder if he might hit out publicly at some of the more blatant culture wars stuff that emerges from within Right to Roam, in order to make proper progress, but I'm not aware that he ever does.

Jon hands over to Paul who begins by telling us about learning, while he was studying law, that trespass is only a civil offence. 'Basically', he explains, 'if you don't obstruct anything, damage anything, or steal anything, you can go anywhere you like and they can't stop you. It's not criminal.' This realisation, he continues, truly transformed his life. Ever since, he's felt that he can just go out and enjoy the countryside or that he can wander into building sites in London, and climb up tower blocks at night, to look out over the city before the flats are sold to 'scumbags'.*

The landowner could technically, because it's a civil matter, try to sue you, he explains, but 'it's never going to happen' because it isn't worth their while. They could, he adds, without a court order, remove you from their property using reasonable physical force but 'that's a massive ball ache'. Paul continues by explaining that 'aggravated trespass', which was criminalised in 1994 to limit environmental protests, could be anything from disrupting a pheasant shoot to climbing onto a racetrack while it's in use to stopping forestry work but if you're not obstructing anyone doing something then it's fine.

Jon takes over to give us some further examples of the best ways to respond when you're confronted by 'an angry landowner'. One of the most successful ones, he tells us, is having an apple ready to hand. Paul steps towards him and puts on a mock West Country accent. 'Oi, get off my land.' Jon looks up nonchalantly and mimes taking a bite of the apple. Paul drops the West Country accent and goes into theatrical panic. 'Well, what are you doing here? Get off.' Jon turns to us and explains that what we've just witnessed is 'apocalyptic relaxation in the face of anger'. There's

---

* It is worth noting that injunctions can be imposed which make climbing up something like a building under construction a criminal offence.

apparently just something about eating an apple that shows you're so at ease with the world. 'It defuses and distentangles the situation.' Jon notes that it doesn't need to be an apple. Any sort of fruit would probably work just as well.

We break off into little groups to give it a go. A Dutch woman, in her mid-thirties, takes on the role of the landowner. She stands up to assert her authority and a girl sitting next me becomes the trespasser. The Dutch woman asks her what she's doing, then tells her she's committing a crime and threatens to run her down with angry dogs. She plays the role so well and so powerfully that by the time the apple comes out, its apocalyptic powers aren't quite strong enough to de-escalate the situation.

Our own group's conflict is still ongoing when Jon stands up at the front again to give us some more advice. You could, he suggests, if they tell you it's private property, reply that you don't actually believe in private property, because there's basically, he explains, conclusively, no response to that. But if they don't set up that particular goal, another 'ballsy play' he likes is using your environmental knowledge to say that sure, you're somewhere you shouldn't be but they are doing something far worse like felling trees or tearing hedges out.

Jon and Paul seem to be pleased that it's all going well and they move on to talking about the last mode of counterattack. The plan is that we identify something of great beauty and we then share our love with the landowner. In short, Jon tells us that we're pitching the joy of nature against 'the parsimonious, oppressive, exclusive' landowning mindset. A girl who hasn't spoken up until now, kicks us off. 'What are you doing on my land?' The Dutch woman shrugs and having not contributed I tell the rest of the group that I'm actually looking at curlew. 'At what?' the girl replies. It isn't, I realise, part of the game – it's just an honest question and we spend a couple of minutes talking about curlew and what they look like. Then Jon stands up at the front and asks how we got on. There isn't much of a response so I put my hand up and tell him about the curlew. 'You could say you went to look at curlew because you love curlew and nobody else around has curlew. It's quite likely to make them feel positive and then you can potentially bond over curlew.' Some of the group laugh but Jon nods and says it has the potential to be a positive conversation because either the person recognises that you love the thing they love or they're interested in hearing about what it is you've come to see.

We stack the chairs away and head off to find a pub. Most of them are closed but there's a bar up the street in the basement of a glass office block. I sit with Jon and a woman wearing a T-shirt with a picture of a cat in outer space on it. I tell Jon about some naturists I've been trying to get in touch with who are worried that those fighting for access don't think of them at all. He smiles and says that's probably fair.

*

The following week at the Court of Appeal, when the judges break for lunch, I head across the courtroom to speak to Alexander Darwall. It's the first time I've actually seen him in the flesh and I want to tell him I keep trying to get in touch but his barrister, Timothy Moreshead, steps in front of him and holds his arm up. Alexander, I'm told by the journalists in the gallery, won't speak to anybody.

The case, according to Sir Geoffrey Vos, the presiding judge, is a complicated one but the whole thing centres around whether 'wild camping', a term which the judges seem to agree they don't much like, constitutes 'open air recreation'. Isn't it fun, Lord Justice Underhill, Sir Geoffrey Vos, and Lord Justice Newey have spent much of the morning wondering, to have a long lunch on a Sunday followed by a snooze? Is that not recreation and what happens if a person is reading a book and they fall asleep (the judges agree they have all been guilty of doing that). Has such a situation ceased to be recreational?

Out on the street, in front of the Court of Appeal, a dozen or so Morris dancers with painted faces, floral garlands, and blue hi-vis vests are gathered in the middle of a growing crowd. I push my way through and find a space next to a lady who is filming it all with a phone covered in Extinction Rebellion stickers. There are people with signs reading 'Dartmoor is our moor', there's a woman with a printout of Oliver Twist on it with the caption, 'Please sir can I have some moor', and there are various people with the same printout of a pheasant that I saw back in January.

On the edge of the crowd in a bright blue polo shirt and sunglasses with lenses to match, I spot the writer Robert Macfarlane and I walk across to talk to him about a poet he knows called Colin Simms. I tell him I tried to find Colin once, in his cottage in the Pennines with its wild garden, but Colin hadn't been at home when I called. Robert and I talk briefly about nature writing and what it means. It's not a label, he tells me, that he likes much. He apparently doesn't want to be a nature writer. Behind us, a queue of people, fans of Macfarlane as nature writer, are waiting to talk to him. 'Well I guess', I reply, 'you could start writing about fox hunting – these guys would drop you pretty quickly.'

About a fortnight later, I'm walking past the lime kilns in Burgess Park when the news alert pings on my phone. The decision is unanimous. 'Wild camping' is 'unambiguously' and 'clearly' a form of 'open air recreation' and is therefore expressly permitted according to the applicable byelaws.

Summer turned to autumn and the Right to Roam campaign went to ground for a bit. Jon Moses is vague when I later ask why, but in spring, in part because the Supreme Court has agreed to hear Alexander Darwall's appeal over the legitimacy of wild camping, it seems like the guys at Central Campaign get back on the horse.

At about the same time, at a party in London Bridge, I bump into Lily, a girl from the London chapter of Right to Roam who tells me it's basically all over. She no longer has anything to do with it and she's not even sure if the London group still exists anymore. In the end she started to think that those running the campaign were really just using it as a platform to grow their profiles and sell nature books. The thing is, she says as we stand at the bar, I just think we realised that nobody cares that much. She went, she tells me, to the We Out Here festival in Dorset and it was the weirdest thing because it was on the young Earl of Shaftesbury's estate and he seemed pleased that everyone was there. 'In fact', she says, as though she's talking about seeing a poodle driving a bin lorry, 'he was DJ-ing.' What Right to Roam is, she says to me thoughtfully, is basically a symbolic thing.

It's a moment when I realise that Right to Roam, as the latest and noisiest iteration of the land access campaign, is a problem. They have highlighted issues that don't really exist and in doing so have diverted people's attention from problems that actually do. People get turned on by the idea that we're only able to access 8 per cent of the countryside and they then end up wondering what all the fuss is about when they actually get out there and realise that in reality things are quite different. Hundreds of thousands of kilometres of footpath and millions of accessible acres could keep most of us busy for many lifetimes but you're not going to say too much about all that if your shtick is that the whole place is out of bounds.

That is a battle we should be fighting. I tell Lily my view that it's not really about access, it's about the quality of access and being able to engage with the countryside. She nods thoughtfully and pays for her beer. The bar is filling up and before I head back to where I'm sitting, I tell her my news about Alexander Darwall and how for over a year I've been trying to get him to speak to me and then just the other day, he replied. 'I'm going to see him on Monday.'

Alexander Darwall puts a teabag in a mug for me and presses the button for boiling water. He is wearing a suit and tie and he tells me as though it is a matter of importance that he will leave me to deal with the milk myself. We sit by the window. There are ferns on the table, there's hardly anybody about, and he asks what I want from him. I suppose, I reply, that I've spent over a year talking to campaigners and people who make placards with pictures of him on them and say wild things about driven grouse moors on Dartmoor and I'd quite like to hear his thoughts. He leans back and looks at me. I ask him whether it would be okay to write in my notepad. 'No', he tells me, 'I'm not right for your book.' He says it as though I've offended him very deeply and I put the notepad down on the table. We talk about the fish in his river on his estate in Scotland instead and how large they are in spring. Access isn't too big a problem there apparently because they don't have a Munro.*

We talk for half an hour or so and he says again, apologising this time, that he's not right for my book but like me he says he worries about how the world is changing. The country, he tells me, is in a mess. Darwall says very little in the end. What I need to look at, he suggests, is the impact of people on agriculture and I need to go and speak to other landowners. Those who are too frit to put their heads above the parapet like he has.

I cycle back towards the river. It's cold on Vauxhall Bridge and it's starting to rain. I stop to text my editor and little droplets fall across the screen of my phone – 'Not sure I can use any of that', I tell him. But by the time I'm home an email

---

* A Munro is a mountain in Scotland that is over 3,000 feet tall. They are named after Sir Hugh Munro, who published a list of the 283 highest Munros in *The Scottish Mountaineering Club Journal* in 1891.

from Darwall has landed in my inbox. He enjoyed meeting, he says, but he needs to think about what to say.

Lots of people would like to hear, I'm sure, that he was awful. That he is everything all those thousands of people on Dartmoor think he is. But it's not quite like that. He is a man, of extraordinary single-mindedness, who believes that if you buy a swathe of the countryside, you should be allowed to decide what happens there because what's the point in the whole concept of property otherwise? As landowners go, Darwall is a bit unusual. The access campaign holds him up to be representative but most landowners, I come to learn, see him as being an outlier. He puts his head above the parapet and he bears the scars. Googling his name throws up a slew of vitriol. 'Mega cunt', one Reddit user says. 'Absolute scumbag', according to another, and over on Instagram, in comments on Right to Roam's own page: 'Do him in the absolute cnut' and 'Such a punchable face'. The Right to Roam campaign, Jon Moses later tells me, has created a new culture in which if you try to dictate what people can and can't do on your land, they will create a media shitstorm. 'That's what we're here for', he tells me cheerfully. I'm not sure that sounds, as Martin Shaw put it, as though it's all about wonder and goodness.

A couple of months later, on rereading Brooke Jarvis's piece in the *New York Times Magazine*, which was widely shared by people like Robert Macfarlane, I write to Alexander to ask about a detail that stood out. Brooke wasn't there on Dartmoor but the piece quotes one activist as saying that the protestors marched up a two-mile 'right of way' to Darwall's land while 'private security guards' flanked the crowds on either side 'holding dogs'. That two-mile right of way was actually a public road and we were not flanked on either side by security guards with dogs. Brooke's piece, some paragraphs earlier, mentions 'attack dogs' being used by gamekeepers, in the early twentieth century, to keep ramblers off the land. These gamekeepers, and there were armies of them, according to Brooke, were hired 'to kick the ramblers out'. Clearly they weren't hired for that purpose. They were hired to protect gamebirds and happened to be there on the ground and there weren't 'armies' of them. Those details aside, it is interesting that dogs feature in both Brooke's retelling of the twentieth-century fight for land access and in her account of the protest on Dartmoor.

Alexander replied to suggest that I give American newspapers a 'wide berth'. Brooke, at the time of writing, hasn't come back to me at all in regards to my request for clarification. It might seem like a quibble but it does matter that there weren't dogs flanking the protestors that day and in claiming there were, a thread is sewn, that connects Dartmoor to a very different fight on Kinder Scout a century previously.

*

The Earl of Bathurst, looking more like a prying neighbour in deep suburbia than a man who owns 15,500 acres, leans on a metal gate while watching us gather. A fortnight previously the news broke that the Bathurst family, for the first time in 326 years, was going to start charging £4 a go to access Cirencester Park, which runs to 3,000 acres. The announcement had gone down predictably and a 'Fayre for All' had been organised in protest. Dancing, music, and poetry were promised, as well as talks on everything from botany to slavery, and as ever there would be puppets.

We would 'technically' be trespassing, an email from the central campaign noted, but that, it went on, highlights the 'absurdity of this situation'. One moment you're simply out for a walk and 'the next you're labelled a trespasser'. Happily, though, the new passes that would eventually need to be bought at the gate hadn't actually arrived yet.

On the other side of the drive from the big house, beside a row of worker's cottages, Peter Clegg, the estate company's chief executive, is staring down at his phone. He tells me when I walk over to him to wait just a moment while he finishes sending an email then he puts it in his pocket. What it is, he explains, when I ask, is that the money will go to the 'maintenance of the park, and biodiversity projects'. Most of the crowd here, he says, are 'just interested people like yourself'. He looks around and then continues by telling me that it's not 'a mass movement'. We chat briefly about the difficulty of trying to charge people when the estate was, as nobody tries to deny, bought by Benjamin Bathurst with the proceeds of slavery. Peter shrugs and says it's not brilliant as a starting point but 'that was then'. Most aristocratic estates, he reasons, have some thorny history and all they can do is what they believe is right in the present.

In comparison to other estates, Peter feels that they are being very reasonable. 'Try going to Westonbirt', he suggests, where Forestry England, which runs the famous arboretum there, charges a £16 entrance fee. Peter also points out there will be no fee for locals – the community, he explains, will get free passes to walk 'with their friends'. There is, though, a deposit that needs to be paid of £10. 'What if I die?', a dog walker I meet asks. 'If I die, does my family get that ten pounds back?'

While the crowd builds, I drop a quick message to the Head of Land and Property at an estate in the Midlands. 'Bathurst', he replies – just as Jon Moses picks up a megaphone and picks his way through the crowd to stand by the ticket booth – 'is an idiot. Is a twenty-thousand-acre estate really that short of cash that they need to charge people to use a park that's been free for hundreds of years?' The whole thing, he goes on, doesn't paint landowners in a good light and 'it stinks of greed'.

The crowd quietens when Jon Moses starts speaking. Jon touches on 1,800 acres of the park being transferred to a trust held in Bermuda, which by the Earl's own admission was a capital gains tax dodge. Jon mentions 'hundreds of thousands pounds' of agricultural subsidies, made up of taxpayers' money, that are awarded to the Bathursts' farming business each year, and he talks about the children who will need to bring their family pass with them when they are cutting through the park to go to school. 'As taxpayers', he calls out to the crowd, we have already paid but we are 'now told we must pay again'. A cheer goes up and then Jon goes in for his knockout blow. 'If', he says, in mock sympathy, 'the estate can no longer meet its obligations and there's no room in their ample accounts for the park's maintenance, we'll take it. Please, by all means, give it back.' The crowd hoots with delight.

When we all make our way up the hill, I fall in beside David Watts, a local amateur historian who tells me about a little book he wrote on the history of the park. It struck him, one morning, while he was out running that he didn't know, despite visiting the place for decades, how one family came to own so much of England. It might be worth, he suggests, having a look at it. A couple of weeks later I do. It's a sort of vague and fanciful history of land ownership. It begins by noting that the system of landholding in England 'based on social hierarchy' was introduced in the eleventh century, as opposed to land simply 'being owned by the people who worked it'.

The crowd, halfway up the slope, is herded off to the right where Dr Jessica Moody, from the University of Bristol, addresses us from the steps of a neoclassical folly. I'm half listening to her and half being talked at by a man who wonders if I'd like to get involved in sabotaging the badger cull. 'Over two hundred thousand they've killed', he tells me. 'They're clever, are badgers.' Moody lectures on collective memory and public history and has written on Britain's amnesia around the slave trade. She's interested, she explains, 'in how the past is used and abused for various political ends and how that changes over time'. What she wants to speak to us about, she goes on, is *forgetting*, and how forgetting the connection between slavery and landed estates has taken work. It has been reliant on unremembering and reframing.

The Bathurst family has, she outlines, a longstanding connection to the Transatlantic slave trade. Benjamin Bathurst, who was the progenitor of the current dynasty and who died in 1704, was both a governor of the East India Company and the Royal Africa Company. We've historically, Moody notes, been keen – or the owners of these estates have been keen – to highlight things like literary connections and big houses getting turned into hospitals during the war, rather than the truth about how wealth was generated. Moody doesn't make the link explicitly but the connection is clear. People owned by the Bathursts worked themselves to death to pay for the purchase of Cirencester Park and now the public is being asked to pay in turn.

A little girl with a knitted fox hat is wandering among the crowd handing out leaflets for the South West Hunt Saboteurs. Her mother spent the speech calling out 'disgusting' and 'shameful', and most of the crowd hold their hands up in polite refusal as though the girl is begging.

It was never going to be an easy announcement for the Bathursts – the Earl came out as saying that he gets it – people don't like change. He himself, he reasoned, is not a man who likes change either but 'unfortunately, to keep the park running, we have to have some change here'. He added, echoing his chief executive, that they are far from the only place that charges for entry.

It's also very easy to get excited about the ticket cost at the gate but it's perfectly possible to let people in for nothing, while making money out of them and out of nature elsewhere. The famous Knepp rewilding project doesn't charge for access, Jon Moses points out, and he's right but it's £750 to stay in their Peregrine Treehouse for three nights and the prices at the farm shop there are well beyond most people's means.*

---

* In 2000, Charles Burrell and his wife, Isabella Tree, 'rewilded' their 3,500-acre estate in Sussex. It has become something of a poster boy for rewilding in Britain.

At the top of the hill, where a Right to Roam banner has been draped across a 16-foot-high bronze sculpture of a horse's head, we stop to have lunch, and Daniel Grimston, the campaign's self-styled 'poet-in-non-residence', reads something that he later tells me he wrote the previous evening. 'This place, that house', the fourth stanza begins, 'was built from screams.' While we eat I chat to two boys in their early twenties who are in a band together and who seem a bit unsure about the whole thing. They totally get, they tell me, that people need to maintain their gardens 'but the thing is, does this park even need maintaining?'

After lunch, a girl in tartan trousers and wellington boots from the group SISTER (Stroud International Solidarity Together for Earth Repairs) reads a speech from her phone. 'Coloniality', she explains, has everything to do with the 'degradation of normal people that has been happening since the Romans arrived'. Jon Moses holds a megaphone for her and looks down at the grass. 'Once these lands', she continues, 'were held in common. Once they would have been used for the food, water, medicine, and the livelihood of many, many people.' The girl pauses and glances up at the crowd. 'Over hundreds of years, the elites have taken the land that belonged to us all and have violently demanded that they have the right to own and control it.' The 'elites' the girl goes on, made servants of us. 'You and me along with the descendants of the enslaved peoples and their communities in Africa.' It's really quite something. When she's done a burst of applause goes up and then a lady plays the lyre and sings a song about breaking the spell that keeps us down. Some of us close our eyes.

Usually when writing about people you become more and more sympathetic to their cause the deeper you go, but I started to realise that there was something odd, and curiously cultish, about Right to Roam. They were promoting a simple solution to a problem that they were either misrepresenting or didn't really seem to understand while ignoring the problems that their proposed solution would cause.

In trying to inspire a mass movement, it was becoming clear that they weren't targeting those who actually use footpaths and who understand the history of access in the countryside, because their messaging would strike anybody well-versed in it as being absurd. You could say well, who cares? If people want to make big puppets and big claims about being locked out of the countryside, go ahead. But the trouble is that there are real issues and when the noisiest people are immensely creative with their messaging, there's a danger that the problems we do face don't get solved. It's a little like Hilaire Belloc's Matilda who told lies and was burned to death. If the loudest and best-connected of access campaigners shout about things that aren't much of a problem, decision-makers are unlikely to listen when quieter campaigners, with less clout and cultural capital, start pointing out things that actually are.

3

Great Estates

*Are the masses locked out of England's
great estates?*

I can only assume, when the invitation lands via WhatsApp in mid-December, that somebody has dropped out. Would you, the conservationist Jake Fiennes asks, like to come and shoot at Holkham in three weeks time?

Jake, who was a gamekeeper in his younger years, has been involved with all sorts of nature restoration projects. He helped rewild Knepp in the early days, he worked at Raveningham for the Bacon family, and at Holkham, the largest private land-holding in Norfolk, he gets involved in everything from reviving water meadows to restoring hedges. It might seem odd to some that a person who is in love with wildlife also likes to shoot it and eat it, but man's relationship with nature is more complex than people like to admit. Our ancestors drew mammoths on the walls of caves because they revered them, then they hunted them with spears. Sir Peter Scott, who founded the Wildfowl and Wetlands Trust, devoted his life to birds and he painted them beautifully, but he shot them and ate them too. Jake Fiennes, as far as I know anyway, doesn't paint, but I'd put him in much the same category as Peter Scott, as a shooting, nature-loving man.

'If you let me know if you can come', the WhatsApp ran, 'the Earl of Leicester's secretary will send further details.' I don't paint either but I do love the creatures I hunt. I love snipe in sundrenched winter meadows and it's never really autumn, I think, until the teal are in.

The email comes the following week. We are to park on the right hand side of 'the lions' – which were commissioned by the second Earl of Leicester in 1872 – because the people doing Parkrun, which happens every Saturday morning at Holkham, will be parking on the other side. There are usually over a hundred runners and the 5-kilometre route passes various interesting features, such as a thatched seventeenth-century ice house and an obelisk built by the first Earl.

We meet on the gravel. As well as Jake and the current Earl, there is a French financier, a local seaweed farmer, a big cattle man from Cumbria, the estate's director of farming, and a young land agent who works nearby. As we head off, the Earl tells me, while rolling a cigarette, that Parkrun is a brilliant thing. He always likes to do it on Saturdays if he's not busy shooting and he confesses it gives him great pleasure to beat farmers on the estate who are half his age.

The whole day is pretty lush. We see some very impressive woodland, we see lots of parkland deer, and the keepering team wear bowler hats (which their predecessors were supposedly given to protect their heads when they were attacked by poachers). The wind is cold, the big Norfolk sky is almost cloudless, and at about three o'clock, when the light starts to go, the headkeeper tells us all that we'll get one more drive in and that will be our lot.

He places me between a gatehouse and a belt of trees, and almost as soon as I've got my gun out of its slip, birds start to break. There is a partridge that comes low, two jays screech through the oak canopy and then just as the pheasants start to get up, the keepers' radios crackle. Three dog walkers are coming down the track. When they appear in the middle of the woods, they look slightly annoyed by the whole thing, as though their pleasant late afternoon wander has been disrupted by people doing something they disapprove of. They nod curtly and then when they're gone, shooting recommences.

After the horn is blown, we wander back to the trucks and while we're standing there, waiting for the last of the Guns, a paramedic appears on a bike. He's pedalled over, on his rounds, one of the beaters explains, as though it's the most normal thing in the world, to say hello. He's always about, apparently, in case a visiting member of the public trips in one of the greenhouses or has a heart attack by the fountain.

Clearly, I was there as a guest but there was a very real sense that Holkham is a place – albeit a place with car parking fees – both for the local community and for interested tourists, some of whom come a very long way. Many of those who had done Parkrun seemed to hang around all day and it was really something to see a shoot on one of England's great estates happily pause to let three dog walkers wander through a drive. While I was standing there, I remembered the speech that was screened in the shadow of Kinder Scout about 50 million pheasants being released each year. It was suggested there needs to be less space given over to pheasants and more room for 'us peasants'. It had gone down very well. But that evening, while I was driving back to my flat in Camberwell, South London, I found myself thinking that at Holkham there seems to be room for shooting and for dog walkers, as well as for farming, deer management, picnicking, commercial forestry operations, and for nature. Jake Fiennes, who is respected by almost everybody in conservation, is only there because it is a large, wealthy estate. The wildlife that the public gets to see at Holkham is there, in part, because of Jake and Jake is there because Holkham is a success. It's also worth saying that lots of the people in the beating line that day were local and working class. They were engaging with the countryside (as well as earning fifty quid or so) not in spite of shooting but because of it. My happiest memory of the day was standing behind a hedge with a local beater and his young daughter. His first love, he told me, was wildfowling down on the marsh.

There is almost no 'access land' at Holkham, by which I mean that according to that well-worn 8 per cent figure, the public has nothing. They are, as some would put it, locked out. But according to Jake some 20 per cent of the 25,000 acres can be enjoyed by the public.* The more I looked the more it started to seem as though compelling narratives around large landowners being parsimonious bastards don't always stack up.

*

Upon seeing signs for Reading and realising that the bus I'm on is going back the same way we came, I head downstairs to speak to the driver. 'Yes', he says, in an uncanny way that suggests he was expecting me, 'you ought to have got off four stops back. What to do is get off at the next one and wait on the other side.' He pulls in a couple of hundred yards further on and I grab my bag before stepping out into the spring sun. It is late April and it is the warmest day so far of what has been a grey year.

The garage that was meant to be changing the brake pads on my car hadn't been able to get them in as quickly as they'd hoped, so the only way to actually get to the Englefield Estate – some 45 miles west of London – was by bus, train, bus again,

---

* The Nature Reserve at Holkham makes up about one-fifth of the estate, about 80 per cent of which is open to the public. The park is 3,500 acres, which the public can enjoy. Alongside this, there is a network of public rights of way, which allows the public to view the farmland. The beach frontage at Holkham contributes to the accessibility. In the past century, Holkham (as with many other English estates) has reduced in size by about half.

and then on foot. It was supposed to be a little over two hours but by the time I sit down at the café next to the bus stop, it's been almost three.

Somebody has stuffed a leaflet about signal crayfish into a flower pot next to a plastic cup full of cigarette ends and I read it while drinking a pint of Cruzcampo (Spain's number one draught beer). In the past ten years, according to the leaflet, the Reading and District Angling Association has removed 100 tonnes of signal crayfish from the River Kennet. They eat fish spawn, they eat invertebrates, and they displace silt.

The bus, appropriately for a day full of disappointment, comes ten minutes after it's meant to. There is a mother with a push-chair, an old lady with shopping bags, and two grey-faced men arguing loudly about going to 'score'. I get off where I was meant to at the Theale Green School stop, then I turn right onto the A340 where the traffic comes at me fast and the strimmed verge is no more than two feet wide. After a couple of hundred yards, I cross the road and find, unexpectedly, a small wooden gate with 'Englefield' on it. The house is seemingly much further on and I hadn't quite appreciated how big the estate is.

Behind the stone wall, there is a sign that reads 'Welcome to Englefield Community Woodland'. It is a place, apparently, for butterflies, reptiles, commercial timber growth, the public (if they keep their dogs under control), and horse riders who have bought an annual permit from the Estate office. 'This woodland is', the sign promises in the top corner, 'a fantastic place for wildlife and people.' And then in the bottom left corner, there is a plea to 'follow designated trails'. I head on, keeping the A340 on my right and on my left, somewhere in the pines, a squirrel barks.

The Right to Roam campaign has Englefield, which has been owned by Lord Richard Benyon's family for hundreds of years, fixedly in its sights. In 2022, a group of 150 campaigners, including the obligatory Morris dancers and people dressed as woodland spirits, descended on the estate to call on Benyon to open up his 14,000 acres to the public. 'We want the joy of meeting in the commons with music', Nadia Shaikh, a co-organiser of the campaign, explained to the *Guardian*, 'so we are acting as if we already have that freedom.' It's clear that over the past couple of hundred years, people have been treated roughly at Englefield. Common land on the estate was enclosed from the early 1800s, houses were moved to create a deer park, and there is also, according to the Ramblers, a lost footpath that runs across estate land. But I wanted to know how bad things really are – I wanted to find out whether locals stand at the gate, yearning for access to the manicured dreamscape beyond.

At the end of the wood, there is a small poodle running busily in and out of the wild garlic, and when I tell the lady walking behind it I'm writing about land access, she laughs and turns to her husband who is dawdling behind her. 'That's him you want to speak to about that', she replies. 'Oh right', he says excitedly, 'so you just came down here to get some views on the ground, as it were?' I tell him it's exactly that and he starts running through some places he's lived over the years. 'There was South Oxfordshire, and the farmers there were terrible. You couldn't park in a gateway and if you walked into a field, they were on you.' He shakes his head and adds, in a changed tone, that he is very aware that there are two sides to it. 'It is a difficult one because people walk all over the crops and their dogs do chase pheasants.' The man tells me they drive about five miles to get to Englefield because of how peaceful it is. In fact he hardly ever, he says, sees more than two or three other dog walkers. He pauses and looks around over the rim of his glasses then pushes his hands into the pockets of his olive green trousers and says he remembers the trees being planted about 35 years ago. He isn't really sure what they'd have to say if you jumped the wall behind us and walked across the farm-land but you can't say, he doesn't think, that access isn't good. He points towards the direction of the big house in the distance. 'Benyon, who's now in charge 'cos his father died, he seems pretty alright.' The man shrugs, as though to say that life is what it is, then he tells me he's called Ian and that his dog's called Poppy. He doesn't tell me his wife's name but he wanders off down the path after her.

I keep going for a couple of hundred yards then I realise, on looking at my map, that to get to the big house, on paths I'm allowed to be on anyway, I'm going to have to go back the way I came. On my left there is what looks to be newly created and inaccessible wetland habitat, where geese are marching their goslings in the sun and on my right, there is a gate with barbed wire wrapped around the top rung. I climb it, jump down into the field, and then slip quickly into the shadow of a hawthorn hedge. Ahead of me, a rabbit sits motionless on the track and then when I'm 30 yards out it bolts into the cowslips. Out on the left, lapwings on eggs are hunkered down in the earth and lapwing cocks are displaying, their peewit cry cutting through the drone of the M4. There are hares too, lots of them, and halfway down the track a pair of grey partridges, a species that like the lapwing, has almost disappeared from the English coun-tryside, break from the bottom of a stunted oak.

Being there, being where I shouldn't be, is a great pleasure. It's absolutely true that there is more wildlife in the fields I'm not allowed to access and down in the wetland area I passed, than in the Community Woodland but that's obviously not coincidental. If I had a dog trespassing with me, the lapwings and the partridges would soon be gone and it would be perfectly possible to see most of the things in the fields from behind the wall back in the community wood.

The Englefield Estate sits just under seven miles from the centre of Reading and some 15 miles from Basingstoke, which together have a combined population of almost 300,000 people. It was interesting to hear from Ian that the Community Woodland is hardly ever busy but at the same time, if the entirety of the estate was opened up to local Berkshire residents and their dogs, there would be big consequences for wildlife. In 2009, Englefield was down to just two breeding pairs of English partridges, due to predators, a lack of habitat, and modern farming practices. Happily, that number has now risen to 82 pairs – if dog walkers were present on the ground where the partridge restoration project is taking place, achieving results would be difficult.

At the end of the track, where somebody has fly-tipped four PVC windows, I hop another gate and then carry on along Bostock Lane before getting to the start of the long drive that leads up to Englefield House. It isn't entirely clear whether the public are welcome but the side gate is open so I slip through. There isn't, on a Friday in late spring anyway, much of a buzz at Englefield but two people are walking down the drive and they stop to chat. David, as he tells me he's called, lives on the other side of Reading but he's originally from Ghana and it's the first time that he and his wife have visited. 'First time here today', he says, 'and it's like wow.' He holds his hands up as though he is a preacher, then he points along the drive to a herd of fallow deer that are grazing behind the fence and tells me he's never seen anything like it. 'There is', David continues, 'nothing like this in Ghana.' They do, his wife explains, have National Parks, but 'nothing like this'.* If there was anywhere like this, he says, 'it would be private and we wouldn't be able to access it'. Then he tells me a little more about the deer and asks if I've seen deer like that, before interrupting himself to say that really he is just 'so grateful to have the opportunity to

---

* There is some evidence that local communities were displaced in Ghana to create national parks, which are popular with tourists.

access other people's property'. He did wonder, he says, suddenly looking very earnest, if you are able to go into the fields at the side of the drive but 'we thought', his wife cuts in, that 'maybe this is for the farmers only.'

It is 18 degrees and I take my jacket off before walking on. Further up the drive, just by a 'Private' sign in front of manicured lawns by the house, a young boy is riding a polo pony. He swings his mallet theatrically and glances away as though he and his pony are the only two creatures in the world and before I get a chance to speak to him, he trots away. Pangbourne Polo Club, located at Englefield, which has two fields and 70 stables, is apparently popular with the London polo crowd as it isn't really so far to drive but driving, crucially, a bit like polo, isn't available to all. I don't imagine many members of Pangbourne Polo Club get the bus with their mallets but if they did they'd discover that it is expensive and very slow (£54 for me in the end, not including those Mini Cheddars and the pint of Cruzcampo).

A little further on, by the estate garden centre, which is run by a charity that supports people with learning difficulties who work alongside the staff, I chat to three South Carolinans who are buying climbing roses. 'I really wouldn't know anything about that at all', the old man says when I ask him about land access, 'because we just flew in this morning.' He gestures to his wife and then says they are visiting their daughter who lives nearby and have never been to England. 'We come here all the time', the daughter tells me, acknowledging some partner who isn't present. They only ever, she continues, walk up and down the drive and go to the tea room and the garden centre but she thinks it's kind of 'amazing'. Her dad tells me again that he really wouldn't know anything about access at all and then goes into a long tale, the point of which is that people in South Carolina are very protective over their trout streams. If your foot even touches their property, he says severely, they'll be out there.

I tell him it's odd really because the States is such an expansive place. 'Oh yes', he replies cheerfully, 'you can drive a long way but you can't get out your truck.' His wife then tells me that they're going to see some other big houses, 'some National Trust properties', and her daughter nods. 'Yes, mom, but the National Trust is different though.'

In the estate garden centre, a slightly miserable older lady sells me some radish seeds and tells me she's not really sure about where the 1,700 acres of 'land available for public access' that gets talked about on the Englefield website are, but she suggests with disinterest that I could ask at the shop. I head across there and the lady behind the till makes me a cup of tea and says that walking isn't really her thing but to her it's 'a community'. Did I know, she asks, that they do concerts 'up there in the big house?' I tell I didn't and she nods in thoughtful appreciation while squeezing the teabag. 'You remember Caroline Flack', she says, 'from the telly.' I nod and say that yes, I do sort of remember.* 'Well, they did a concert for her.' She suggests I can sit down, to rest for a bit, if I'd like to. And while I sit and drink the tea, most of it spilling out under the plastic lid onto my lap, she tells me about fish and chips in the village hall. 'It's the lady who owns the tea room who organises the fish and chips.'

Outside, two elderly ladies are sitting at a table eating sandwiches. I ask them about access and they ask me to repeat the question. 'Oh', one of them eventually says, not really giving me much confidence that she understands what I'm asking about. They are actually only really interested in the tea room, they tell me. They want to walk to the tea room but there is the school though, they add. 'The little school and they do

---

* Caroline Flack was a TV presenter and actor who died by suicide in 2020. Events were set up after her death to raise funds and awareness for mental health.

events on the playing fields.' They look at me suspiciously, as though I'm trying to catch them out in some way and then they return to their sandwiches.

I head out onto the street that runs through Englefield Village, where almost all the buildings have dark blue doors to denote that they are owned by the family in the big house. At a Right to Roam event, not long before I went to visit Englefield, Nadia Shaikh had said, while standing up at the front, that it's sometimes hard to articulate but you just sometimes know 'something doesn't feel right'. There is, it's true, sometimes a slightly odd atmosphere on large landed estates. I suspect some casual visitors like the mood but that mood is dictated by one family and has often been created over a very long time. They are generally monuments to a family's immense wealth and are both classy (in an English cultural conception), while simultaneously being immensely vulgar. Does a person really need their coat of arms chiselled into the wall outside their bedroom window and must a family paint all the doors of their cottages the same colour? It all feels a bit like a five-year-old saying 'that and that and that – all of this is mine'. It is difficult, I think, to visit somewhere like Chatsworth or even Holkham without feeling small, and I guess that making other people feel small is sort of the point of making your house and gardens quite so big. Many of these places would have maybe felt a little less odd when they were busier – when there were more gamekeepers, more shepherds, and even more domestic staff but there can be something ghostly about them now, there is a kind of malaise, a very palpable presence but also a sense of absence. I feel the oddness that I think Nadia Shaikh was evoking but I'm not sure anybody else whom I speak to at Englefield does really.

Beyond the nursery in the village, there is a path that looks as though it's not often used. In the woods on the left of the path there are little dens that look to have been made by children, and at the end, the path opens out into meadows that connect with each other, maybe a hundred to a hundred and fifty acres in total, all bounded by a stream. I call the Estate office to ask them where the other 1,700 acres are and the girl who answers tells me she's not really that sure. The gardens, she confirms, are closed today but if I give her a moment she'll just 'look up a map'. There is the community woodland, she says eventually, and the meadows I'm on and then there are lots of walking routes. 'You'll see the signs around.' I get the impression it's not a question she gets asked all that much but I thank her anyway and I continue. On the other side of the meadow there is a middle-aged woman running and as she nears the stream, a duck dips into the reeds with her ducklings disappearing behind her.

I head back to the village and then leave the interior of the Englefield Estate to wander back towards a bus on the A340. There is a stop on the other side of the road but the sign is almost completely overgrown with ivy and under the heading 'Quality Travel for West Berkshire', there is a note that says 'operates Mondays and Wednesdays only: no smoking'. The transport problem is a very real one. I struggle to find anybody at Englefield who wants more access but nobody would suggest, I think, that it's actually easy to get there and walking on those verges is pretty dangerous. It seems fair to say that getting people to the countryside who don't have cars, without having to pay a huge amount for public transport, is a bigger concern than them actually being able to wander when they get there.

I've been walking for about fifteen minutes, when I pass a newly-refurbished wooden building with a sign on it that reads 'The Movement Barn'. I head in and find that there are only two people there. 'Excuse me', I say to a young guy in the squat rack, 'I was just wondering if I could ask you a few questions about land access.' He is much more forthcoming than I expect him to be and he calls his friend over who is working away on his lats in front of the mirror. 'There is a loop we run round', they confirm 'but it's only short and there's this big road.' The two guys, who look to be a bit younger than me – both of them in very clean sports kits – seem to know the area well. The thing is, they continue, the access is good but it's quite disjointed. 'There's a bit here and a bit there.' In fact the estate is so big, they tell me, that they don't really know what there is. What they'd really like is a longer running loop. 'So yes', they conclude, with some uncertainty, 'maybe access could be better.'

In Theale, on the recreation ground there is a funfair and children, in their school uniforms, eat candy floss while queuing for the dodgems.

*

The Right Honourable Lord Richard Benyon, wearing dark jeans and a blue woollen jumper, leans forward in his armchair and passes me a little plate of biscuits. 'Would you like milk with your coffee?' He is softly spoken and thoughtful in a vaguely paternalistic sort of way. 'Please', I reply, 'just a little.' He pours the milk very carefully then passes me the white china cup.

We are sitting in his immaculate office, underneath a large painting of what he tells me that he thinks is the Lake District, with cattle grazing in the foreground, but he doesn't seem all that sure. Behind us, his secretary is typing and beyond the window, in the parkland, there is the happy sound of a group of little school children running around. I wrote to him, after I visited, telling him about the bus, the boys at the gym, and David, who was so keen on the deer, and he suggested we should chat.

Richard looks up and asks his secretary if she has a copy of 'that letter'. He crosses the room to get it, then sits back down, telling me that it came last week from somebody local who is involved in 'access issues'. He starts reading it but pauses after a couple of sentences and says that it's about a new book, a book called *Wild Service* written by Nick Hayes. 'He came to see me', Richard continues, while carrying on reading, 'when I was an MP, in one of my surgeries, by saying he was a constituent, when he wasn't and he taped the meeting.' I tell Richard I've actually got a copy of the book with me and I wanted to ask him about it. He nods and says it's all there 'on the first page'. He starts to run through the errors: 'Thirty thousand acres? Well that would be nice. We are big here. It's 14,000 and we've got 7,500 in Scotland.' I look down at my copy to follow along and he continues aloud: 'but for a few stunted footpaths that trace along some field margins, the rivers, lakes, woodland, and meadows of his vast domain remain shut, at all times, to the public.' He glances up at me and shakes his head in what appears to be very genuine confusion, then he goes back to reading the letter.

The prologue in *Wild Service* – a collection of essays written by high profile figures from the Right to Roam campaign – kicks off by noting that while St Mark's church at Englefield, which sits halfway up Richard's drive, is 'open to all', the estate itself is forever closed. 'The grace of God', Richard continues, 'and the meanness of man, side by side in the little village of Englefield.' Richard's secretary has stopped typing and is listening in. He puts the letter down, shrugs, smiles and then says in a nonchalant sort of way, 'It makes us out to be . . .' he pauses for a moment as though trying to find the right words, 'it makes us out to be ridiculous.'

His 91-year-old mother, he explains, fondly, opens St Mark's every single morning and closes it again at night. The prologue in *Wild Service* points out that people don't have to pay to go to St Mark's, which is true, but its upkeep is paid for by the Benyons and it is sort of incorrect too that you 'don't need permission' to go there because getting there relies on the drive being kept open as a permissive path, again by the Benyons. St Mark's, he gives me the impression, is his mother's thing but access more generally is his concern. 'Of the however many people that live within forty-five minutes of here, how many of them want more access and can't actually get it? Either on designated footpaths or on the access agreements we've made.' He reaches for a chocolate biscuit, breaks one in half, then tells me in detail about the 1,700 acres that people can walk across, including a three-kilometre walk, a five-kilometre walk, and Pamber Forest, a 500-acre nature reserve which they run with Basingstoke and Newborough Council and the Hampshire and Isle of Wight Wildlife Trust, something he tells me proudly works 'very well'. He looks again at the letter and I tell him that if the stuff about the public being locked out really is completely incorrect, it's potentially libellous and he should write to Bloomsbury, the publisher, to have it changed. He makes a vague noise as though to say life is really too short for all that.

Back in 1999, when Richard was an MP, and the Countryside and Rights of Way Act was being debated, he sat on the Country Landowners' Association council and he thinks that in retrospect they got it wrong. They were saying, he tells me, that greater footfall in the countryside 'is going to be a disaster and yet here we are in a triangle between Reading and Basingstoke – we open up large areas of the estate and we have very few problems'. People, he goes on, can walk extensively, they're allowed to picnic, and if they're somewhere they shouldn't be, there's lots of other places they can be. 'I just think there's so much rubbish talked about access and I think there's a huge opportunity for more of it.'

All his life, Richard tells me, he's campaigned for the public to be able to benefit from getting out into the countryside, and lately he's become very interested in 'social prescribing'. He explains that if somebody in Mortimer, a small town of about 8,000, just outside Reading, is overweight and has diabetes, their doctor can prescribe them a walk three times a week around the woods in Englefield. Richard tops up my coffee then says that they haven't got round to it yet but they are thinking about putting an outdoor gym in and maybe a longer running route as well. One of the benefits of access, he explains, is that it also supports various businesses that they rent premises to.

When they are creating new paths, Englefield thinks that the best approach is 'to start from the bottom up'. They invite the local Ramblers' Association to come and tell them where they would like to go. In some instances, they've found that where people would like to go gets very muddy so they've put in some hard surface. What it's all about, Richard feels, 'is getting people to go where they want to go and where you want them to go. Not where they probably don't want to go and where you don't want them to go.' It wouldn't, he says, work to have 'untrammelled access' over 'a ground-nesting bird project'. Part of the motivation for getting local people to help them devise routes and paths is that it gives them a sense of ownership, which is something he tells me he is keen on. He points to examples of 'nature volunteers' who help with conservation work and who will then call up if somebody is lighting a fire where they shouldn't or if a car is being smashed up. Not, Richard adds, something that happens very often but their proximity to urban areas means that it isn't unheard of.

Leaning back in his chair, Richard asks if I knew that Right to Roam had come to Englefield to trespass a couple of years ago. The night before they turned up, they had been hosting a music festival and there was a sign, he tells me, on top of the hill that said 'Welcome'. They had a policy, he explains, that nobody was to confront them. 'It infuriated them because they want confrontation.' He pauses then says in awe that 'they looked extraordinary, creatures of the forest and face paint. You know, I almost like that. I like the eccentricity of it.'

As Richard sees it, Nick Hayes only uses him as a sort of pinup of a local landowner because he lives nearby but he doesn't feel that Nick has really taken any time to try to understand Englefield. The children playing outside are the last little group of the 1,700 who have visited over the past week. Twenty years ago, Richard travelled up to Chatsworth, which hosts 14,000 children from Derbyshire every year, showing them various rural and agricultural activities. They decided they could do something similar. 'We made a few mistakes along the way and we changed it and then we created something a bit bigger.' He tells me that the children come from Basingstoke, Reading, Newbury, and then his secretary stops typing and adds 'Windsor'. Richard nods earnestly, 'Windsor, of course.' He explains that they visit the house, they go around the church, but crucially they wander around the grounds. There are stands run by the gamekeeping team, West Berkshire Archaeologists, a waste company teaches them about recycling, the building team talk to them about roofing, and the carpenters 'teach them how to make bird boxes'. His secretary stops typing again and looks up, 'And the bats and bees.' Richard nods. 'Of course. This place has just been full of the noise of children.'

His phone, which he has placed on the footstool in front of him, rings and he turns it over. He tells me that when he was at Defra he learned that one in four children who live in Plymouth has never been to the sea. 'I want them to have a nice day out from the classroom here.' The conversation, at this point, feels a little strange – Richard has that public school, military togetherness about him but it feels as though this really matters, like on some level just below the surface of us chatting, there is real emotion there. 'I want young people to understand', he continues, 'that the countryside doesn't just happen, that there are skilled people who make it happen.' He wants them to understand too about where food comes from. The cost of having them, he tells me when I ask, is 'big' but he adds that 'we now have parents and teachers coming who came here as kids'.

He turns his phone around to look at it briefly, then puts it back face down. Before I arrived, he was having breakfast with the guy who runs his farm shop but I don't get the impression he's got to rush off. I want to know whether he thinks that all these people on his doorstep are a burden or a business opportunity or a frustration. He supposes, he says after some thought, that it is 'a responsibility'. His mother and his father, he explains, always wanted to be welcoming. 'My father set about putting large areas of the estate into full free public access, with no income from it.'

Richard concedes that in a way the game has changed; he is very aware that if he set himself against the public his life would be 'a misery'. He is also, he tells me thoughtfully, fully aware that people are going to take a 'pejorative view' of Englefield before they take 'a positive one'. All the polo that goes on out the front does, he says, look 'a bit elitist' but at the same time anybody local with a horse can hack around the park for a year for the price of a new set of horseshoes.

Surely the editorial team at Bloomsbury do their homework when an author puts the boot into somebody in a book that they reportedly paid a £45,000 advance for, a book that promises to inspire a mass movement.

As we head down the stairs, overhung by a large Grecian tapestry, Richard tells me that he recently discovered that there's a man who lives in his woods. 'You should speak to him.' Richard says he's a stonemason and he's a friend of 'that guy Nick Hayes' who wrote the book but he apparently seems to believe Nick's quite wrong about Englefield. I ask him if it's legal to camp in the woods at Englefield and Richard shrugs: 'Probably not', then he goes on to say, as we head out into the courtyard, that he'd hate for anybody reading my book to think that he wakes up in the morning worrying about anybody like that stonemason making their bed on his land. Who he worries about, he says, 'are young families in Mortimer or Reading'.

We stop in front of a very modern glass-fronted extension. 'What, as in you want them to know they can come here?' I ask. 'Yes', he replies, 'I'm worried about them. I want them to know.'

*

For a campaign that is pretty vocal about minority groups in rural Britain, and the way they are perceived, Right to Roam, as a collective, seems curiously sure that landowners and farmers are exclusively male yokels or toffs, Old MacDonald or Mr Darcy. At every meeting I attend, whenever a landowner is imagined for the purposes of a discussion, some sort of role play, or is referenced in a story, they are always squarely male and they generally own vast parts of the country, which are almost always inherited. On Dartmoor, I heard it said twice, completely erroneously that Alexander Darwall inherited every acre he owns. I guess, to some, the only thing worse than people earning lots of money and buying land is people owning it who haven't done much work at all.

It's true that most landowners are men but certainly not all of them, and minorities matter. Jane Heathcote-Drummond-Willoughby owns vast tracts of Lincolnshire as well as two castles; Lisbet Rausing, of the Tetrapak family, has 57,000 acres in the Highlands; and Miranda Rock, the granddaughter of the 6th Marquess of Exeter, runs Burghley House in Lincolnshire. Rock's mother was the custodian of Burghley House before her, which sits among 15,000 acres. These are not rare examples – right across Britain there are female landowners and women who sit on the boards of estate companies.*

The point is it will not always be a man with a triple-barrelled name or a man who can't spell who chases you off the land. It

---

* Those who get hot and bothered about estates seem to think they are owned by one man, but they are often held in trust or are companies with multiple beneficiaries.

might be a woman with a triple-barrelled name, or even a female farmer who lacks the literacy and social wattage of the campaigners who knocked together *Wild Service*.

At 9.30 in the market square in Ripon, it is already 14 degrees and by ten o'clock the local rock choir is standing beneath the Hawksmoor obelisk singing Whitney Houston's 'I Want to Dance with Somebody'. I finish my onion bhajis just as they're getting started on Dolly Parton's 'Jolene', then I drive to Crambeck, on the edge of the Howardian Hills, to see a couple who feel that their lives are being made impossible by trespassers.

Louise Pollard lifts a cigarette to her pink-lipsticked mouth, makes a little kissing noise, then exhales. 'The thing is', she tells me, glancing over the rim of her tortoiseshell sunglasses, 'we aren't from money.' Her husband, Richard, who is sitting at the other end of the patio, in Hawaiian shorts, a black polo shirt with an upturned collar, and a beige bucket hat, is fiddling with his vape. Richard and Louise moved to Crambeck in 1999, and just over 15 years later they borrowed some money from Louise's mother to buy a field that adjoins their garden. Up until that point, many of the people in the village, which is made up of some 60 households, had wandered in the field with little thought about who owned it but as soon as the sale went through, the Pollards stuck fences up and put a couple of sheep on the ground. The move went down badly but then in 2021 when they finally managed to buy a block of woodland next to the field from the Castle Howard Estate – after making, according to Louise, about 50 approaches – things got much worse.

Louise tells me that part of her motivation for buying the 17-acre wood was because she wants to protect it. The footfall, she thinks, was far too high, there was rubbish everywhere, people were chopping down trees for firewood, and the place was covered in dog shit. We finish our coffee and walk round to the front of the house where the Pollards' white golf buggy is parked up out of the sun. Louise explains, as we pass through large electric gates, that at points in her life, she's had almost nothing and what she really wants to do is leave something behind. She wants to feel that a well-managed patch of woodland in North Yorkshire is her legacy.

The grass in the meadow comes halfway up the buggy's wheels and Richard tells me that as soon as his sheep are clipped, they'll be out grazing. It's not easy though, he admits, to find somebody who will actually come and do the work when you've only got two. He parks the buggy at the top of the field in the shade of a large sycamore and we climb out. Beneath us, on the other side of a barbed wire fence, there are 120 caravans, with black plastic roofs. We walk down the margin towards the wood where a large barricade has been fixed across an old entrance. As Richard and Louise see it, they were fighting a war on two fronts. They had hundreds of caravanners – mostly 'from West Yorkshire', Louise tells me – who were spilling out into the woods on one side and then on the other they had everybody from the village.

The owner of the caravan park was reportedly relatively understanding when Richard and Louise said they were going to shut his customers out but the people in the village rallied against them and they are now no longer on speaking terms with dozens of their neighbours. One of their great misfortunes, as they see it anyway, is that Amy-Jane Beer, one of the organisers of the national Right to Roam campaign lives in a house at the bottom of the village.

Louise tells me, almost mystically, that it's really just such a weird coincidence that she ended up owning a wood in the same village that Amy-Jane lives in. Almost every time Louise says her name she follows it up with something about Amy-Jane's pink hair before saying, 'Get out my face, Amy', whereupon Richard glances at her and shakes his head in frustration. It has all become very bitter and deeply personal. Louise is keen to show me footage of Amy-Jane's husband wandering through their wood. Louise, in the clip, comes across as mildly hysterical but there's a sense too that he is enjoying the whole thing.

For two years now Richard and Louise have wanted to start felling some of the trees in their wood but due to ongoing issues with trespassing they haven't been able to start. 'I'd love that', Louise replies when I suggest they could get horses in to pull the timber out (Louise works as a racing photographer) but until the conflict over public access to the area is resolved, they tell me that there's nothing they can do. It wouldn't be safe for them to have machinery in there while people are still wandering. It's important to note that at both Burghley and Englefield, they close the woods while they are carrying out forestry work.

Louise and Richard want to show me where a path, previously worn away by countless feet, is 'rewilding' because of the recent exclusion. 'It's amazing', Richard says, in seemingly heartfelt wonder, looking down at the dock leaves and the wild garlic. 'It's just all coming back.' As we start to head round towards the house, Richard tells me that when they first put fences up, the words 'Land is not ownership, land is love', were scrawled in chalk and hexes were hung in the trees. It doesn't, Louise admits, make much sense, but they suspect that some of the locals are keen on a sort of pseudo witchcraft.

Every Sunday, Richard orders a roast from the local pub and we drive to pick it up in his Land Rover Defender. He was always, he says, as we turn out onto the main road, with a plastic model of the late Queen bobbing on the dashboard, a Discovery man but then they brought out the new Defender and that all changed. The diesel, he admits, isn't particularly fast but he loves the hybrid. The Pollards have one of each.

We turn left, across the Derwent, and Richard tells me it's strange in a way because when he was growing up in Oldham during the Thatcher years, it was all about owning your own house and getting on. Now, though, that he's actually got on – through building power plants – and has bought a bit of land, it's as though people around him reckon he's done something disgraceful, but he wonders if they are actually representative of the nation or if they just shout the loudest. If Labour does carry on with the Right to Roam, he suspects it would be political suicide.

As we sit at the bar, waiting for the paper boxes to come with our lunches in them, Richard suggests that maybe they ought to say that large estates, places like Castle Howard, whom they bought the wood from, should make 20 per cent of their land accessible but he supposes it would have an impact on wildlife, although quite what sort of impact, he isn't sure. I offer to buy him a half pint while we wait and he looks at the taps but then he shakes his head and says that if we start, we'll be drinking till Wednesday.

When we get back, Louise has laid the table and has placed a mat over every glass in case of flies. While we eat, Richard tells me about the man next door who invited him over when word got out that they'd bought the woodland. 'Religious', he says, 'very religious.' The man asked Richard, when he'd summoned him, what his intentions were for the wood. Richard puts his cutlery down, looks at me, swallows, then says 'It's none of his business, though, is it?' Richard apparently had to tell him to stop raising his voice. The man wanted to remind him that they lived in the biggest two houses in the village, which comes with responsibilities. At the close of the meeting, the neighbour apparently told Richard he was going to pray for him. Richard tells me he didn't really feel he could leave but nor did he just want to sit there so he stood while the man prayed.

Louise, when she's done, lights a cigarette and turns to face me. What upsets her the most, she explains, about Amy-Jane is that she's forced her to become conservative. She was never like that in her younger days, and certainly not when she was at art school, but she is feeling more and more that we've got to stand up for tradition and laws and boundaries. Because, she explains, if we just let people go wherever they like, where does it end? We'll raise a generation, she thinks, who'll want the cars off our drives as well as wanting to access our land. She finishes her cigarette, then goes to see about some ice cream.

Richard takes me out through the garden past the stables and stops to tell me that during Covid, it seemed like half the village would stop by the end of their garden to go for a pee when they walked past or would stand there 'rubbernecking'. A little way up the track, there are a couple of hundred hedge whips that haven't long gone in. He crouches down to push a couple of them back into the ground and tells me proudly that there are about six different kinds of hedging plant in there and that it didn't take him long at all. We carry on down the path and Richard explains that when they bought the wood, 'all this propaganda' was spread through the village about how they were going to keep everyone out of the wood and that they were going to make a narrow path. He spreads his arms out then tells me they had no intention of making it narrow. 'It was just all bullshit.'

The fence posts along the path have been covered in black anti-vandal paint and there are 'No trespassing' signs every fifty metres or so, as well as warnings that you are filmed. Richard looks up at them self-consciously then says that he thinks they've maybe gone a bit over the top but they are currently relying on the Definitive Map officers to come up with a new official record of Rights of Way for the wood and the officers are very interested in the history of signage. We wander on and then we stop where somebody has run their finger across the vandal paint before writing on one of the posts. The words are faint and it takes me some time to make them out: 'Wanker Dickes'. I turn to Richard. 'Is that you. You're the Wanker Dicke?' He looks at it for a moment, sadly, then nods and tells me it's a very West Yorkshire phrase. 'But probably not Amy-Jane's work', I reply. 'No', he says, 'probably not.'

On the way back up the path I stop beside a big oak and ask him if he'd mind much if a child climbed it? He looks up at the tree and then tells me he wouldn't, not if they didn't break it. We walk for a while in silence and then just as we turn back into the garden Richard says to me that the thing is, it's not like the Castle Howard estate. He knows almost every tree. The wood, to him, is almost like a garden.

We eat our ice cream and Louise talks about Amy-Jane. The problem, as she sees it, is that Amy-Jane is just so credible. Everybody knows, Louise thinks, that she writes for the *Guardian* and she advises people. Just as I finish, Louise goes and gets two articles that she herself has written. She's thinking about sending them to the *Guardian*, in the hope that they might print them and then people could see things from her perspective. Amy-Jane, she tells me, has written loads on trespassing. She's even encouraged people to do it but what, Louise wants to know, what about us?

Just before three o'clock I drive south. The traffic is light and two hours later I'm at Grantham North services, pulled up at the petrol station, drinking watery coffee and reading Louise's dispatches. They are good in parts, surreal in others, and at points, very vivid. In 2020, she writes, before they bought the wood, bags of 'dog shit' hung from the branches of her beloved trees. They were 'like ball sacks, like male scrotums'.

*

About ten months later, I am sitting beside a fire on the edge of the Thames with almost all of the Right to Roam campaign organisers. Jon Moses is there, Nadia Shaikh, and Paul Powlesland. We jumped the gate at the top of the stairs and set up camp on the sand. It is cold for late April and the lights on the side of Waterloo Bridge cast the rising river in purple and green. Between Daniel Grimston reading a poem about buried bodies and herring gulls and a Scottish folk singer singing an eerie and beautiful song, I ask Amy-Jane, who is sitting on the other side of the fire to me, about the Pollards. Feelings are clearly mutual and complicated. Louise, she tells me, is miserable and a sociophobe.

The Pollards, it's fair to say, do not wear landownership lightly. And yet, for all that I feel sorry for little children in Crambeck who can't climb the fence in the wood without returning home covered in vandal paint, the situation is tricky. Since the sixteenth century, when the Duke of Norfolk's fourth son, Lord William Howard, married his stepsister, the little wood was owned by an immensely wealthy family who probably knew almost nothing about it at all. I've met landowners, even self-styled progressive ones, who've told me, off the record, that there are parts of their estates they've never been to. I've walked with people who admit, quite merrily, that really they have no idea where their place ends and the estate next door begins. Meanwhile, Richard is there in Crambeck, puffing away on his vape, while thinking about every tree in that wood. Many would tell you that no man has the right to own a wood, but if a man must own a wood, isn't it better that he knows all the trees and loves them? Louise's favourite tree, she told me, is one she's christened 'Jack the Green Man', an apparently all-seeing and previously-neglected sycamore.

In Guy Shrubsole's 2019 bestseller, *Who Owns England?*, he trots out that line about a few thousand dukes, baronets, and country squires owning more acres than all of middle England lumped together. It's an arresting thought but what about those who own England's 'micro-estates', as Richard put it grandly. Will nobody spare a thought for middle England done well? A couple of months after going to Yorkshire to see the Pollards, I met one of Shrubsole's hated few thousand at a party. 'The thing is', he told me, noting that Alexander Darwall has got it 'very wrong indeed', landowners are never going to beat the public, 'you really ought to look on them as an opportunity'. The point he was making is that car parks, cafés, and shops selling artisanal ham and cheese can be lucrative but that's not much good if you've only got twenty or thirty acres. As we stood chatting, I was reminded of Richard's passing comment, while we waited for our Sunday roast. Maybe the onus should be on the few thousand to do their bit, while small-scale land-owners might be permitted to create sanctuaries for wildlife. Certainly there are woods in sparsely populated areas where a bit of footfall causes no issues but in Crambeck, hemmed in on one side by the caravan park and by the village on the other, it's inevitable that the wood and the wildlife that lives in it would suffer without those fences. By Louise's own admission, before she owned the land, she too used to let her dog shit there without picking it up. 'We all did', she told me, sucking thoughtfully on a Marlboro Light, 'but we didn't know any better.'

There are people, again people who fit squarely into Shrubsole's few thousand, who have gardens and grounds that are much bigger than Louise's beloved wood. A landowner told me recently that what he wants to know 'is how far this Right to Roam lot will take it?' His concern was that he charges people to visit his parkland, the proceeds of which pay for the gardener. He supposed, he continued, in what felt like an effort to calm himself down, that even if some sort of Right to Roam does come in, his parkland would probably be considered 'curtilage', meaning it might be exempt from any access designations, as is the case in Scotland. Thank goodness, I thought, that lawn won't mow itself. But is it right that the very wealthy get to turnstile their Capability Brown-designed expanses while somebody with a woodland half the size must throw it open? I'm sure there are lots of people who, on paper, would welcome the idea of the hardworking middle classes buying land from aristocrats, from that 'few thousand' and protecting it but now, Louise feels that she has become 'the enemy'.

Whether we like it or not, it generally seems to be the case that the bigger the estate, the better the public access. Holkham, for example, is surrounded by much smaller estates where the access is nowhere near as good. Put simply, you probably wouldn't want a family picnicking on your croft but there's almost certainly room for them on 10,000 acres and all the better if they buy a few sausage rolls at that expensive farm shop or a couple of pints of the estate's raw milk.

Across the Irish Sea, large landowners, on both sides of the border, have generally been done away with. Aristocrats (many of whom were installed as the result of policies devised by Lord Burghley, Miranda Rock's forebear, in the sixteenth century) were dispossessed and their holdings were broken up. In other words, the public beat 'em, but now what? There is essentially no guaranteed public access there. Farmers and their families have often been involved in violent conflicts to secure what they've got and it now seems as though they aren't willing to give an inch. Ownership and control is about possession in the aftermath of the plantations and it has a very real bearing on recreational access.

There is also a useful comparison to be made across the sea, when it comes to the size of land holdings, in the wake of redistribution. For a 2017 study titled 'The trouble with accessing the countryside in Northern Ireland: A comparison with Great Britain', Dr Linda Price interviewed several owners of 'smaller holdings' who suggested that because they only have modest acreages, access is potentially a greater problem. 'In GB', one landowning interviewee told her, 'you sometimes have thousands of acres – whereas in the Mournes (a mountain range in County Down) it is only fifteen hectares.' Accordingly, footpaths would remove a larger area, proportionally, from agricultural production and any damage would be felt more greatly.

It is notable too that none of the acts of parliament that have created greater access in Britain, such as the Countryside and Rights of Way (CROW) Act 2000, have applied in Northern Ireland – in short, no rambling after radical redistribution.

There is a degree to which access and ownership in England and Wales have been separated. You can't, for example, keep people off an upland estate because it's likely that it would constitute access land. You can't keep people off public rights of way that run through your meadows either and if your farm runs down to the beach, there will be dog walkers. Clearly ownership has a bearing on some types of access but to entirely conflate the two issues seems like a deliberate attempt to toxify a situation that needs, urgently, to be detoxified if it is to be made better. It isn't easy to persuade landowners to create more space for forest schools or to give over land for village allotments if people are being bussed in to shout at them.

*

It took me a couple of days to track down Andrew Hood and when I drove to his studio, at the back of an old farmyard, it was unseasonably cold. He was standing there, barefoot, out of the rain, in shorts bleached by the sun. If sedentary indoor lives make us fat and torpid, Andrew's life, a life lived among the trees, seems to have made him become more animal. He is wiry and strong and he looks years younger than he is.

In the corner of the workshop, down on the ground, opposite a plastic jug full of disposable razors, there is a large stone bust of a Reading tramp, with big ears and a tattered pork pie hat. There was a festival, Andrew explained, celebrating Reading and he was thinking about all of the people whom the town is associated with, people like Kate Winslet and Mike Oldfield but you never actually see them. He wanted to make some work for the festival that celebrates Reading as it is. 'So that', he said, as we stood looking down at it, 'was my contribution.'

It's been about eight or nine years since Andrew started sleeping in the woods each night. He had a flat for some time and he rented a studio on the Englefield Estate but when his marriage broke up he realised he could only pay the rent on one of them. The choice seemed to him to be pretty obvious and he's been on a sort of ceaseless wander ever since. Every night when he was at Englefield – before recently moving to the Hardwick Estate on the other side of the Thames – he'd lock up, take a tarpaulin sheet with him, and he'd just go. If it's raining, he looks for somewhere sheltered; if the land is flooded, he tries to find somewhere elevated; if there's a gale he avoids wooded areas because of the possibility of trees falling on him, and he always likes to be upwind of any motorways. His movements around Berkshire are dictated by the noise of the M4 – if you end up in the wrong place, the constant rumble means you can't sleep.

He showed me some of his work, a sculpture of his mother, painted stags' antlers, and mosaics. Then we went through to his office where he makes bird boxes, devises squirrel traps, and weaves rope from nettle fibres. He has, he believes, become more human in some way because of the way he lives his life and it feels true. He has nothing, by his own admission, but sleeping in the woods has made him hear better and listen out for other creatures. He has, he thinks, won things back that most of the human species lost, through lack of use, long ago. It is something that we should want for everybody, particularly for young people. Being able to sleep out is something that landowners should facilitate.

The whole thing obviously began out of necessity, Andrew explained, as he made me a cup of instant coffee, 'no milk I'm afraid', but in time the ritual of locking up and heading out became 'sacred'. Every night was a different act of trespass and every morning he awoke, not looking at 'a plastered ceiling', but at the grass or at the tree canopy above him.

In all the time he's been living his vagrant life, Andrew has only been caught three times, twice on the Englefield Estate, and in both instances, he was found by gamekeepers as he was getting up in the morning. The trouble is, he told me cheerfully, surrounded by bowls of conkers and squirrel pelts, is that he quite likes to sleep in until 9 a.m. most mornings when the whole world is already 'up and at 'em' – there really is, he thinks, very little chance of getting caught on your way in or during the night. He never cooks or uses a torch but the risk comes when you're packing up. It was never, he thinks, a hostile, 'this is private [. . .] staring down the barrel of a gun' sort of situation. The first time, the keeper simply told him he should be careful because they are often out shooting at night and the second time round, another keeper hung about for 45 minutes discussing all sorts.

Andrew's relationship with private land on large estates in the Home Counties is pretty illuminating. Rural Berkshire is his bed and he thinks the benefits of engaging with the countryside are so immense and numinous that they are almost impossible to understand. He believes we are meant to sleep on the floor and we are meant to forage and to hunt but he doesn't think that the land should be thrown open. 'To allow everyone unfettered access to the countryside', would be, he reckons, 'a dangerous thing'. From his own experience he recognises that what little remains of the natural world is in a precarious and much-diminished state. And – which is really what I want to know – it is also wrong apparently to paint Richard Benyon as a man who has locked his gates to the world. Richard couldn't, he thinks, have done much more to welcome the trespassers from Right to Roam when they came, short of actually making them cups of tea.

On the table, in front of us, were a stack of old diaries, with tattered covers and the paper gone yellow, in which Andrew records every night that he spends sleeping in the woods. He writes about the weather and the creatures he sees. He passed me the one on the top of the stack, then he went to make another cup of coffee. It is strange, he thinks, because for all that he likes trespassing he tries not to sleep in woods where the public are actually allowed. It is, he said jokingly, a little selfish but private woods are often in a much better state and you don't wake up looking at a discarded bag of dog shit.

In the space next door to Andrew there is a project called Path Hill Outdoors, which connects young people who are struggling in mainstream education with the countryside. They skin rabbits, they make fire, and they cook outside, but isn't it a bit sad, Andrew said as he sat down in his office chair and folded his legs, that it's just for badly behaved children and not for every child?

We drank our coffee and talked a little about how he feels. Life for Andrew clearly isn't that easy and yet he sometimes feels, he told me, as though he is the most content person he knows. He's sort of resigned himself to having very little, to making objects he wants to make, and every night he goes back to the trees. All he really seemed to want, it emerged when we talked, is to design a better squirrel trap. His current model has not been all that successful.

When we were done, we walked back through the studio, and stood beneath a tarpaulin next to a table of chisels, and we looked out at the rain which was coming down on the fields. I asked him, just before I went, where he was going to sleep that night and he turned to look up at the grey sky. 'It depends on the weather', he replied, 'where I sleep depends on the weather.'

*

It is such a seductive idea that aristocratic landowners are determined to keep the masses out, but in all the time I spent researching this book, I couldn't find one person on the ground, with the exception of those at protests, who really believed it. There are two obvious points though. My great-grandfather worked as a civil servant, his son worked in advertising, and my father worked in mining. I suspect I'd be no good in the civil service. I'm not really sure if I'd be useful in advertising, and my father, unlike me, is a heavyweight on Microsoft Excel. If my great-grandfather had been a landowner, it's possible I would be a landowner. There's every chance I'd be a good one but there's also every chance I could be a totally shit one and therein lies an issue. Just because somebody's dad was a good lion trainer, it doesn't mean they are going to be able to get a lion to stand on its hind legs and roar too. Five generations on, a once capable lion-training family may have lost any sort of ability with big cats at all.

It might upset some people to hear it, but there are plenty of examples of landowners who do a very good job. Yet at the same time, if every landowner had to reapply for their job and the role was opened to all comers, there are probably very few of them who would regain their role. Across the country there are landowners who don't know what they own and have no interest in property, rural enterprise, or farming. Always off the record, for obvious reasons, land agents will tell you all sorts of stories about some of the bosses they've had and their wild ineptitude. The trouble usually comes, Richard Benyon told me, when people end up taking on an estate after a career of doing something completely different or after a lengthy period of doing very little at all. Richard Benyon worked as a land agent and ran a farm (not all that well, he reckons) – but he's undeniably done the groundwork.

Some people will say, what's the problem? If your great-grandad was a drain-cover magnate and you're now squandering that once-buoyant business, then so what. The issue though is that we are all stakeholders when it comes to land and its resources. We all eat, breathe, and drink. Andrew's life is a testament to the tremendous power that the land can have on us psychologically too. If only landowners understood that, he told me, they would probably provide more opportunities for engagement. Except, of course, for 'the ones who don't care'.

Humans and the land are inseparable and landowners have an immense responsibility, and as obviously happens at Englefield, that responsibility needs to extend to connecting people with nature in its fullest sense. 'The trouble with the public', I've heard landowners and farmers say a thousand times in various different ways, 'is that they don't understand the countryside', to which the answer must be 'Yes, you're probably right but what are you doing, as somebody who really can make a difference, to change that?'

One afternoon, in Lincolnshire, after I'd been wandering across the Burghley Estate, asking people what they made of the access (the answers were resoundingly positive), I visited the Bull and Swan in Stamford. On the wall there was a letter dated March, 1908, which had been sent to the then Lord Cecil by the pub's landlord. 'My Lord', the letter ran, 'may I take the pleasure of fishing in your lake [. . .] I should most earnestly like the occasion.' There was no response beneath it and the barmaid told me she didn't know if Cecil had ever replied. But the letter illustrated a fundamental point. Because of their assets, landowners can give people (be they pub landlords or local schoolchildren) the opportunity to do things like fish, make fires, and collect mushrooms. That need is greater today than ever. The ancestors of little children in Stamford dug that lake over the course of three years. Surely that gives them a claim to cast a worm for the pike that now swim in it?

*

Over the weeks that followed the publication of Right to Roam's *Wild Service*, it got fairly limited coverage. There was a fawning piece in the *Guardian* and Richard Smyth took a swipe at the sentimentality of the whole thing in Engelsberg Ideas but nobody seemed to pick up on the errors in the prologue. It might be outrageous that Richard Benyon is as rich as he is, it might make you sick that he inherited a large bit of Hackney, but the truth matters when you're trying to make things better. Facts before facepaint.

It was a late August morning when I cycled across the Thames with my own copy of *Wild Service* to go to the Bloomsbury offices. It must have been 10 a.m. when I arrived and I stood for a moment on the steps outside that smart blue door in Bedford Square. The leaves on the plane trees were starting to turn and a man with an oily mess of black hair, was lying on a bench with his bare feet sticking out beneath a blanket. The door was locked but a lady answered almost as soon as I rang the bell. I told her what it was, that there was a book they'd published with a prologue full of pretty egregious errors. Obviously, I continued, we should try to get these things right because they do matter. She sounded quite sympathetic but told me there was no way I could come in. The editorial team doesn't just make time for people wandering by. 'So no access?' I asked. 'No access', she replied. A bin lorry passed by and I crossed the road. There were parakeets screeching in the trees and the man on the bench nodded at me as though to say good morning.

For weeks, I didn't hear back from Bloomsbury and then just before I went to press with this book they sent me a smiley face emoji and a note to say that the editors can't get back to every query. Then, some days later, a junior editor got in touch. She had, apparently, discussed my queries with the authors who knew nothing about the 'Community Woodland'. My follow up email offering to take any of the editorial staff down there to show them the extent of the access went unanswered, so as far as I know they have every intention of publishing the same mistruths when the paperback comes out in spring :(

*

I learned just before this book went to press that Andrew Hood died very unexpectedly. He was a fascinating man and we stayed in touch after I went to see him. We were talking about turning his 'Night Diaries' into a book of some sort. It would have been something about the effects of sleeping out in the woods and how all of those nights had made him more human.

4

Conservation

What access means for nature and how it can be managed

We are in Dominic Buscall's sister's hatchback heading west towards the sea. Since leaving Eton, a little over a decade ago, Dom has been working things out. 'I was obsessed', he tells me, 'just waking up every day on my gap year and thinking, well, I own five guns.' Dom did it all – he shot ducks, he shot pigeons, and during his teenage years, the other landowning kids in Norfolk reckoned he was the best pheasant killer in the county. It wasn't that he woke up one day and suddenly thought the whole thing was absurd. It was more, he says, running his hands through a mess of blonde hair, a gradual thing. 'The truth is that when I met Shah, I just got a totally different perspective. That's quite helpful, just meeting someone from another world and they're like what is this shooting thing?' As he speaks, his own sense of certainty seems to come and go, and then forty yards down the track, a French partridge runs across the mud in front of the car and disappears into the grass. 'A survivor', Dom says dismissively, 'or it'll have come in from elsewhere. I just think eighty per cent of shooting is fucked up and I mean when I see a pheasant now, the thought always crosses my mind that there's a strong case to just try and eradicate them.' Dom thinks

110

that in many ways, landowners trying to keep the public off their ground is a hangover from the golden era of wild bird shoots. Places like Ken Hill, he explains, were, along with lots of other Norfolk estates, 'keepered up to the nines', and footfall posed a genuine risk to ground-nesting grey partridges but now that most game birds are simply reared in captivity and released, Dom can't see that the public pose the same threat. 'It's a legacy thing', he shrugs.

The March fields ahead of us are sodden and the big eastern sky is a wash of grey. Dom's family has been on the Ken Hill estate, in West Norfolk, which is currently a sniff under four thousand acres, since the 1870s. 'Some dude invented something called an economiser', he tells me, 'which sits in an engine. They were industrialists.'* But the 1870s, he adds, in the context of English land ownership, isn't all that long ago. A truck pulls past us with a girl in the passenger seat. That's Hetty, Dom nods, she's the conservation manager, 'she's learning to stalk deer'. The track we're driving down was once a railway line and in 1962, just seven years before it was closed, John Betjeman, later the Poet Laureate, took a trip from King's Lynn to Hunstanton, which became a film about the wonder of branch lines.

We pull up by an old concrete platelayers' hut, with smashed windows and mossy walls. Jessie, my new spaniel puppy, who has been sleeping at my feet, jumps out and runs round and round in circles, with her nose to the ground, picking up cow dung. 'It's all organic', Dom says, as I fail to call her back to me. Further inland, five figures are standing beneath the trees, looking at something at the far end of the field in front of us. 'That makes me very happy', Dom says, as he watches them through his binoculars. 'There are five piglets rooting there and

---

* In 1845 Sir Edward Green, the son of a Yorkshire ironmaster and an ancestor of Dom Buscall's, patented the 'economiser', which recycled heat from boilers and consequently reduced fuel consumption.

they're taking photos.' The piglets are part of Dom's conservation strategy. When they root around they unearth seeds that are trapped in the soils, which creates a diversity of sward, and he tells me that people seeing the pigs in action is a great thing. 'They might see those piglets and work out what it's all about or they might go home and read up on it.'

We walk to the door of the hut and Dom tells me that from a pretty young age, he realised that owning a slice of Norfolk was a tremendous responsibility but that it took him some time to come to an understanding of how to meet that responsibility. 'The vast majority of us are like, hugely privileged, like unfairly privileged and I think that you have a responsibility to provide spaces where people can get onto the land.' Over the past ten years, Dom tells me that he has come to see that what he has is the ability to connect people with the countryside and to give them an understanding of 'climate change and nature loss as being existential threats to humanity and society'. Access, he believes, leads to understanding – it causes people to reflect and to realise 'there's a need for less degradation'. The floor of the hut in front of us is covered in beer cans, sun-bleached agricultural rubbish from Ken Hill's past, and spent shotgun cartridges. Dom is waiting for a structural survey to be carried out in the hope he can turn the platelayers' hut into accommodation. For the past three years, he's been working on a plan to turn Ken Hill into a busy ecotourism business.

Dom often comes across young landowners who are still, as he puts it, drinking the Kool-Aid but Ken Hill, he thinks, is proof that there are better ways to make money than just looking at every field and thinking it should be turned into a golden expanse of wheat. Already, because of environmental grants, Dom tells me they're making more money than they did when they farmed conventionally and with their plans for ecotourism chugging through countless sluice gates of bureaucracy in the right direction, it looks like they're going to carry on making money, and then Dom continues, 'We'll probably make even more money than that.' They have put in for 70 pitches a night, he explains, but they'll take as many as the planners will allow. A year on, the Ken Hill website is full of details about wildlife tours you can go on. £37 for 'the wildlife watching tour', same again to see the beavers, and £250 for the one-day regenerative farming workshop.

In principle, an Etonian with countless acres fencing in some beavers and charging people to have a look isn't very Right to Roam but we should surely applaud landowners who take fields out of intensive agricultural production to give them over to nature and promote the appreciation of it? It would be sensible to suggest that monetising tent pitches and charging people to learn about wildlife is a positive alternative to ploughing everything up. But what's the difference then between what Dom's doing and what Alexander Darwall suggested doing? Both men would like to charge people to camp and Dom, for his 'glamping' proposition anyway, would, I suspect, like to charge more. Admittedly, Dom's vision comes from a more positive place and Darwall is hopeless at PR but the difference isn't as big as people might like to pretend.

We get back into the car and Jessie crawls beneath my seat. The amount of work they're going to have to do, Dom admits, to make sure that all those people don't go off and shit on the beach is massive but he thinks that through engaging, it's all possible. He does, he tells me very slowly as though he's trying to work out exactly how the words will land, have a problem with people being able to wild camp wherever they like but in creating designated zones you can actually control the situation and divert people away from sensitive areas.

The hedges on either side of us, bramble and thorn, rise up to three times the height of the car and specks of rain are blown across the windshield. A small group of woodpigeons drift over the track ahead of us then settle further up in an oak. Dom, when we pass a gap in the hedge, tells me that the field to our right was sugar beet until four years ago and then they stopped farming it and put Exmoor ponies down to graze instead. 'We went from something like just eight species of plant in 2019 to 48 in 2022. Grazing it just completely transformed the sward.'

The Snettisham Caravan Park clubhouse is closed for the season and large sandy-coloured rabbits, grazing among the statics, watch us as we drive past. Dom thinks the idea that people and conservation aren't compatible is just 'fucking stupid'. The very notion of conservation, he believes, is a human concept that we apply to our role in the environment. 'Maybe true, utter wilderness and people . . .' – he turns right into the car park before he finishes the sentence, and then picks up elsewhere by telling me that he doesn't see why we should be afraid of making money from tourism and putting it back into the landscape. I later learn that the land the caravan park sits on was once part of the Ken Hill estate but they sold it. It's a lovely idea that those who wrestle patches of land away from the rich might do something special with them for nature, and sometimes they do but Ken Hill is a good example of a wealthy landowner being able to afford to think differently. The caravan park, beyond the rabbits and a single magpie, is lifeless.

We park up by two bird wrecks, white breast bones coming up among the black feathers, and then we walk along the dunes. Jessie bumps along at Dom's feet before realising she's got the wrong person and slips back, looking quite ashamed, to trot beside me. Dom doesn't think there's anything particularly wrong with private land ownership in theory, but, pulling his hat down against the wind, and raising his voice, he tells me there is an issue he believes with 'highly concentrated ownership. It's not necessarily a problem that ninety-two per cent of the UK is privately owned but I think it is a problem that within that ninety-two per cent, a very small number of people and organisations own vast amounts.'* He shrugs and says that if you think about it, it is sort of totally nuts – people's access to the local countryside is basically 'dictated by whether some guy is a twat or not – just the whims of one man'.

On our left, out over the mud, a group of sanderlings are flying low in the thin winter light. Last summer, behind the dunes, there was a great fire and Dom tells me they won't ever know what caused it. It could have been a cigarette, a disposable barbecue, or just a piece of glass magnifying the heat of the mid-summer sun, but in just a few hours it ripped through 80 acres. The blaze killed reptiles and amphibians, late-nesting birds, and destroyed three turtledove habitats, a species which is almost extinct in Britain. 'Cooked', Dom says, passing me a burnt sloeberry from a charred blackthorn bush, 'and those turtledove habitats won't come back.' I squeeze the berry between my fingers and it collapses onto my palm. It was the third fire in four years and Dom suggests it's probably not a coincidence that it's the only part of the farm with permissive access. Most of those who use the path that runs behind the dunes are dog walkers and as we carry on along it, Dom says he guesses that 'the Darwall reaction would just be to fence it and say shit luck mate. Fuck off.' But he doesn't think that in reality that would actually solve the problem. Instead it would just move the problem somewhere else. The dog walkers will always walk their dogs and the only way is to engage. 'It's not like all the people who go to Dartmoor are just going to stop camping. It's not very collaborative.'

In a clearing, a man in a hi-vis jacket stands talking on the phone. He ends the call as we approach and puts it in his pocket. 'How you doing, Bob', Dom says cheerily. The man smiles and then points back towards the car park. 'We got a

---

* It's not very clear where Dom takes this number from – I assume this is his own take on the Right to Roam campaign's magic 8 per cent figure.

truck keeps coming in the car park and I tell him to get out and he goes up the other way. Same truck was around when they had that diesel stolen.' The man shakes his head, then says he knows they're dodgy but there's nothing much can be done. Dom listens patiently, nodding along, but says very little about it. 'But anyway', the man says, changing the subject. 'You're going to do some speaking at the village council meeting, is that right?' The man speaks to Dom partly with deference and partly as though he's a little boy. Dom nods and says he's very much looking forward to it and then thanks Bob 'for everything'. As we turn right to head back along the sea wall back to the car park, Dom explains that Bob had told him he was fully behind his ecotourism plans and had written a letter of support to the planning committee.

The wind rises and below us, back inland, a group of teal are strung out across the sky. There is still some wildfowling that happens on the other end of the marsh, Dom says to me, as we stand watching the birds with the sea to our backs but it will have to go in time. He will have to, he says, as though he doesn't have much choice, 'Wild Ken Hillify' everything. He stoops down and picks up Jessie. 'It's the direction of travel. There'll be a moment when it's no longer acceptable.' For a couple of years now, the BBC have filmed *Springwatch* at Ken Hill and when they come Dom admits that he wrote up 'lines of enquiry. In case they asked about the wildfowling.' The reason he had up his sleeve, he tells me when I ask, was that they 'don't want to exclude people from the countryside'.

At the end of the track a muntjac buck edges out of the burnt scrub, nose down, and walks quite carefree across the grass in front of us. The wind is right in our faces and the creature is totally unaware of our presence. Jessie watches it, her nose in the air. Speaking quietly, so as to not disturb the buck, Dom asks if I'm going to write about health and safety. 'People love reading about health and safety', I reply. He laughs and tells me it might be one of the only justifiable reasons to limit land access. 'What about farm equipment or the need to control muntjac at scale across the UK, which is fundamentally dangerous?' The buck stops, looks round at us with its black eyes, then bounds away into the undergrowth, its white tail held high in alarm.

Dom is popular with the land access campaign. He seems to fit their conception of what a landowner ought to look like: nature-focused, softly radical, and slightly uncomfortable about being set to inherit thousands of acres. But, for all that, Ken Hill is hardly a free-for-all that's been wrestled from the hands of 'the elites' to be enjoyed by the public, whenever they fancy it. Like Knepp, it is an ecotourism business pitched at the well-heeled. For the cost of one of Dom's regenerative farming one-day workshops, which comes in at £250, I could join Heacham Wildfowlers (with a current membership rate of £100 for the first season and £70 thereafter) for over three seasons. Who knows. Perhaps that would take me right up to the end of their time on the marsh at Ken Hill.* It is challenging to justify a well-heeled ecotourism business muscling out local generally working-class men, many of whom are in their twilight years.

But for all that, and for all that Ken Hill wouldn't work as a business if a robust Right to Roam act was passed, Dom does something that a lot of landowners don't do, in that he works hard to connect people with nature and to give them a greater understanding of the landscape around them.

At any get-together of British landowners, the sort of people whom Dom would describe as having drunk the Kool-Aid, from an Atlantic Salmon Trust lunch to the Suffolk Show, you'll

---

* While fowlers around Britain can generally go out on the marsh itself, which is owned by the Crown, their access to it is limited by landowners. (See chapter 5: 'Water'.)

meet people who'll tell you that the public don't know anything about conservation and the fragility of wildlife. They're right, but Dom is using his privilege to change that. It seems right to suggest that what really matters is the quality and richness of the experience rather than being able to wander where you like and Dom is creating those experiences. I just hope that he can extend them to those who aren't able to pay, and perhaps the wildfowlers might also get a reprieve. After all, it was Dom himself who said that the trouble with land ownership in Britain is that the whims of one person, or perhaps the journey they've been on, dictates how everybody in the locality gets to interact with that person's slice of the countryside.

On the way out of Snettisham, heading east towards Walsingham, there is a drake mallard lying on the road with its feet tucked up beneath it. The duck must have been clipped by a car and the tarmac around it is covered in blood and feathers. I stop and get out. But when I'm fifteen yards away it stands and hobbles away up the road towards the grey church, with a wing trailing behind it. The bird stops just before an oak tree and then tumbles into the ditch where it's carried away by the stream.

That evening, I'm meant to be calling in to the weekly meeting of the Birmingham Socialist Workers' Party. They are discussing the Right to Roam and the need for working-class action but I get waylaid talking to a local landowner. When she was little, she tells me, as we sit eating pasta in the same house she's always lived in, little boys would come every Sunday to fish. They would knock on the big door with their rods and write their name in the book, then a farm worker would take them up the river to catch trout, but they don't come anymore. 'Not sure what they do now', she says, 'probably stay in their rooms playing on their computers.'

I make it along, virtually, to the Birmingham Socialist Workers' Party meeting the following week. They are discussing how to plot their way from protest to revolution. There are only about eight people there, and three old men are the only ones who seem to say anything but they are all in agreement that the French do it right. When they want something they go out and take it and until we learn to rise up and do the same, we will remain ground down.

The following morning, after breakfast, I head to Holkham, and on my way out of Walsingham, I pass the charred remains of the village hall. The pantile roof has caved in and a mound of concrete blocks lie on the grass. It had taken many years to fundraise for the hall to be built and it had been the site of countless weddings, birthday parties and village dances.

An old man, who lives across the street, told the local newspaper that he stood in his living room and cried when it went up. Three days after it happened, they arrested a 13-year-old boy on suspicion of arson.

*

Andy Bloomfield, who has been watching a great white egret, cutting low over the grazing marsh out in front of us, puts his binoculars down, looks at me, and laughs. 'How does Dom Buscall know about that then?' I tell him I guess it's just the sort of thing that gets round. 'That was in the late eighties I was doing the wrestling', he replies. 'It was local circuit mostly, but I used to go down to Essex a bit and I went up to Yorkshire.' The egret is hovering in the wind, just above the reeds on the other side of the fence and Andy shakes his head, as though wondering at the passing of time, then lifts his binoculars and turns towards it again.

During the peak of the feather-trade, towards the close of the nineteenth century and the dawn of the twentieth, millions of egrets were hunted for their skins. But the popularity of hats declined and naturalists started to realise that irreparable damage was being done. In recent decades, great white egrets have made a notable recovery in Britain and it's six years since Andy first recorded them nesting on the reserve at Holkham. 'Dom told me they called you the Snake or something.' Andy smiles. 'That's right. There used to be an old landlord at the pub and I used to do a lot of running up and down the road to get fit and he passed me one morning, leant out the car window, and said "you look like a fuck rattlesnake, boy".' Andy tells me he never did ask him why or anything like that but he'd been thinking about a new ring name for a while and he thought it would do nicely.

It was perhaps inevitable that Andy would become the warden on the Holkham Nature Reserve. When he was a boy, his father was a shepherd on the estate and he spent much of his childhood helping him. 'I'd always be out with dad in the lambing yard. My family have been here since the 1700s and I just love this landscape and the wildlife and I'll do as much as I can to protect it. It's in my blood, you know. The soil is in my blood.' Whenever he wasn't helping with the sheep, he'd head out to watch birds, but in the 56 years he's lived on the North Norfolk coast, almost everything has changed. On Sundays, when he was young, in the winter at least, Andy remembers hardly seeing anybody at Lady Anne's Drive, now the main car park for the beach at Holkham. 'We used to go down there and watch snow buntings and geese and grebes and things like that. There'd maybe be the odd wildfowler but they didn't even charge because there'd be no one about. You compare that now with a sunny winter's day.' Currently, 800,000 people park up at Lady Anne's Drive each year. 'But don't forget', Andy adds, 'that's just Lady Anne's Drive. There's Wells and Burnham Overy too.'

It's all part of a great change and Andy reckons hardly a month goes by without one of the Sunday papers running a piece that encourages Londoners to head east. 'Everything's been ripped apart in regards to the local scene. Norfolk once was that sleepy Norfolk and everybody had views of it with fishermen in smocks leaning outside the cottage and all the rest of it, but the reality is that's getting eroded away bit by bit.' When he was a young man, he was bitter and often angry about it but he's older now and at some point along the way he started to realise it's just the way of the world. One of the great issues, Andy thinks, is that houses are continually getting bought up by wealthy people who hardly ever visit and inevitably they decide to start renting them out for short-term lets. There's no doubt, he admits, that they spend money and lots of local people work in tourism but all those visitors head to the beach in droves and managing their impact falls to Andy.

He breaks off and turns to the right. 'Oh look here, look, sand martin.' The little brown-and-white bird, journeying across the field, has only just arrived back from Africa. 'Sand martin', he says it again, as though marking the occasion in his mind, 'first of the year.' A large lady in lycra is walking down the path towards us with her phone in her hand. 'Sand martin', Andy calls down to her, 'first one for me.' She draws level with us, looks out over the fields, then glances back at her phone. 'Now I've never heard of it but this app says I just heard a Cetti's warbler. I'm just a towny with an app, I'm afraid.' Andy nods. 'You might have heard one', he replies. 'They've got a very loud sort of strident call. Sounds a bit tropical.' The lady smiles. 'He was only just down there.' Andy looks down the track towards where she's pointing. 'You would have done', he says in a matter-of-fact sort of way. The lady hoiks her backpack up onto her shoulders and looks towards the marsh. 'Well, good to know it's a thing. I'd never heard of a Cetti's warbler.' She lingers for a moment and tells us briefly about some of the birds in her local park in London with her app, swans mostly, then she continues on her way.

'Nice lady', I say to Andy when she's gone. 'She was', he replies. Andy tells me we could sit out all day and not hear a local accent. But what amazes him even more is that when they're handing out leaflets, a huge number of people seem to be visiting Holkham for the first time. He says it as though it's a kind of almost unbelievable natural phenomenon, a great migration. In a way he thinks it's a great opportunity to educate people but there are just so many of them. He tells me that, without a doubt, the key for the environment is education. He pauses for a moment and looks back towards the marsh where a pair of sand martins have appeared and are crisscrossing down a ditch. But the reality, he adds, is that lots of visitors turn up knowing almost nothing at all and try as they might, it is impossible for staff at Holkham to educate everybody.

We climb into Andy's truck and head up the track, back towards the coast road. 'Thing is', he says, watching the ground in front of us, where the verge drops away steeply, 'there's no point being angry. There's always been change on this coast. People have always come to Norfolk. We might be sticks in the mud but without that change, where would we be in modern times?' A small herd of belted Galloways graze away on our right – the estate was told they would eat the rushes right down but that was ten years ago now and the rushes remain. Andy separates the correct key from the bunch for me and I climb out to open the gate. They are all secured with heavy locks. When I get back in he tells me that you realise as you get older that there are two sorts of people, and it doesn't matter where they've come from really. There are good people and there are arseholes.

Two spoonbills, out beyond the remains of an Iron Age fort, are half hidden in a dark tangle of willow. Andy admits, nodding his head as though he's trying to keep an open mind, that he's never been to anything like a protest for access to the land but he supposes people there 'are gonna turn round and say why should he up there own all this 25,000 acres and why can't I walk where I want to when he can?' He points in the direction of Holkham Hall. It feels as though he's about to make some sort of point but he stops to watch a muntjac running across the open ground to our left. It trots along as though it isn't particularly concerned that we are sitting watching it. Tacitus records that somewhere near the site of the spoonbill colony, the Roman Army defeated a group of Iceni rebels in 47 AD, and it's also thought that the camp was used by the Danes but it's now a place that few people ever go to.

When the deer is gone, Andy tells me it must have been 1982 when he first saw a muntjac at Holkham. 'You got squirrels, Egyptian goose, greylag, Canada goose, Chinese water deer. All quite dominant in this landscape. None of them should be here.' We sit for a moment and he looks back at the birds on their nest then he turns to me and says he guesses those land access guys are going to say why is he allowed to go and look at those spoonbills 'when I can't?' One of the birds in the trees in front of us is tucked up, incubating eggs on the nest. They first started to fly over the site, prospecting it, in 2004 but it was only in 2010 that they first nested successfully. Since then, 495 fledglings have been born, which has created a British population, some three centuries after they were hunted to extinction.

Andy shifts round so he's looking at me. 'This is their space, you see. The spoonbills need this space to exist. We've got all that space,' – he points down towards the beach – 'and we can travel to the other side of the world if we like. Men have even gone to the moon. So why can't we just give nature one little bit of space, when all around nature's getting depleted?' He passes me his binoculars. It takes me a moment to pick the spoonbills out and when I find them, they are high up busily preening their white feathers. To their left, higher still, a cormorant perches on a thin branch, bobbing up and down in the breeze. Andy tells me that the acidity of their guano has started to kill the poplars and the oaks. He thinks, though, that most people don't realise how beautiful they are. 'There's so much more colour on the plumage than people realise, you know what I meant? You got that green, and look at the face, the reds and the oranges and the white on the nape.' I pass Andy's binoculars back to him and he perches them on the dashboard. 'Can you imagine if you had public access here? Cattle egrets, little egrets, grey heron. They all nest round here. And obviously there's no access. You just wouldn't at this stage in the game, you wouldn't if you had people roaming everywhere, you wouldn't have all this stuff.' There's nothing he says that sounds as though it's just come to him – every question, every observation feels like it's the culmination of years of sitting out on the marsh.

He spins the car round and we drive back along Bone's Drift, a track named after Sam Bone, a long-dead gamekeeper. As Andy sees it, it's quite clear really. You do absolutely, he tells me, need places with good access where people can observe nature. 'If people can't see stuff they'll never understand it and then why would they want to protect it?', but you also need places of sanctuary.

As we head down into the trees Andy tells me that when he started at Holkham they used to have trouble with naturists. There were reported incidents of people getting flashed and the whole thing became a pick-up point for men before evolving into a dogging site for both men and women. 'Not', I say to Andy, 'what you necessarily associate the Holkham Estate with.' He shrugs, 'Not really, no. Not really the image that Holkham wanted.' Andy feels the situation was managed well, in fact managing the nudists was part of the job when he started. Some thirty years on, the nudists are only allowed in a designated section of the dunes and Andy tells me it was a long time ago that he almost ran over that naked man in a tractor when he was working on the marsh. 'Said he was looking for the beach and I just said to him you ent going to find it down there.' We slow to a crawl – ahead of us beach-goers in wellies and jeans, most of them with dogs, are spread out across the track, heading down onto the sand. We turn back on ourselves and head east. Heavy grey clouds are blowing in across the sky.

I lean across and shout at Andy to slow down but he's already stopped. The little black poodle that dashed beneath the front wheels of the truck appears again from beneath us and trots back to its owner, who is still crouched with the dog's lead in her hand. She mouths an apology and Andy nods at her. That's the closest he's ever come, he says as we move off again, to running over a dog. The ground on our left has been cordoned off to create space for shore larks to spend the winter and for ringed plovers to breed. You're not, he realises, going to keep everybody out with a bit of baler twine, a few posts, and a sign but he hopes that most reasonable people will assume that the fence is there for a purpose. Not so long ago, Andy saw a lurcher flying over the dunes after a muntjac. As it stood over the creature, killing it in the enclosure, just ahead of us, terns – who had young at the time – descended on the dog and mobbed it. The lady, Andy tells me, didn't appear until about twenty minutes later and it was one of the few occasions that he's actually banned someone from the beach. 'That's it, I said to her, you're getting banned.' In part, he thinks it's negligence, but it's ignorance too – over the years he's stopped to ask countless people to head a different way who were taken aback to hear that there were birds nesting on the ground. Birds, they'd always reckoned, nest in trees.

On Wells beach we drive along the wet sand below the huts, some of which are old and rotten, while others are newly painted in blues and pinks. Most of them are shut up but outside one or two there are people dressed in scarfs and hats, drinking tea out of Thermoses. Ahead of us, there is another cordon, which has been put up to protect seals. In part, it's there so that people keep their dogs out, but it's there in the hope that it will keep people out too. The trouble, Andy thinks, when it comes to the seals is that people think they're for them. 'They got this skewed view of nature. Some of them want to get over the rope and get a selfie with a seal. They think that's just something there to look at. That is the majority of people's view.'

A family, up ahead of us on the beach, with a fat mongrel dog pulling at its lead, are getting ready to go for a swim. As we drive slowly towards them, I ask Andy what the point of nature is, if it's not just there for us to look at. 'Well', he replies, glancing towards a lone seal, which is lolling on its back on the sand, 'he's got as much right there as what we have. That's his natural place and we need to recognise that and respect it.' The family take their clothes off, and leave them in little piles on the beach. 'What we'll do', Andy says as he heads towards them, 'is we'll just ask them a few things.' They tell us, when Andy asks, that they don't to be honest actually really read the signs. They're local, 'come from Fakenham for the day', and they sort of always think that signs are for all the Londoners. Andy asks them if they're aware that the beach is part of Britain's largest private nature reserve, spanning 9,600 acres and running from the sea itself to a long way back inland. 'Not really', one of the ladies, who has tattoos on her shoulders, replies apologetically. She does though, she assures us, know there's something special about a place if it's National Trust. 'Something worth looking after', her friend adds 'but this isn't National Trust.' Andy confirms that it is not.

The fat dog is pulling at its lead and the man holding it, who has said almost nothing at all, suggests they best get on. The group drop their towels and run down into the sea. 'That's a strange one', Andy says, as we drive away. 'That's almost like they're local so they're entitled to go where they want and they're completely unaware it's a nature reserve.'

It's so often said that if only people were able to go and explore the countryside they would appreciate it a lot more. 'How can they care for what we're losing', the narrative runs, 'if they never knew it was there in the first place?' It's a beautiful idea but aside from people being able to wander much more freely than is often suggested, particularly in places like the uplands where they can see the likes of curlew, lapwings and black grouse, I'm not really sure if people truly take notice. Most of Britain's beaches are accessible and all spring long, around the coast, dog walkers and joggers butt up against terns and waders, but most of them don't seem to care all that much. They still let their dogs wander and if you asked them about the extent to which they'd seen terns decline, I suspect most of them wouldn't really have an answer.

There are plenty of landowners I've met who have no idea about rare birds that are present on land their families have owned for centuries. They get to see the wildlife, day in day out, but it doesn't mean they care about it. Lots of landowners are interested in profit and the tax-efficient long-term store of wealth, just as lots of picnickers are simply interested in whether they remembered that bottle opener and whether their Bluetooth speaker is working. Neither of them notice the chiffchaff in the trees.

At a Right to Roam event, about a year after I go to visit Andy, Nicola Chester, who has an essay in the book *Wild Service*, suggests that even the farmers around her no longer know what lapwings look like. I suspect many of them, the older ones at least, and active farmers rather than landowners, would disagree with that sentiment. But if Nicola's right and even the farmers who work the land don't appreciate the wild-life on their patch, the idea that throwing open access is suddenly going to make weekenders care, simply through exposure, doesn't really follow.

Further along the beach, heading towards Wells, Andy pulls up next to some of the only people on the beach without a dog, and asks them in a way that brings the three of them sharply to attention if they know that they're on a nature reserve and if they know why it's a nature reserve. 'Wildlife, I should imagine', the man replies in a local accent, running the tip of his tongue beneath his moustache. 'And how do you feel about dogs?' The man tells Andy that he's seen the signs, although he can't remember seeing them previously, and he supposes at certain times of year people need to keep their dogs on leads because there are birds nesting. His wife, who is standing a couple of feet behind him, cuts in, in a German accent, and tells Andy that 'they must keep their dogs on the lead and they must pick up after them because they are not always responsible'. Andy nods. 'What about camp fires then', he asks, 'people camping and starting fires on the beach?' The man looks at Andy thoughtfully as though the whole thing is very disappointing. 'Does that happen here?', he asks. Andy confirms that it does. The young man standing with them, who I assume is their son, says that he supposes it would be okay if they practised 'leave no trace'. He says it as though it's some sort of martial art underpinned by an inconceivably complex philosophy and his mother looks at him witheringly. 'They don't though', she replies, the fluency of her English going as she becomes frustrated, 'I understood that this was a nature reserve. They won't do the clearing up and all this.'

The man looks at his wife, then at his son, then tells Andy he knows a bit about the nature reserve – he used to teach children about access when he worked at Alderman Peel, the local school. Andy sits up. 'When was you there then?' The teacher replies that he retired 12 years ago but he was there from 1979. 'Brown', the teacher adds, 'history Brown.' Andy laughs. 'You was my first form teacher. I think you just started that day. Andy Bloomfield.' History Brown tells Andy he'd never have recognised him but he remembers him well. 'You were going out with that young lady.' Andy smiles and says the less said about that the better. 'And the wrestling, you aren't still doing the wrestling?' Andy shakes his head. 'Not for a long time.'

History Brown tells us that he doesn't get back to Wells so often now that he doesn't teach there – he likes it but the property is just too expensive for him so he lives over at Heacham near Ken Hill. Before we drive off I ask him what he thinks about all the plans there, the plans for the café and the nature tourism. He looks at me thoughtfully. 'I am bit worried about that', he admits. 'We're a bit concerned. I assume they're going to try and organise it so that the wildlife and everything is still protected. But you'll get a lot of people.' His wife glances at him and then looks at me. 'They must use it', she says, 'to educate people about how to manage the countryside.'

On our way back along the beach, I tell Andy he didn't really answer my question. How do you justify one man owning such a large bit of Norfolk. It's almost the only question that he doesn't seem to have an answer for. 'I dunno, that's the law of the land', he replies. 'There's laws in the land that we all have to abide by. And, you know, why can't we walk into a shop and steal a box of cornflakes, 'cos we can't.' The wind is blowing the sand towards us along the beach, and it shimmers in the light of the spring sun.

*

Up ahead of us, a silhouetted bird stands on the track beneath the cold dawn sky. Will Morris, his jacket zipped up under his chin and a green hat pulled right down over his ears, leans over the steering wheel of his pickup. 'Oh yeah', he says, as we crawl towards it. 'Oh yeah, this was the original lek but there's just the one here now.' We stop some forty yards out and Will lifts his binoculars. The bird, which has become a bird quite clearly, doesn't seem to notice us at all. Until a few years ago, it was one of a group of some twenty male black grouse but as foot-fall on the track increased, the lek fragmented, and the birds are now spread out across the moor in twos and threes. 'Used to be everywhere, black grouse, and in every county', Will says as he watches it, 'but it's a rare thing now.'

Will tells me that it was during lockdown, after the Government encouraged people 'to get out into the countryside', that it happened. He'd never seen so many people walking and cycling in the Pennines. 'Absolute nightmare. Did a lot of damage.' He puts his binoculars down on the seat behind us and we carry on up the track. 'Litter and gates being left open?', I ask. 'Bit of that', he replies. Then he tells me that the real problem was that somehow they found 'the quiet little corners'. When we are ten yards or so from the black grouse, it takes flight and curls round, towards the moor, over a lichen-covered wall.

Like all moorland, the land we're on, under the Countryside Rights of Way Act, is officially access land (part of that fabled 8 per cent) and the public can wander across it freely. 'We can close the area off when birds are on the nest', Will tells me, 'but the problem is that you can't legally keep people out on weekends and bank holidays, which is when most people turn up anyway."* Clearly, any nesting bird on the moor has no way of knowing that it's a Saturday or that the May bank holiday is coming up and they continue to nest – their calendar, to the

* Will is referencing the 28 days rule. Land can be closed for 28 days in one calendar year but it can't be imposed on Bank Holidays, Christmas Day or Good Friday, or on across more than four weekend days or on any Saturday or Sunday in the summer. You can't close moorland off on Good Friday, which is about the same time that lapwings start nesting, with curlew nesting a little later.

extent that they have one at all, is not the same as ours. But as ever they must work around us.

We drive through a gateway and then head out over the fields. Up ahead of us, light seeps into the sky and somewhere below us a curlew cries in the cold. Will nods when I say to him it's been a pretty shit spring really. 'Rain every day.' He nods again and says, when I ask him if he ever just feels like heading to Costa Rica or somewhere for a bit that it would be nice. 'But I'd soon get bored.' Will has been the head gamekeeper on the Barningham Estate for seven years and prior to that he did 12 years in the Peak District. He had, he tells me, a good boss and it was a great moor but in the end he just couldn't put up with it. The land he was on was near Sheffield and he felt that everybody in the surrounding area was opposed to his work. 'Everyone's against you down there. Makes it difficult.' He starts telling me about his decision to take the job in County Durham and then stops. A bird, maybe a little over a hundred yards out, is flying across the field. 'Grey hen there,* you see it? Probably flying up to the new lek.' With the windows down we head left slightly and as we crest a rise in the field, I start to hear it, a rich bubbling, long and low, and then a noise like cats fighting in the night.

They are spread out, the three of them, around a patch of rushes by the wall – displaced birds from the lek on the track. Tail feathers white carnations and black eyes staring up beneath red wattles, they run with their chests to the grey grass. Will's problem is that people either seem not to care at all about the black grouse or they care too much and they harass them. He had mountain bikers who would tear through the middle of the lek at twenty miles an hour and he now has 'rogue birdwatchers' who set their hides up in the middle of the night and 'wait for it to come light, then it's out with the lenses'. The trouble, Will thinks, is when they start trying to get closer and closer and

---

* A female black grouse is called a 'grey hen'.

eventually the birds won't come back. 'They can be a bit selfish, those guys.' It's only fair, he tells me, that people want to see the black grouse but you've got to respect them too. It's a really interesting point – it is perfectly logical that people won't respect nature if they never see it but some birdwatchers see huge numbers of birds and they know a lot about them but they don't really seem to care for them. It's about ticking a box. It sadly doesn't necessarily follow that to know that something is there inspires you to want to protect it.

Will reaches into the back, past his rifle, and grabs a flask of tea. He asks if I want a cup then passes me a mug with teddy bears on it. We sit there for a bit, sipping the tea and listening to the birds. Will doesn't say much apart from 'curlew' when a curlew drifts by, and then 'redshank', a while later when two of them fly across the lek. 'Just love them', he says when they're gone, 'Always have. Just love the look of them.' Ahead of us, on the edge of the reeds, two cock birds are facing off. The one on the left stands square and the bird on the right stands awkwardly at an angle, edging away as the dominant bird stakes its claim to the hens. As we watch them, Will tells me that in the Peak District he had a terrible time with fell runners. 'They were just proper hardliners, some of them. Just all of a sudden you'd get thirty of them running right through the middle of the moor in nesting time. You can't tell me they're not doing any damage. Nests get trampled. With a lapwing nest you can more or less stand on it before you've even seen it.' Will thinks that as much as anything they did it just to wind the keepers up and because they're anti-land ownership. 'They're just anti-everything. You'd think they'd look at this', he gestures across the hill, 'and think, Christ we need to be preserving that not trying to break it – but people are so obsessed with just kicking the landowner in the backside.' He stops and holds his arm out as though to cut me off and points to our right, 'Eh up, mating with her. Do you see? She'll go off and lay an egg now. Come back tomorrow. Mate again tomorrow. Each day until she's laid a clutch then she'll start incubating.' Will tells me that it's when they're on the nest that they're particularly vulnerable. Walkers with dogs are meant to stick to the paths but they often don't and Will has previously found grouse with brood patches on their chests, meaning they've been incubating, that have been crushed by dogs. The birds will sit tight in order to protect the young until it's too late and the dog is right on them.

Reaching across, Will pours me the last of the tea, and then asks a few moments later what it is they actually want. 'The people who want more access?' I reply. He nods. I tell him I guess they don't want to be told where they can and can't go because psychologically, that doesn't feel like freedom. He raises his eyebrows as though weighing the whole thing up and then tells me that as he sees it, they've got enough ground to go at already. 'When the Countryside and Rights of Way Act came in, that changed things. People would say it's my right and all that. But there's some hardliners who will just keep going, wanting more and more. I object to some things that are in law but I'm not trying to change them.' Will takes my cup and puts it on the back seat next to the rifle and then spins the truck round and we drive towards the top corner of the field. As we go, he tells me, with faint resignation, that in reality we are only going to end up with more access, and more access, he reckons, will mean more disturbance.

At the top of the field, we turn right and head along the lane between two dry stone walls. There are rabbits mooching on the verges, grey partridges are scratching in the fields, and thin clouds sweep across the pale blue sky. From time to time he tells me that he gets campers pulling up in motorhomes and he thinks it's best just to let them be. The image of a gamekeeper, he admits, often isn't a particularly good one and he thinks it pays to be aware of that when talking to the public, which has increasingly become a big part of his job. Not so long ago, Barningham village and villages like it were mostly populated by keepers, farmers, and estate workers, but that has changed now. With Newcastle only an hour away, the local area has filled up with commuters who seem to know almost nothing. 'We do all that', Will tells me, with pride, 'like talking in the village hall.' People, he thinks, don't really realise how much work goes into conservation and how much damage they can do. Although he admits that some game-keepers are probably better at talking to the public than others.

At the top of the lane we turn left down a track. There is thick fog in the bottom valley and lapwings are calling in the stillness. On our left the blackened remains of a large building, sit on a raised plot of scorched earth, and Will tells me when I ask that it was a pig unit. 'Burned down a year ago. Blew up. Pretty grim.' He shakes his head then adds that he was told they mostly got gassed rather than burned. I ask him what happened to the carcasses. 'They took them away. Gone into dog food I think.' Further down the hill, the ground is rushy and a cock grouse sits on a mossy knoll, its feathers wet. 'Doesn't quite look himself', Will says as he slows the truck. He sits there looking at the bird. 'He doesn't look himself, does he? He'll have just been sat out here in the cold.' Above us on the horizon, a grey hen is sitting in a hawthorn. I ask Will about it and he tells me he's thinned those trees out for them a bit, as he thinks they like to be able to see, but he keeps watching the cock bird, then he purses his lips and whistles. The bird looks up and then walks towards us. 'That's a grouse chick noise, see. He doesn't look so bad when he's up and moving.'

Down in the village, except for the rabbits in the car park, and a bay horse that trots towards me across the field, nothing is up and about. The white umbrellas outside the pub are all folded down, and the crest of the Milbank family, who have owned the 7,000-acre Barningham Estate since 1690, is fixed to the wall above the bin, a lion's head on one side and a crown on the other.

*

One Tuesday morning, just after breakfast, while he's out walking his poodles, Chris Packham rings me on WhatsApp to give me a quote for a piece I've been asked to write about whether game shooting needs to be more heavily regulated. There was, I say to him at the end of the call, one more thing. I'm writing about land access, I explain, and the impact of people on nature. We talk a bit about his poodles and their behaviour. Apparently they are mostly quite good but they don't always come back when called. He walks them on the beach in winter but not in the spring when birds are nesting.

The thing is, he says to me, in his reasonable, matter of fact, sort of way, it's only possible for RSPB Minsmere to have over 100,000 visitors a year because access is pretty tightly controlled. It's only because of the boardwalks, he explains, and people having to stick to them that wildlife flourishes there.

Chris would probably not be a massive fan of Will Morris, although I suspect he'd have really enjoyed being out with us on the hill looking at black grouse and I sometimes wonder if he's more open-minded about gamekeepers than people think, but it doesn't seem unreasonable to suggest that Barningham too should have a boardwalk system. It's patently ridiculous, when they are working night and day to save the black grouse, which has disappeared from so much of Britain, that they aren't allowed to cordon off what birds they have left during bank holidays. It feels like a particularly absurd example of privileging human life over animal life. Is our right to wander with our dogs or go fell running in large groups greater than the right of black grouse or lapwings to exist?

If thought about purely from the perspective of declining biodiversity, there are places where access, at certain times of the year, should be restricted. Andy Bloomfield, at Holkham, said to me the idea of going dog-free is an interesting one but he just doesn't think people would stand for it. Again, the right of my spaniel to have a good time seems to matter more than the right of shorebirds to breed successfully.

*

Down in the basement, at the British Ecological Society, beneath the white glow of halogen lights, ecologists, PhD students, activists, and mental health practitioners are gathered round a table with pots of coffee, bananas, muffins, and sandwiches cut into triangles. Everybody seems to know everybody else. It's midday and we're all there to hear about different sides of a growing problem. Nature is good for us. It makes us better and happier, but too many pairs of boots on the ground seem to be contributing to the destruction of rural Britain and the things that live there.

We break off into little groups and sit at tables around the room. It's a gathering of informed and inspired people and it all feels very collegiate. Sarah Howes, a lecturer in mental health nursing stands up at the front. She speaks quietly and everyone listens intently. There is a growing body of evidence, she tells us, that makes it clear that investing both time and money in providing access to nature is an investment in our collective wellbeing. It took some time, she acknowledges, for the immense benefits of 'green social prescribing', such as community gardening and getting out into the woods, as Richard Benyon is keen for people to do at Englefield, to be recognised but such prescriptions are now on the rise. In part, it was due to Covid. During the pandemic, 41 per cent of people agreed that nature was more important than ever for their wellbeing.

As she talks, I remember my mother texting me most days when she was recovering from bone marrow cancer and a stem cell transplant. Every morning she would set off towards a pond that I'd dug out, in a field in front of our house, some years previously. At first she could only make it 50 yards or so and then 75 and then 100, but as time passed, she grew stronger, and eventually she made it to the water's edge. Almost every morning she would message me to tell me what she'd seen there. She saw mallard and teal and geese, and occasionally in winter, a woodcock would get up from the rushes. The pond was a locus of life and it felt as though going there and hearing and seeing brought her back to life, in a way. But I guess that even as a frail woman, tottering down there over the grass, she was causing disturbance. It's lovely to think that other people might have gone there too, in search of recovery, and it being Scotland, anybody could have done in theory, but I wonder how long those woodcock and teal that gave my mother such joy would have stuck around if people had turned up three times a day.

The following speaker, Beth Collier, a nature-allied psychotherapist and ethnographer, tells us about her work in southeast London that supports people of colour in exploring their relationship with the natural world. It's interesting to hear that although a lot of people who come to Britain are deeply connected with nature in their heritage countries, they lose that connection when they come here. Cities become safe places. A lot of Beth's work centres around training black and Asian nature guides in order to make others feel more comfortable.

Beth and Sarah Howes' presentations would be almost impossible for anybody to disagree with. Clearly, spending time outside is good for us but Dr Durwyn Lilley, who comes after Beth, has spent his life considering the reality of time spent outside and his findings are stark. He shows us pictures of Burnham Beeches, in Buckinghamshire, not far from London. On paths accessed by just 5.8 people a day there is moss and leaf litter. There is vegetation around the bottom of the trees, habitat for all sorts of little creatures, which in turn provide food for animals and birds that feed on them. He puts some pictures up of paths accessed by 187 people a day – the pictures show a muddy deadland, where the earth is compacted, and tree roots struggle beneath.

In a way, it's a dispassionate talk. Durwyn isn't an activist – he's just a guy with the facts and he delivers them in a fairly straight-forward way. In places where access is high, he explains, those out walking spread the seeds of non-native trees which compete with British flora, and horses make the situation even worse. Durwyn suggests that when it comes to dog walking, we should stop thinking of nature reserves as being good places to go. Over the years Durwyn has been involved in surveying visitors at National Parks and other key wildlife and has found that up to 80 per cent of them are out to walk the dog. The consequences don't just involve the relatively obvious, such as the disturbance of nesting birds. Things like flea treatment and shampoo leaching into water when dogs swim can have a terminal impact on aquatic fauna.

One solution is designated dog parks but Durwyn also makes it clear that we can't just blame it all on our pets. At Snettisham, in Norfolk, very near Ken Hill, Durwyn carried out a survey which found that ringed plovers avoid places where there is human activity. He also found that the accidental trampling of nests by human feet contributed to their plight. Ultimately, they concluded that a complete absence of human disturbance would cause a population increase of 85 per cent and if footfall was to double, the ringed plover population at that point would decrease by 23 per cent.

The numbers provide the next speaker, Amy-Jane Beer, author and naturalist, Right to Roam campaigner, and beloved neighbour of the Pollards in Crambeck, with a pretty tough task. When we've seen the harm that humans can cause, demanding that access becomes a right rather than a privilege is tricky. Amy-Jane starts by noting that the Right to Roam movement recognises the need to protect landscapes but she wants us to move away from having to ask for permission. Her point that the problem of people would be diluted if we were granted access to vast swathes of the coun-tryside rather than just 8 per cent makes logical sense – but do we really just head to the same places because we aren't allowed to go elsewhere or do we go to those places and because they are easy to get to, because they're beautiful, and because the pubs are good? In Scotland, you can go where you like, but the Isle of Skye in August is back-to-back caravans, while in Dumfriesshire, in the summer, there are very few people at all. On Skye I've struggled before to get a restaurant booking, while in Dumfriesshire you'll struggle to find a restaurant anywhere.

Amy-Jane's second point is a more abstract one. What we need to do, she suggests, is to stop requiring people to ask permission because that makes them visitors rather than making them one with nature. If we feel like visitors in nature, she suggests, rather than actually 'being nature' we won't take responsibility for protecting it and restoring it. It sounds great but does somebody fishing who has paid for a permit feel less 'a part of the place' than they would if they could just fish for free. It also seems problematic to suggest that we would do better by nature if we are truly able to be 'part of it'. It's arguable that we are good at conservation because we are not on par with the animals. I like foxes, for example, but they are no good at conservation and corvids simply won't be told that those lapwing eggs they are about to eat, if they'd only leave them be, would hatch into a bird species that's almost extinct in Britain. Does our understanding of ecology make us distinct from animals? The fox would happily eat the last oystercatcher but we as humans – some of us anyway – would be deeply upset if we were down to the last fox. Is it our realisation that we must conserve that means we are related to nature but are ultimately distinct from it?

When the Q&A rolls round, I decide not to ask about being human. Dissent feels like it might go against the ethos of the event. There are questions about creating spaces for invertebrates, and there is a question about wild zones in urban parks. Someone cheerily points out that lots of animals do well where there are people. It's actually just some animals that don't. At the end, I put my hand up to ask whether sacrificial zones where we put people and their dogs first are acceptable. The panel nods sympathetically. 'Sometimes', they tell me, 'sacrificial zones are a price we have to pay.'

After a couple of glasses, a few of us head to the Narrowboat on the Regent's canal. We sit around a table and talk about what a success the event was. And in many ways, it was. I get chatting to Jon Moses. He is tired because the previous evening he was sleeping out in the woods after listening to nightingales. He awoke early, he tells me, because of the pheasants crowing in the trees. As the conversation continues, I tell him that I guess, in many ways, fox hunting is much easier to defend than driven pheasant shooting. He prefers it too, he replies, because there's 'a higher chance of toffs breaking their necks'. He looks at me after he's said it, and laughs uncomfortably, seemingly not sure whether to pass it off as a joke or a moment of great radicalism.

About a year after the seminar at the British Ecological Society, I head to Mid-Norfolk for a workshop on pond restoration. There are people from the Norfolk Wildlife Trust, the National Trust, and various farmers' groups. I am – I realise quite quickly – the only person who has turned up, unaffiliated, just because I like ponds. When the first morning of lectures is over, we head out into the fields to look at various Norfolk Ponds Trust projects and we are all told that we have to dip our boots. When I ask what it is they are worried about, the list goes on and on. There could be eggs of invasive crayfish or killer shrimp on our boots; there could be the seeds of things like Himalayan balsam or New Zealand pygmyweed, which outcompetes native plants; and there could be the spores of chytrid fungus, which has the potential to eat the skin off our great crested newts. In short, your boots, worn on a foreign birdwatching trip and then worn again in Norfolk a fortnight later or even just worn across Britain, have the potential to cause untold ecological damage through introducing things many of us have never heard of.

*

In the yard outside the head gamekeeper's cottage on the Arundel Estate, West Sussex, a little girl's pink bicycle lies on its side, blue streamers on the end of the handlebars blowing in the wind. 'Well, I wouldn't suggest you go in there and tickle them,' Charlie Mellor says, with a smile, 'but you'll be alright'. I walk towards the kennel and stand in front of a sign that reads 'Dogs on the loose'. Behind the gate, on the tarmac, there is a half-crushed metal bowl. I wait for a moment and nothing happens then I suck at the back of my thumb to make a noise like a rabbit in distress and a Belgian Malinois comes barrelling out of the kennel up at the back, gathering pace, and then leaping up off the ground. The dog thuds its head against the wire roof, then it crouches and bares its teeth. 'That one was found wandering the streets of London', Charlie shouts across. 'We know nothing about it except it's got foreign plates.' One of Charlie's underkeepers pops his head out from the shed. 'Foreign plates?', he says to Charlie. 'She drives on the other side of the road does she?' Charlie laughs and corrects himself. 'Meant it's got a foreign chip.'

Charlie comes and stands next to me and the two dogs wag their tails, open-mouthed. Hare coursing, he tells me, used to be a bit of a problem in Sussex but most of the keepers have big dogs now. 'They've had a few bites over the years, and the word apparently gets out pretty quick.' I follow Charlie into his cottage through the side door and then I sit at the kitchen table. 'Coffee?' he asks. 'Please', I reply. He looks up above the kitchen cupboards at a few rectangular cardboard boxes and then says that if I like he can try to make me a caramel latte.

At the door to the hall, a small teckel* peers through at us and in the corner a young black Labrador looks anxious. 'You alright mate', Charlie says, on walking over to it. 'You look a bit hangdog. You alright?' There is something very neat about Charlie. He is

---

* A teckel is a working dachshund. It is sometimes used to track deer.

short but strong and his beard is tightly curled and ginger. He has been a keeper on the Arundel estate for 14 years except for the one year when he went to Australia. 'Split up with my now wife and thought fuck this. Then came back and got back with my now wife.' He slurps at his coffee and laughs.

Charlie's brief at Arundel is to lead a five-man keepering team in restoring wildlife across a previously nature-depleted landscape. The work involves habitat restoration, patience, a lot of money, fencing areas off, and what some locals call 'extreme predator control'. The previous day, Charlie came across two people from the village, 'a lovely couple actually. I know them pretty well', who were out with their dog off the lead. 'First thing I noticed was this black thing about 300 yards up the track. It was a cocker spaniel. I just said to them, "Come on, guys. You must have seen the signs."' The couple apologised and said the dog really was having a lovely time and a pleasant and very open conversation followed in which they admitted that the dog had caught a hare that morning in a gateway. Charlie looks at me and shakes his head. 'Probably had leverets', I told them. 'And they said, oh right' – he puts on a posh voice. 'Leverets. Is that so? We didn't know hares got a disease.'

Charlie tells me they have twenty miles of paths running across the estate and the footfall wouldn't bother him so much if it wasn't for dogs running loose among ground-nesting birds and those who take it upon themselves to smash up traps. 'If people were respectful, I wouldn't mind open access but most of them aren't.' Just a fortnight prior to me visiting, Guy Shrubsole posted on social media about trespassing on what he thought was the neighbouring Angmering Estate, and releasing a crow that was serving as a 'call bird' in a Larsen trap.* What Guy didn't realise,

---

* A Larsen trap is a cage trap with two compartments, which is used to live trap corvids. A previously caught magpie or crow is kept in the decoy compartment, which attracts territory-holders that see the decoy bird as an intruder.

according to Charlie, is that Angmering is now part of the Norfolk Estate and wildlife recovery at Angmering is part of Charlie's brief. A back and forth between Guy and Charlie broke out online. Charlie accepts that the whole thing is complicated – the piece of land Guy was on only came back into the Duke's possession a couple of years ago after being separated out but surely, Charlie adds, he should be in the know. After all, Charlie adds, he claims to have literally written the book on who owns England. 'He'd just done a bit of googling, and had totally surmised something. And he could have asked.' After a long morning of Guy saying 'no, I wasn't', and Charlie saying 'yes you were – I've lived here for fourteen years', Guy rounded it all off by telling the many thousands of people who were following along that he will always take the opportunity to release crows from traps. Some cheered – while many conservationists who work on the ground felt that Guy was standing there naked.

Leaning across the table, Charlie runs through pictures of all the traps that have been smashed up over the previous weeks. 'Literally every day. This morning Dom, one of the underkeepers, sent me this.' He shows me a picture of a trap with the arm snapped off. 'As well as the impact on wildlife, the cost runs into thousands of pounds. Every Larsen trap's £150. I mean, if I didn't work for a duke, my boss would probably go hang on, this is getting a bit silly.' Beyond the window a woodpigeon, its chest puffed up, is sitting in a pine tree, sheltering from the heat. I watch it for a moment and then I say to Charlie that I guess Guy's point is that if this landscape was ecologically balanced, you wouldn't have to use these traps and you wouldn't have to worry so much about people smashing them up. He nods. 'And Guy's right. Completely true. I'd agree with him but what are we going to do? Just wait for it all to balance itself? That's never going to happen. The curlew will be extinct before then, the grey partridge gone, the lapwing will be extinct. We all want a utopian world but unfortunately it's not gonna work.' He picks up his mug, swirls the coffee round in the bottom, then drinks the last of it and we head outside. On the way out, above the door to the utility room, two bridles hang from a nail. His little girl had a small pony, Charlie tells me as we pass but sadly he got colic and died.

The lads are still out in the yard, one of them standing by a ferret hutch and the other looking quizzically at the washing machine. 'You ever used a washing machine before?' Charlie asks him. The boy smiles and Charlie tells me they've been washing curlew beds then opens the door to a small building next to the keeper's shed. Inside there is a strong smell of bird shit. 'That's just the droppings beneath the heat lamp', he says as he closes the door behind us and crosses the concrete floor. In the corner, there is a black plastic basin with 11 curlew chicks, small balls of yellow and black fluff, their big feet wandering awkwardly beneath little jutting heads. Charlie reaches down to pick up the nearest of them. He clasps it in his right hand and massages its neck with his thumb. 'This one's just got a bit of muscle spasm. They call it a wryneck. Normally they come right to be honest, we had two last year.' He puts the bird back and watches it as it looks cured for a moment before its neck gives out again. Charlie tells me that they've got a licence to bring 120 eggs down off a northern moor, which they then hatch and release. The hope is that eventually they'll end up with a breeding population again. Half the trouble, he says, as he shows me some eggs is the disturbance. 'Again, it's the dogs. Whatever anybody says, the very last thing you want is dogs where you got ground-nesting birds.' He lifts an egg and holds it up to me like a priest giving me communion. He doesn't say anything but he runs the nail of his forefinger next to it in the air to show me where the little bird is starting to push out into the world.

The lanes that crisscross the Arundel estate are chalky white and the Land Rover kicks up a cloud of pale dust as we head down the hill, away from the cottage. Charlie slows as we pass a sign that has been nailed to a mossy wooden post above a clump of nettles. 'I put these up to try and educate the public but not sure they notice.' There are four pictures on the sign, a lapwing, a skylark, a corn bunting, and a grey partridge, with the words 'Critically endangered ground nesting birds breed here during the spring', running above the pictures and 'Keep dogs on a lead' below.

It is the hottest day of the year so far and the land looks thirsty. 'On this bit alone we put twenty miles of new hedges in', Charlie says, gesturing out to our right where cow parsley runs up into blackthorn. 'No grant either. The Duke paid for all of it.' Charlie's phone rings and he looks at it, lets it ring out, then pushes it into his pocket. We drive on for a bit, then I ask Charlie if he thinks that in a world beyond dukes, a more equal world, we would still be able to have all of these hedges and wildflower margins through some other publicly funded means. He looks at me and shakes his head, 'No, mate. We wouldn't.'

Just a couple of days after Guy visited the Norfolk estate, Lewis Winks, a prominent Right to Roam campaigner who works in the Geography Department at the University of Exeter, called for access, for the public, to field margins. This would, he suggested, 'help address inequalities blighting our access to the countryside'. In real terms, he calculated that the move would allow people to enjoy a further 38 per cent of English soil. The land on both sides of us is Edenic, 'sort of like 1930s farming', Charlie tells me merrily. But it's double-fenced and a small strip down the side of the lane has been strimmed to create a footpath. 'Why would they want to walk down the margin though?' Charlie says when I mention Winks. 'All they are going to do is stand on nests. That's my argument. What's wrong with walking on the bloody track?' We drive through a gateway and the ground kicks up sharply. 'I guess it's about a sense of immersion', I reply, 'and being in nature rather than just looking.' He shakes his head, and tells me that it is all a bit funny. 'Without those fences, the youngsters don't stand a chance'.

In front of us, little chicks trip and stumble ahead of the truck as they head for the long grass. 'Nice few lapwings about', Charlie says as he watches them. Every nest is marked with a post so that keepers don't run over them. 'So yeah, on here we'd have about twelve pairs of lapwings. And they would bring off probably about twenty-four young each year, two per pair. And that is largely down to predator control. Obviously, the habitat's here, but without the predator control it wouldn't happen.' At either end of the lapwing patch there are two crow traps that get moved around all year. The hope is that anything flying in or out is caught. He watches the ground as he talks, telling me that he does understand that Guy thought he did the right thing by letting the crow out but it's ignorant. 'People's ignorance never fails to astound me. People just walk around with their eyes shut. I tell you, that's the trouble.'

One field over from the lapwing patch on the other side of the hedge, two skylarks fly upward, beating their wings frantically as though trying to escape the pull of the earth. As he watches them, Charlie tells me they've got five hundred pairs of skylarks now.

It all started for him, he says, as we drive off, with birdwatching. 'I was mad keen when I was little.' His dad was in the navy and his mum would let him and his sisters out in the morning and they'd come back for tea. As he got a bit older, Charlie thinks he probably became the most prolific poacher in his village. 'I went from watching the birds to watching them and shooting them.' It was when he was about eight years old that he finally, after plucking up the courage, knocked on the door of the local keeper's cottage to ask if he could go with him on his rounds. 'Well Charlie', he says, 'if you're with us, at least we'll know where you are.' He laughs nostalgically after he tells me the story and then says that for him, the whole job of a wild bird keeper has to start with knowing all of the birds. 'You've got to love the birds.'

Charlie's phone rings and the man on the other end asks him where the tractor is. 'Just up at my house on the drive. You'll see it.' As the conversation goes on, the list of things wrong with the tractor grows and grows. 'Oh and none of the dials work either. Is that a big job?' He puts the phone down and then tells me that's the thing about tractors. It's driven by twelve or so people and it was always somebody else who broke it. We drive through a farmyard and Charlie tells me that if I've got time he'll take me to the place where Guy let the bird out of the trap. One of the things that he found most telling about the exchange was that Guy kept insisting that the land is covered in pheasant feeders. 'They're bloody wild partridge feeders. They've got wire guards round to stop the pheasants getting in which is hilarious really.' Angmering, he explains, is a work in progress; there was a pheasant shoot on it for a while when it was owned by the other side of 'the family' but he likes to think that most people could see that there's been a change of approach. 'Seventeen miles of new hedging gone in.' He often thinks, he says to me reflectively, that it's a good thing people take notice of what the likes of his boss have to say because those in charge won't listen to gamekeepers. Guy didn't even accept that Charlie knew about the land he lives on, a landscape he knows better than anybody. 'I'm out on this bit of ground every day of my life. Surely I know what I'm talking about. You'd hope so. You know what I mean? Maybe it's 'cos I don't have letters after my name.'

Beneath us, just beyond a barn, two men are stooped over a fence, next to a small digger. 'Guy's point', Charlie explains as we head down the hill, is that the field he was on 'is actually Right to Roam' but the land around it isn't. I ask him why and he shrugs. 'I don't know, to be honest. To be honest that's one you'd have to look that one up.'* As we pull up in front of a gate to Angmering, where some sheep have been penned in, Charlie tells me that the thing is, if anybody wrote to the estate office or got in touch, and asked if they could go and see the orchids or they wanted to have a look at a wood, 'The answer would be yes. Course it would.' The men look up and one of them wanders over to us. 'But I suppose that would create a sort of power dynamic. Where they are subservient.' Charlie laughs. 'It is what it is. Everything's owned by someone.' The two old boys shuffle up to the car. 'Alright Kev', Charlie says to one of them, who is wearing a woollen hat in spite of the heat. The three of them say hello to each other in at least seven slightly varying terms, and then Kev moves the conversation on by telling Charlie he got two magpies yesterday. 'Oh well done. You got a couple of magpies down there did you?' Kev nods. 'They just come down on the rabbits.' He looks at me and Charlie explains by way of intro-duction that I'm writing a book on Right to Roam. Kev sniffs. 'Oh right, this Right to Roam? Ban it. Yup, ban it.' We drive away and I watch in the rearview mirror as a cloud of dust blows up behind us and the two men go back to hammering in posts again.

What Guy Shrubsole got up to that day is unforgivable. It's unforgivable because to destroy the infrastructure at a place where they are trying to save endangered wildlife is madness. We are talking about interfering with the fight to save a bird that is on the verge of extinction in the Home Counties. It is maddening too, though, because it throws a

---

* The land is an access island, as referred to by Caroline Lucas – the little patch itself is access land (these access islands make up .2 per cent of the 8 per cent) but it isn't accessible unless you trespass.

spanner into the works in terms of trying to foster greater relations between those who would like more opportunities to engage with wildlife and some of those who can provide it. And what really stands out is the arrogance of it all – sure, Guy fucked up but Charlie's just a gamekeeper, so it's perfectly conceivable that Charlie doesn't actually know much about the world around him and the land he calls home, and Guy must surely be right, in the end, anyway. In the months that followed, I spoke to Jon Moses who told me, pretty frankly, that it hadn't been a campaign highlight. Nor, I suppose, was it a good day for nature, and it was a disaster for rural relations. That said, it was a very busy time for Guy Shrubsole's social media profile. The pictures he took got a lot of likes and that, depressingly, is often what campaigning is really about.

In early September, at a party in East London, I bump into a friend of a friend who has been at almost every Right to Roam meeting I've attended. 'You should come to my trespass', she says excitedly. 'We're going to go to Arundel.' I tell her I was there not so long ago and they seem to do some really interesting things. 'Do they?' she says, smiling sweetly at me in a way that suggests I've been duped by projects that were probably only ever undertaken, to the extent that they are undertaken at all, in order to be able to put up signs to keep people out. 'They really do', I reply. 'Obviously the Duke is hugely rich and we can object to that but they do some impressive stuff.' I explain about Charlie the gamekeeper and his love of songbirds and about the grey partridges and the lapwing plots. I tell her about all the new hedges and I show her videos of the curlew chicks underneath the heat lamp. She makes appreciative noises, then says that they 'aren't going to go there'. They are heading for the farmed areas. A couple of weeks later, Right to Roam puts out a message calling for protestors. They are going to

Arundel, the note reads, to bear witness to the 'ecological destruction' that goes on behind those fences.

*

One of the great inequalities when it comes to life on earth is that we get to decide, albeit in an often long and drawn-out way, the fate of the animals. Do we want curlew in Britain, do we want shorebirds on Holkham beach and do we want capercaillie in what remains of pine forests?

Or, instead, do we want Holkham to be a place for dog walking and picnics, and would we rather have mountain biking trails as opposed to capercaillie leks? Do black grouse matter? We can, if we are sensible about it, have both. For instance, it would be entirely logical to suggest a ban on walking on the beach after five consecutive days of freezing temperatures – the wintering birds, at that point, are starting to starve and they can't put up with energy loss as a result of disturbance. It would be perfectly sensible but would humans forgo those cold winter walks?

We can, if we were more thoughtful, have most of what we need while still giving other life forms, the beautiful and endangered, a chance to exist too. And that existence ultimately benefits us. The countryside would be a far poorer place without birdsong or the flash of sanderlings flying over the mud. What we clearly can't have, though, is a free-for-all. With a population that has increased almost 30-fold since the year 1500, we need to be intelligent. We can't walk through every field margin and every wood, all year round – particularly given that the public can't be trusted not to do destructive and irresponsible things. It is not accurate to say that if only we can see everything, we would love it more. If we could see everything, all the time, there would soon be less to see and less to love. What about those birdwatchers on Barningham disturbing those black grouse? They appreciate them, in a sense, but they harass too.

What Dom Buscall has done at Ken Hill should not be underestimated. Sure, he has the means but he has used those means to create a place for humans and for nature. What he's done couldn't be replicated everywhere – clearly, we need to farm. We must still eat – but it is a great example of the sort of thing we need more of, opportunities that have been created to engage with the complexity of nature and the countryside rather than just to cross it. But, at the same time, what he's done wouldn't be possible if the countryside was thrown open. He is effectively capitalising on there being limited access while monetising a high quality alternative.

It must be said that landowners, as well as having a responsibility to create engagement opportunities, also have a responsibility to ensure that, at certain times of year, endangered species won't be disturbed although this is something that access campaigners and access legislation make very difficult. It is also made challenging by landowners who think about footfall in their beachside café, rather than redshank numbers on the shore.

In the weeks before I finished this book, I received a message from a professor of ecology who lives not far from Middlewick Ranges. He wanted to give me some background on a current battle going on down there over some land owned by the MOD. The 107-hectare site, next to Colchester, is used as a firing range but it is also one of the best nightingale habitats in England. The ecologist, speaking to me off the record, explained that the reason it's so good for wildlife is because the public, due to the land being a firing range, don't have unfettered access. The issue the MOD were facing, though, as he understood it, is that campaigners were starting to call for access to be opened up. The army doesn't apparently care much about nightingales but due to public exclusion they happen to be sitting on a remarkable nature reserve. However, they simply don't want a range that people want to be able to walk across whenever they like – big guns and dog walkers are best kept apart. The irony, my contact suggested, is that the same people who were making a big noise about the destruction of the habitat (because the MOD has now sold it to be built on) were the very same people who had been calling for more access. As humans we want our cake and we want to eat it too.

Some months after I bumped into that girl who was heading down to Arundel to bear witness to all that ecological destruction, I bumped into her again. It had been, she told me, a good trespass. They had seen a lot of those hedges, they couldn't find the ecological destruction, and the strangest thing had been that nobody seemed to care much that they were there.

It is, on many levels, grotesque that some people own millions of pounds worth of land they've never set foot on while other people in Britain starve. Dom Buscall didn't seem comfortable with it and I can see why. But the wealth of some of those people, Dom included, means that they have been able to create engagement opportunities as well as funding conservation. The stuff is there because of them and people are able to see it because of them. What we need to do is to make all landowners recognise the power they have.

5

Water

What impact does access have on Britain's rivers, the sea, and all the creatures that live there?

Down on Chelsea Embankment, an old man in a pink sun-bleached cap casts a worm out into the Thames, then he leans against the railings in the heat. It is a Saturday, mid-afternoon, and the streets are quiet. When I ask him what he's fishing for, he looks at me uneasily. 'Eel', he eventually says, 'but I don't speak English.' For a while he stares at his float, then he reels his line in, seemingly to check whether the bait is still on the hook. He glances at me, then turns back to the river, pulls his cap down over his face, and casts again. The worm, as it lands, makes a small plop and while he's reeling in the slack I ask him whether anybody can fish for eels or if you need some sort of permit. He shrugs and smiles. 'Just eel for me. The river for everybody enjoy.'

From building cities on the sea to netting rivers for salmon, humans have long been drawn to water. Water sustains life and provides food and a means of travel, but access to Welsh and English rivers is relatively tight. The water itself doesn't actually belong to anybody but access to that water is limited by who owns the river bed. Whoever owns the land abutting the river, generally owns the bed out to the midway point. But that isn't always the case. Ownership of the river bed can sometimes be retained when the land is sold or it might be owned by a fishing club for instance. Clearly the ownership of the bank, whether the proprietor owns the riverbed or not, still has a bearing on a person's ability to access the river. Rowing down the river Thames through Surrey is very nice but when I did it some years ago, I ended up mostly sleeping in public parks because the smart gardens that run down to the river tend to have 'No mooring' signs. Quite how much access to our rivers exists is contested. Some activists claim that the public can hardly dip a toe in England's major rivers but as ever the reality is complicated. There are some 42,700 miles of inland waterways in England and Wales, of which 2,920 miles are available for navigation, either through the existence of public rights or access agreements.*

Down the years, a number of campaigns – led by groups such as the British Canoe Union – have tried to get access opened up across our waterways but there has been resistance from conservationists, landowners, and anglers. 'It's no good', a dour fisherman told me, a couple of years ago, after I'd been speaking at the Glasgow Book Festival with the Scottish author, Malachy Tallack. 'When the weather's warm, the ladies do their wild swimming and you can't cast a line.'

I never did find out if Malachy accepted the guy's invitation to speak after their end of season dinner. 'You'd need to wear your black tie', the old guy told him. 'We're the oldest fishing club in Scotland.' Malachy seemed pained by the thought. But the man had a point – him and all the old guys like him had paid chunky season ticket fees to go fishing whereas 'those ladies'

* It is worth noting that the beds of tidal rivers are generally owned by the Crown.

(as he bitterly put it) hadn't paid anything at all. 'And they contribute nothing', the old boy went on – and he went on and on – 'to the upkeep of the lochs.'

*

On my way to Hayfield, for a mass swimming trespass in Kinder Reservoir, I come across a man in a crumpled suit, holding a tattered bag, standing at the side of the road with his thumb in the air. I pull over to ask him where he's going. He tells me, very earnestly, that he would like to go to Hayfield. He climbs in, puts his bag down in the footwell, and I turn the heater up for him. His name is Muss and he came to Britain from Alexandria, he tells me, almost twenty years ago. He was, he says, as a young man, 'a great athlete – world championship, Mediterranean championship, Egyptian championship. I had them all.'

He likes Derbyshire, he says, and it took him a very long time to be allowed into the country. 'A lot of investigation. Always a lot of investigation.' The police, he explains, want to know everything about you if you come from an Arab country – they want to know who you are and who you're related to. But he tells me, thoughtfully, that it's better to be safe. 'Police here are good.'

Down below us, the fields fall away steeply, and ewes are grazing beneath the cold sky. Muss tells me he loves Derbyshire. He loved Hayfield, when he used to live there, but it became too expensive for him and he had to move out – the trouble, he thinks, is that lots of people from London got jobs in Manchester, working for the BBC and they all decided to live in Hayfield. They are, he thinks, 'lovely people. Some very famous. Some are *Coronation Street* but they are not my people.' He explains that he likes to live among ordinary people so he applied for a council house out of town.

He asks me where I'm headed and I tell him I'm a writer and I'm going to swim in the reservoir on Kinder Scout for a book I'm working on. We talk for a bit about writing and he asks what Kinder Scout is and I explain that the land all around the reservoir was owned by a rich man once and the people couldn't access it at all and now they can, for picnics and things, but they can't swim there legally. Muss shakes his head. 'That's wrong, isn't it?' Muss asks if the rich man gets paid now for people to walk on the land. 'He doesn't own it anymore', I reply. 'He's probably dead.' Muss nods. 'So the public get it?' I tell him that essentially yes, the public can go there now. He nods as though he is giving it some thought. 'That is fantastic', he says after a bit. 'That is really fantastic.' I drop him off by a white sign that reads 'Hayfield', buttressed inexplicably on both sides by large wooden cutouts of Mickey Mouse. He shakes my hand then walks on up the road. For some weeks, I poke around online but I never do find any record of Muss or any of those great wins.

The path up to the reservoir is narrow and muddy and there are signs reading 'Erosion control: please to keep to the track' running alongside it. I fall in between a group of Pakistani men who tell me, after asking why there are so many people, that they won't be going swimming and a group of young Communist Party members who tell me they aren't there for the swim either. 'Communists can swim though?' I ask the boy at the back who is holding a flag. 'They can and they do', he replies, but they are heading for Kinder Plateau, the highest point in the Peak, some of them in hiking kit and some of them in braces and black boots.

When we get to the reservoir, three ladies who are bathing in the reedy shallows, shout over to the communists to ask what the flags are all about. 'Young Communist Party' a few of them shout back in harmony. The ladies nod thoughtfully and agree among themselves that Young Communists are alright. At the northern end of the reservoir, a group of some three hundred people have gathered. There are people in wetsuits, there are people who look like they have no intention of getting in, and there are people in swimming costumes, many of them middle-aged ladies. There are a few vaguely radical-looking kids in their late teens and twenties, including a small group in woolly hats and fleeces, who are singing along while one of them strums out Ewan MacColl's 'Manchester Rambler' on a guitar. It's mostly pretty sedate: flasks of tea, sandwiches wrapped in tin foil, and poodle-cross dogs. Except of course, we are there to do something illegal. The reservoir belongs to United Utilities, the water supplier, and while cycling, walking, and having a picnic is absolutely fine, swimming is not. According to the company, the reservoir is deep, cold, and full of 'hidden hazards'. There are also, apparently, 'strong currents below the surface' as the reservoir constantly supplies Stockport. The offence we are there to commit is a civil one rather than a criminal one and presumably, in the interests of seeking to avoid negative publicity, nobody has turned up to stop us.

It would be wrong to suggest that wild swimming, as swimming in open water is now fashionably called, is completely risk free. Every year about 400 people drown in Britain and about a quarter drown while swimming recreationally, a proportion that is growing. Between 2018 and 2021 there was a 79 per cent increase in deaths related to wild swimming and coast guard call-outs doubled but as the Open Water Swimming Society rightly points out, with over four million people swimming in rivers, lochs, lakes, and the sea each year, those numbers don't make it a high-risk activity. In 2022, for instance, in England and Wales, almost a thousand people died due to overdosing on cocaine, while almost one hundred people died due to being hit by cars while cycling. Cocaine, we can probably agree, is something we can do without, but wild swimming, like cycling, is a positive thing. 'Wild swimming saved my life' a girl with a mullet, standing in front of me, has felt-tipped onto an A3 sheet of paper stuck to her backpack and below it, there is a number to text if you are having suicidal thoughts. Incidentally, about 200 people drown themselves each year in order to take their own lives. Water gives and takes.

It's increasingly recognised, and the Kinder Reservoir trespass has been in the firing line in the past for this very reason, that a large number of people entering the water with sunscreen on is not a good thing. There are even parts of the world where there are signs on beaches prohibiting certain types of sunscreen being worn by swimmers. The impact of oxybenzone and octinoxate, two common ingredients in sunscreen, both of which are photoprotective, cause deformities in coral. It's estimated that 14,000 tonnes of sunscreen are released into coral reefs each year. The effect on marine life is the most widely-acknowledged consequence of sunscreen but it is increasingly understood to have an impact on freshwater fish too. In 2021, a study carried out by the University of York and Seoul National University found that compounds in sunscreen damage freshwater fish reproduction, as well as their kidney function and hormonal balances. There are mineral sunscreens, without damaging UV filters, but clearly public awareness around the products they are using and the impact they could potentially have is limited. It is not just products for human use that pose a risk. Dogs dosed with flea and worming treatments can be hugely harmful in ponds and rivers. In 2021, neonicotinoids were found in two-thirds of UK rivers. 'Imidacloprid', one of the most common types of neonic found, is banned for use in agriculture so the most likely source of its transmission is our beloved dogs. In other words, they don't only wreak havoc on the shore, among colonies of ground-nesting birds, but dogs, when we throw tennis balls into the water for them, are killing aquatic life too. Troublingly, my own spaniel loves to swim at every opportunity.*

* Rosemary Perkins, Martin Whitehead and Dave Goulson. 'Dead in the Water: comment on "Development of an aquatic exposure assessment model for imidacloprid in sewage treatment plant discharges arising from use of veterinary medicinal products".' *Environmental Sciences Europe*, vol. 33, no. 88, 2021.

There is something cultish about wild swimming – like people who have sourdough starters or go to the Tate Modern, in London, on Saturday afternoons, its advocates can be homogeneous and tribal but the science is compelling. Dr Mark Harper in his book, *The Cold Water Swim Cure*, writes about an NHS study he was involved in that resulted in some 15 per cent of participants noting an increase in wellbeing after six weeks, in relation to work-related burnout. The Scandinavians have been very aware of the cathartic impact of cold water for centuries. I once spent some days in Finland with a group of old men who spoke very little except to endorse the positive impact, which we tried again and again, of sitting naked in a sauna and then jumping into a cold forest pool.

Landowners often tell you that the reason they don't want children swimming in their ponds is because of the liability if one of them drowns, but in practice there is very little chance of that happening. The courts, over the years, have made it clear that swimmers swim at their own risk and those risks, they have ruled, are obvious. The only thing that landowners are obliged to do is to make would-be swimmers aware of unexpected risks, such as a plough submerged just beneath the surface or unexpected currents. In 1957, the Occupiers' Liability Act placed a duty on landowners to take action to prevent visitors from harm – it didn't include trespassers but they are included in the 1984 Occupiers' Liability Act. However, that act didn't extend to those doing something obviously risky – you have no duty of care, for example, to a trespasser skating across two inches of ice. The trouble, of course, as those who spend lots of time on social media will know well, is that access campaigners often claim that signs warning of the unexpected are used by mean-spirited landowners who simply don't want the kids to swim. In truth, the reality is more nuanced – farm ponds are often full of detritus and climbing out of a lined irrigation reservoir can be difficult.

Out in the water, about three hundred yards away, two mallard watch us. There are people with flowers in their swimming caps. There are ladies with orange inflatable 'tow floats', and a couple have their fingers clasped together and are muttering some sort of prayer or incantation.

I sit for a bit next to a lady with a collie dog in a neckerchief that keeps barking – he isn't allowed in, she tells me, but he wishes he was. He likes to swim and he sees no reason that he shouldn't. She asks me after a while if I've been in yet and I tell her it's not really my thing. I can swim but I don't swim but I did bring a towel just in case. 'You must', she replies, 'now that you're here.'

In the west, above the Peak, there are rain clouds moving in, and the air is turning cold. I take my clothes off, button up the fly on my boxers, then push myself into the water. I swim, messily and out of breath, until I'm ten yards out, then I tread water for a bit, getting a duck's eye view across the reservoir to the old gamekeeper's cottage on the other side. Back on the bank everybody has started cheering and when I turn around, I see that there is a group of naked women heading for the water. They jump in, then swim out and float together on their backs, nipples and toes breaking the surface.

It seems pretty absurd that people can't swim in Kinder Reservoir. One of the main appeals, in an age when raw sewage is literally dumped into British rivers hundreds of times a day, is that reservoirs are very clean. The purity of the water, given that it will end up in our taps, is a priority for the likes of United Utilities. It is true that reservoirs, of which there are almost three hundred in the UK, are often in remote locations, relatively out of reach for the emergency services, but danger is part of life and signs directing people to the most appropriate places to swim would be better than a society where swimming in reservoirs is banned completely and people often just swim anyway, taking their chances, wherever they fancy.

There are a few reservoirs, such as Carding Mill Valley in

Shropshire, and Harthill in Rotherham, where swimming is permitted. Risk assessments have been carried out, swimming areas are designated, there are wild swimming clubs you can join, and the banks have throw lines with life rings on them. In many ways, this is access at its best – neither totally denied, nor a complete free-for-all, but instead it is managed in a way that's beneficial for local people.

The great trouble with claiming that all water is dangerous is that you end up sounding a little like the boy who cried wolf, and it becomes tricky when you really do need to say to people 'No, this bit actually really is dangerous; you could end up getting stuck in a pump like Augustus Gloop in Roald Dahl's Wonka Factory.' The other great benefit of many reservoirs, such as Kinder, is that given they are very deep and they don't tend to have shelved banks or wetland areas around them, they are often oligotrophic (the nutrient content is low) and consequently their benefit as habitat for wildlife is comparatively limited. Whereas, on small ponds, in a lowland farmland setting or on a shallow bit of water by a river meadow, the impact of human access on nature could be far greater. The obvious major advantage of access management, no matter what the body of water, is that you can shut people out during spring, if ducks are on eggs, for example, or even during winter if it's freezing and wildlife is struggling.

There are, it should be noted, reservoirs that are full of life, such as Rutland Water, which hosts internationally important wetland habitat but access there is controlled, with courses for wild swimming marked out by buoys. You can even hire a wetsuit at £5 a go.

*

A little boy in front of me, who appears to be visiting Hunstanton Sea Life Centre with his mother and grandmother, runs towards a fish tank sandwiched between the café and a big rack of fluffy mermaid toys. 'Grandma', he shouts, in wonder, 'there are just millions of them.' The child presses his face against the glass. 'Oh my God', he continues, before calling for his grandmother to come 'straight away' to look at what can't be more than about thirty small blue fish. When they pull him away and head for the main entrance to the aquarium, his mother tells the attendant that he doesn't need 'a welcome photo'. They come, she says wearily, most months.

The lady behind the desk tells me that the curator, Sophie Negus, is on her way down and I watch as an elderly couple, both with walking sticks, decline a welcome photograph too. Sophie arrives from the office just as a group of schoolchildren from Norwich appear – 'Yes, we will be able to see the turtles', their teacher tells them, 'but first we all have to go to the toilet.' Even, she stresses, 'if we don't feel like we need to go' because when you're in there, she explains, that's it. 'No toilet till you're out.'

Sophie, who is in her later twenties, tells me, as we wander past the large aquariums, that Hunstanton Sea Life Centre has a sort of dual function. It's a visitor attraction in part but her main focus is on looking after seals at the Sea Life Centre's 'Seal Hospital', after they've come to harm on the Norfolk coast. Sometimes, she continues, against a backdrop of sweet aquasonic music (which gets switched off apparently when autistic children are visiting) seals get caught in fishing nets but very often they come to harm because of interacting with humans. Except for a small population of orcas, usually in Scottish waters, seals don't have any natural predators so they tend not to have much natural fear of people and dogs, which can create problems. It's not that they won't ever flee from people when they get too close – they can and they do – but at the same time they don't flee at the first sight of humans as a roe deer or a rabbit might. Seals tend to get mixed up with people.

In the first pen at the seal hospital, there is a little male pup, who stares up at us with big black eyes set into a little dog-like face. Sophie explains that in spite of appearances, they aren't actually related to dogs at all. They are, in fact, much more closely related to bears. A mother pushes a pushchair towards us and then lifts out a small chubby child who squeals with delight, on seeing the seal, and kicks his legs around as though he is swimming.

The seal pup was found, Sophie tells me, without enough dentition to eat fish by himself but slowly she has been teaching him to feed and his teeth have now come through so well that he has a herring in the tank with him, which he will hopefully get round to eating at some point over the course of the day. Lily, in the pen next door, was just four days old when she was found on Brancaster Beach. It's never totally clear, according to Sophie, why the pups have been abandoned but quite often it's because their mothers leave them somewhere they think is safe but the pup gets spooked by crowds of people and tries, instinctively, to head off somewhere quieter and when the mother returns, the pup is gone. Another possibility is that the mothers themselves become frightened and they abandon their pups in order to seek safety for themselves. Sophie thinks that we often have 'a much larger effect on everything than we think we do'.

As we move on to the Pup Recovery Pool, Sophie explains that because she is the only person who feeds the pups, they don't associate all humans with food. In fact everybody else just stares at them, then moves on, and they end up thinking that humans in general are boring. The ideal scenario is that they get released back into the wild knowing how to find food for themselves, rather than looking to people to be fed.

Outside, where some of the older resident seals, who aren't suitable to be released, are swimming round and round there is a large blue board stuck to the wall with some backstory about Pippa, who has, it reads, 'a beautiful silver belly'. Pippa was found on Old Hunstanton Beach in 2012, heavily dehydrated and exhausted. Members of the public kept on trying to get her to go back into the sea when all she needed was rest. It's sort of reassuring, Sophie thinks, that the public cares so much but they often appear not to know what to do when they find a seal that really does need help, or they think they've found a seal that needs help when actually it's completely fine. Lately there has also been a spate of people trying to take pictures with seals, which are more inclined to bite while on the land as they feel vulnerable when out of the water. There was even an instance, which the seal hospital ended up involved in, when a man put his toddler on a seal's back, as though the child was riding it, for a photo.

Every time one of the seals rises up out of the water in front of us and then rolls over on its back, Sophie greets it like a friend but there is something reassuringly unsentimental about her. Access, she tells me, is always about balance. Behind the pool, a duck is sitting on a platform and behind the duck, a large white block of art deco flats rises up over the sea. Hunstanton is full of slot machines, caravans, dodgems, and fish and chip shops, but on Mondays, except for fairground workers and children visiting the Sea Life Centre – sometimes as many as a hundred a day – the town is quiet.

The thing is, Sophie says to me, as we retrace our steps, back past the pups, she doesn't think that anybody heads to the beach with their dog, willing it to attack seals, but they just don't think about it. The beach, it seems, for lots of people, is really only about giving their dog a run. It's a place for humans and our pets because humans, in the Anthropocene, always come first. One of the other things they often see at the seal hospital are seals with frisbee rings around their necks. People take them down onto the sand to play with and they end up in the water, where they get carried out to sea, before eventually ending up suffocating some poor marine creature. There have been a number of campaigns to make people aware of the harm they cause. In a way, Sophie thinks, it probably seems like there are so many rules now and guidelines about what we can and can't do on the beach but the truth is we are really only just becoming aware, she tells me, of the damage we cause.

We stop, just before we get back to the café and the shop, to have a look at the guitarfish. Sometimes the guitarfish die, but it apparently tends to happen at night, so they can be pulled out the following morning and are disposed of before opening time.

Over the following weeks, I return again and again to the little videos I took of the seal pups. I loved the seal hospital. It seems to bring so much joy to local children; no doubt everybody leaves knowing more about the marine world, and I liked Sophie too but at the same time, the whole place is a little odd. It's strange, when you think about it, to have a sort of saccharine distillation of 'sea life' just up the beach from the sea, which is run after all by Merlin Entertainments, which also owns Madame Tussauds and Legoland. Those seals were there to recover, but also as an attraction. Yes, we'll disturb you and your babies and then when you abandon them in fright, we'll put them behind glass next to the promenade for us to have a good look at. The seal hospital does great work, that's undeniable, but it is also a late-stage example of the solipsism and unthinking might of man.

*

One of the things that generally separates humans from the rest of the species with whom we share the planet is our love of moving into other habitats. Lobsters never make it up onto the sand and giraffes don't go to sea but we have a seemingly insatiable desire to experience and colonise everywhere and all the places in between. A long list of creatures across the British Isles rely on the sanctuary of coastal zones to escape us and yet by kayak, jet ski, dinghy, and increasingly on foot, as the popularity of 'coasteering' grows, we find them. Seals are very unlikely to haul themselves up on our beds but it's pretty common that a human traipses across theirs.

It is notable that those who agitate for more access to the land and to waterways often take very confident positions on the impact of footfall. We aren't the ones who cause issues, the consensus at most pro-access meetings I attend seems to be. It's the farmers and landowners who cause all the trouble, whereas we, the people, are actually trying to make things better. But scientists and zoologists like Sophie, those who have actually spent years studying the impact of access, usually tend to be much less certain. All around the coast, there are seabirds and shorebirds that are doing badly. The stark decline of species such as the kittiwake has the potential to be made worse by disturbance caused by recreational access. Typically, birds respond when humans come within 100 metres of them but some species have been recorded taking evasive action when humans are seen over 200 metres out. Clearly, if you are a seabird roosting on a cliff edge and two coasteerers plunge into the sea, from on high, next to your nest, it would be likely to trigger panic among your colony. Professor Tom Cameron, at the University of Essex, who researches aquatic ecology with a focus on predation and disturbance, believes that more work needs to be done to gauge the real impact of disturbance on birds. There are times of plenty, he explained to me, when he thinks the impact is limited and there are times when food is scarce that the impact can be immense. The question he posed, though, is whether the public would respond well to having their freedom limited when wildlife is either vulnerable because of breeding or is up against it because of the weather. Many of us, he thinks, probably just don't care. As ever, the need for education and opportunities to engage is stark.

It isn't just birds and mammals that are of concern around the coast; fucoid seaweeds, such as bladderwrack, won't withstand much trampling, which goes too for lichens. Bladderwrack provides habitat for snails, which are in turn eaten by crabs. Across Europe, it is a seaweed in decline because of the acidification of the sea. There are places around the UK where coasteering has become so popular that paths across the rocky shore have been worn away by cold wet trainers. This might sound like a marginal issue but marginal places are essential for creatures that are struggling and it illustrates the impact of man at play in habitats that, in an ecological sense, aren't ours. It's quite something to think that many of us will have disturbed pupping seals in a cave that we can't see and that we aren't aware of but, in truth, our impact on the creatures we share the world with is almost impossible to quantify or to understand. Tom Cameron mentioned the concept of ghosts of disturbance (something he coined himself when we were speaking). All up the east coast, there would be, he believes, seal colonies that simply aren't there because of how busy the beaches are.

Many activity centres avoid coasteering in sensitive areas during bird-nesting season, from the beginning of March to the end of July, as well as during seal-pupping season, which is quite long and runs across the UK from August to the end of January. But surely it follows that back on dry land, we should also close off the uplands when there are critically endangered ground-nesting birds breeding in spring? You can put a dog on a lead but what if that lead is extendable and there is a curlew nesting not far from the path.

In the context of birds, seemingly innocuous activities such as windsurfing and kitesurfing, which are participated in by about 150,000 people a year, have the ability to cause disturbance at distances of up to 700 metres. The fast and apparently random movements of a windsurfer or kitesurfer mean that 'single events' have been found to have large displacement effects.

Clearly, motorised vessels can cause significant harm, and often death, to seals when there are collisions and they can cause disturbance at a greater range but at the same time, because of the noise that they make, seals become aware of a motorboat's presence much earlier. A number of studies have found around 50 per cent of paddled craft cause 'hauled-out' seals to flush into water, compared to just 10 per cent of motorised vessels. In part this is because things like kayaks travel close to the shore but it's also believed that their appearance looks, to a seal, like a shark or an orca, both of which, as predators, are pretty terrifying when they emerge from the dappled sunlight, almost silently, ten yards out. The very worst thing kayakers can do – and of some 1.5 million participants every year, a number of them set out to look for wildlife – is to surround seals, which gives them a sense of having no escape from predation.

The list of activities that people participate in and the potential consequences runs on and on. Basking sharks, for instance, are perceived to show negative responses to groups of divers and at the gentler end of marine recreation, shallow rock pools see a decline in biodiversity when they are trampled at busy beaches. It would be a little extreme to suggest that we should shut down the seaside but the consequences of our presence are real and worsening, as species decline and the popularity of activities like coasteering and windsurfing increases.

It's often said that if only we were able to access the countryside, we would be able to see all the wonderful creatures there, and our relationship with nature would change. Even if it were true that the countryside is out of bounds, that argument crumbles because of the inconvenient example of the coast. Clearly, most of the English seaside is accessible and the public rub up against birdlife and seals but it doesn't seem as though the experience gives them some sort of glorious love of marine life. It doesn't need to be repeated that in many instances we treat non-human life on the coast pretty terribly – evidently to see seals is not to understand them. Nobody in Britain lives more than 70 miles from the coast but how many people really appreciate that there are two different types of seals in the UK and how many people can tell you about gull ecology, in spite of having seen them?

Currently, a coastal path is being constructed around the UK, which will allow people to circumnavigate the whole of the country. It is a good example of the inaccuracy of the narrative that access is being restricted. The process of creating the path has been a tricky one – various landowners have objected but steadily it's getting there. It will be, it's claimed, one of the longest continuous walks in the world. There's no doubt it'll be brilliant for dog walkers and the public will get to venture into even more habitat to rub against even more endangered wildlife.

*

One of the things that coasteering, kayaking, and windsurfing all tend to have in common is that they aren't really about engaging with nature. They put people in the presence of it, in often genuinely wild spaces, but the nature we disturb is just collateral while we have fun. It would be like a couple of seals, quite oblivious to you, hauling themselves out in your garage and then pissing all over the floor. Wildfowling, like fishing, or collecting clams, is different though – it's not just that nature is there, you are actually pursuing it, engaging with it, and harvesting it.

On the banks of the Humber, a thin wind blows among the reeds and Paul Upton, his gun over his shoulder, walks ahead of me, threading a path through plastic bottles and driftwood towards a small oak, just visible in the dawn light. He retired some years ago, after working at the docks in Hull, and with his brother, Dave, he now goes out for a goose most mornings. He is a short man with strong broad shoulders and he does everything with a sense of urgency. He always wanted to go to sea with the cod fleet, he tells me, but his mother wouldn't let him. It can be rough off Svalbard, and over the years lots of boys from Hull have drowned in the Barents Sea.

The redshank cry first and then the curlew call. It's too early for geese and ducks but that's not really the point and Paul doesn't like to shoot ducks, anyway, during the last few weeks of the season when they've started pairing up. He goes out on the marsh, he tells me, just to be there as much as anything. Wildfowling is about getting something for the table but he does it too because he's always done it, and his dad did before him and now his nephews have become wildfowlers. 'It's just that little bit of freedom', he says, unscrewing the lid from his flask and pouring himself a cup of tea. 'I don't know any different. It's that freedom to go when you like.'

Under the oak, to our left, Paul's young Labrador is sitting with his nose turned to the sky and as he drinks his tea, Paul runs his hand through the dog's coat, telling me he's just the sort of dog he likes, strong but not too big and with thick fur for when the sleet rolls in. When Paul's dad was a boy, the marsh was a free-for-all. Across Britain, below the high water mark, in the early twentieth century – particularly on the east coast – there were lots of places just like it. The mud and saltings belong to the Crown and anybody, in theory, could shoot there. Things have changed, though, and to go wildfowling on the north bank of the Humber now, you need to be a member of the club and the land is leased from the Crown. 'Only £140 a year', Paul tells me, 'so it's not too bad for the working man.' The club was established, in part, due to outsiders with money who would come in their rubber dinghies with engines and head out to where the geese roost. The formation of the club meant that access could be restricted to those who lived locally, abided by the rules, and passed a bird recognition test. 'We don't', Paul says as he packs his flask away, 'want anybody thinking a cormorant is a Canada goose. We can't have accidents.' But as well as keeping the trigger-happy away from the roosting grounds, the club fights hard to ensure that wildfowling remains possible for men like Dave and Paul.

Some days before I went out with Paul, I spoke to Ken Arkley who is originally from the North East but came to Hull to work as a trawlerman. Ken has been a member of the Humber Wildfowlers for over twenty years and in that time, he's served as both Secretary and Chairman and a lot of his time is taken up with trying to preserve access. He isn't, he admits, an out-and-out wildfowler – he fishes too but he realised, when he joined the club, how much fowling meant to people like the Uptons and how passionate about it they are. At times he has, he tells me, felt like 'packing it all in' – the amount of grief has been unbelievable and the fight just to keep things going feels endless. But then when he sees 'who he's doing it for' and 'how much it means to them', he just feels he can't walk away. He thinks that to give up would be to let people down and abandon them. These days, Ken doesn't often get out on the marsh himself anymore but it's not, he says, about his own wildfowling. It's about people who without the ability to go out on the marsh to shoot geese, wouldn't really have anything else.

Part of Ken's challenge over the years has been trying to persuade Natural England, who oversee much of the Humber Estuary, that wildfowlers aren't just 'bird killers'. Ken thinks that lots of people would have them off the marsh tomorrow if they could but he wishes they understood that men like Paul and Dave go out after the geese at dawn because of the intimacy it gives them with nature – 'they can't get any closer to the natural world'. Many of them, according to Ken, could hold their own next to the keenest birdwatchers and when the season's through and spring comes round, they head out onto the marsh without their guns, just to watch and to listen.

Across the river, out on the roost, the geese start to call and then, just before seven o'clock, small groups of them lift and start to fly inland to feed. By February, a lot of them have been shot at already and most of the skeins fly wide of us, over ground that the fowlers aren't allowed onto. Every time a skein does pass anywhere close to us, Paul tells me to keep my head down and to stay tucked into the reeds but they aren't close enough and he tells me he's 'not in the business' of wounding birds.

The strange thing, according to Paul, is that when they established the sanctuary out on the roost, it was done with 'birdy people'. In those days he doesn't think there was so much conflict and misunderstanding. Among farmers, ramblers, ornithologists, and wildfowlers, 'there was a live and let live attitude'.

When the light comes up, we move further down into the reeds, where a winter flood has washed timber and glass onto the land and we stand among the debris with Paul holding his gun against his chest while listening to a lone pink, flying high above us. Most of them by February have returned to their breeding grounds in Iceland and Svalbard. During the summer, like many other clubs across the country, the members of the Hull Wildfowlers carry out conservation work. They clear rubbish, they dig and maintain ponds, and they put up nesting tubes for ducks. The idea, Paul tells me, that they threaten duck numbers when what they really want is to see them increase, is frustrating.

Just before eight, Paul's brother, Dave, who is out on the marsh a few hundred metres east of us, gives Paul a ring. 'Now then', Paul says when he picks up. They talk, for some time, about the morning, without really saying very much at all. There've been geese, they both agree and there've been a few ducks, shoveller and mallard, but 'nothing spectacular'. They agree to give it another five minutes and shortly after putting his phone back into his jacket pocket, a skein of four greylags flies directly above us. He shoots this time, then swings through and fires again, his finger slipping to the rear trigger. The geese carry on unharmed and Paul shakes his head. When you no longer care about missing, he tells me, that's when you know it's time to stop.

The marsh that we cross, to get back to where we parked up, is now owned by the club. Originally it was part of a farm but the farmer died, his wife moved away, and neither of the two daughters had any interest in taking it on. The club, Paul explains, borrowed as much as they could in order to bid on the land when it came up at auction – they realised that if somebody else got it, a farmer, or a conservation body, the wildfowling would probably be done. Over the years, Ken has spearheaded efforts to buy little bits of marsh here and there – sometimes it's only been a couple of acres but it allows them to get down onto Crown foreshore where they can shoot. It's a bit of a sorry situation, he thinks, that they actually have to buy land to keep being able to do something that people have been doing on the Humber, relatively freely, for centuries but it is what it is. Across the country, there are people in very similar positions – in Suffolk, the National Trust has prohibited wildfowlers from walking across a section of land, to access the Lantern Marsh at Aldeburgh. 'It is strange', one of the fowlers there said to me when I spoke to him. 'The National Trust is there to create access for people but it's because of them that we can't get out onto the mud anymore to do what we've always done.'

Some years ago there was, Ken recalls, a very strange situation when they thought a bit of land belonged to the Crown and they were paying them rent but it transpired that the Crown had actually sold it some years back to Natural England but nothing was being done with it – in retrospect, he supposes, what that showed was that a little patch of mud in the Humber Estuary really only mattered much to the wildfowlers and the birds that lived there, and it mattered to them greatly.

Back where we parked there are two club members who were shooting further along the marsh. They'd been after ducks, they tell us, for their dinner, but they'd only had geese over them and they shot two. Would I, the older of the men asks, on being told I'm visiting, like one of the greylags to take home?

To claim, as some salty old wildfowlers do, that 'the sport', as they would call it (I'd suggest that among the devout it is more of a faith) is a victimless pursuit would be wrong. There's that goose in my freezer but 'direct mortality', as Natural England euphemistically calls it, is not thought to be an issue of conservation concern if hunting is carried out sustainably, which it generally is. It's true though that disturbance, particularly during harsh weather, can result in a loss of foraging time and also energy expenditure for non-target species, such as knot or dunlin. Importantly, though, wildfowling is carried out from September to February so there is no disturbance during breeding season. Natural England's position is that although there is much evidence of disturbance effects from shooting, there is no clear evidence of population impacts due to wildfowling alone. In short, it might seem counterintuitive but those who actually set out to kill wildlife around the coast do not, it seems, have a measurable negative impact on it. Fowlers don't take selfies with seals or clamber into caves where endangered seabirds are nesting. That said, wildfowling is far from popular among the public and efforts to bring it to an end are mounted regularly. In 2017, in Bournemouth, a birdwatcher set up a petition to have wildfowling banned in Christchurch Harbour, citing disturbance to wintering birds, but also the risk to people sailing, rowing, and canoeing, who may have also been – according to Natural England – disturbing wintering birds. It seems like some clear types of disturbance sit well with people but other, less egregious types, not so much.

Despite fowlers being at the vanguard of the fight for access and generally being working class, I have never heard any land access campaigners acknowledging their struggle. While dog walkers are having their access increased, fowlers are having theirs reduced. There has been some concern among wildfowlers that the new King Charles III coastal path might further limit the land they are able to shoot geese and ducks over. It is immensely complex and it's an issue bound up in all sorts of British cultural anxieties and sensibilities but in short, wild-fowling is both inherently related to the access struggle while it's also totally removed from it. Googling 'Right to Roam' and 'wildfowling' brings up no results at all, whereas the internet is replete with stuff on Right to Roam and picnicking, camping, and jogging.

Paul and Dave and I drive into Newport to buy pies at the bakery. Then we sit at the bus stop outside the Methodist chapel to eat them. Dave tells me, while flakes of pastry fall on the pavement, that over the years his father was in regular contact with Natural England (then English Nature) and he had a lot of paperwork detailing agreements about wildfowling on the estuary. He filed it all away and they then found it shortly after he died. It hasn't meant, as Ken explained, that life for the Humber Wildfowlers has been easy but it has certainly been easier than it would have been without the documents. Promises about access to the marsh in perpetuity, Dave tells me, were made. Paul, who is sitting hunched over on the red plastic bench, says without looking up that even with those promises you can't really be sure – they go to all the meetings about access but they are just wildfowlers and there's not all that much they can do when it comes to fighting it out with giants like Natural England or the Crown Estate. He does wonder whether, Paul says as he scrunches up the paper bag his pie was in, if a time will come when the Crown decides they no longer want to be associated with wildfowling. It might eventually be thought to be good for optics, for the Royals, to announce that no more geese and ducks will be shot on Crown land.

Dave heads home and Paul jumps in with me – he wants to drive across to Patrington Haven, on the other side of Hull, to have a look at a bit of land he used to shoot over where the sea wall is going to be breached. The plan is that if they breach the wall and flood some of the marsh, they will reduce the risk of Hull itself ending up under water. It's not totally clear how it will pan out for the wildfowlers – they hope that they will be given some ground as compensation elsewhere but more immediately, the only road across the flat drained landscape keeps getting blocked off by machinery.

The roads across the reclaimed fields, drained by local land-owners some 250 years ago, are lined by poplar trees and the soil is fertile and dark. Paul keeps asking me to stop so he can look out across the marsh with his binoculars. There are waders and hares and church spires in the distance. It is a place that was taken from the sea and slowly the sea is taking it back again.

In 1907 a railway worker called Stanley Duncan took shelter in a small black hut at Patrington Haven when he was out wildfowling and the weather came in. For some time, Duncan, who was originally from Newcastle but had travelled to Hull to find work, had been increasingly aware that his shooting was under threat. In part this was because it was being 'improved' by farmers but wealthy sportsmen were also taking exclusive leases on it. While the wind was blowing and the rain was coming down, with his punt moored up outside, he decided to establish some kind of representative body to defend fowling men's rights. This became the Wildfowlers' Association of Great Britain and Ireland. The black hut itself was washed away some years ago by a big spring tide but Paul wants to show me where it stood. Water is something that should be feared as well as loved and recognised as special but never truly ours.

For decades nobody seemed to know where Stanley Duncan was buried. In later life, Paul explains, when we are driving back across the flat fields towards the graveyard, Duncan set up a tackle and gun shop in Hull but when he died in 1954 there seemingly wasn't any money for a proper burial and there was no headstone. Then, decades later, the Uptons worked out – using local records – where it was that Duncan was buried.

We are the only people in the graveyard and the wind is blowing through the tops of the conifers. 'Headstone's made from granite', Paul tells me when we get to the graves, 'so it should last.' They had a whip-round to pay for it and a couple of other wildfowlers across the country chipped in too. 'Not for one but for all' is inscribed across the bottom in gold lettering and at the top there is a carved goose, wings outstretched, flying across a red sky. It was, Dave tells me, the way that Duncan saw the land, not just for the rich but for all, and particularly for men from Hull.

At the start of the season, when the geese return from the north and shed their primary feathers, Paul and Dave go out onto the mud to collect a few and then they come and lay them at Stanley's grave. 'I'm not a religious man', Paul says with a nod, but it's a tradition now and sometimes he even brings a bit of gunpowder with him too to scatter over the earth.

*

In looking to sea and thinking about lakes, rivers, and reservoirs, so much about access becomes clear. Water, on this island nation, means a great deal to us. It always has but it shows that sadly, it's quite wrong to say that to encounter wildlife is to understand it and love it. Britain's seals and seabirds don't benefit from us continually coming across them. Thinking about the coast also reinforces the truth that there is a lot of access in Britain. It's pretty clear too that at certain times of year, it would be better if parts of our beaches were completely off-limits. A flimsy plastic cordon is going to do nothing to keep a badly behaved lurcher out when birds are breeding.

It's also overwhelmingly clear that the benefits of being able to swim in open water are immense and there aren't great reasons why it isn't possible in more places. Don't ban it, manage it. It becomes clear too, when we turn to the coast and to Britain's estuaries, that some pastimes are more equal than others. I still think of how delighted all those children were about the prospect of seeing the sea turtles in Hunstanton but what about wildfowling? Wouldn't it be wonderful if more children and young teenagers could get out fowling at dawn or get out to collect seaweed or cast a line for mackerel off the beach. Not every child will have the opportunity – that's not possible – but many more children could.

Humans aren't 'nature' in the way that gulls or geese are but to go foraging or fowling or fishing is to truly engage and a lack of engagement seems to be where we go wrong again and again. There is no access crisis in Britain but there is an engagement crisis. It's about the chance to get out there and smell things, hear things, and taste things. It's a cultural shift that makes people realise that there are things out there for them – there are visceral ways of connecting with the land and the land is generative.

When I saw that goose on top of Stanley Duncan's gravestone, I understood that in a way what these men do is a form of goose worship; even the act of eating the geese and the ducks is part of that. I think of Paul and Dave and Stanley Duncan in the same way I think of the Indigenous people who hunt and eat bears in the Russian Far East. Not as a form of man gaining dominion over nature but as a form of worship and as a way of connecting with the natural world. That, somewhere, has been lost and we need to rekindle it.

The poet, Ted Hughes, talked of fishing giving him a connection 'to this whole – to everything. The stuff of the earth.'[*] Hughes told friends that if the UK abolished fishing, he would 'have to leave the country. I'd have to go live in a land where I can still keep hold of the world.'[†] That is what we need to give people the ability to do, to really hold the world.

[*] Quoted in Neil Roberts. *Ted Hughes, A Literary Life*. Palgrave Macmillan, 2007.
[†] Quoted in Ehor Boyanowsky. *Savage Gods, Silver Ghosts: In the Wild with Ted Hughes*. Douglas & McIntyre, an imprint of D&M Publishers, 2009, p. 187.

6
Agriculture

The obvious and often completely overlooked impact that access has on farming

They're mostly profit-driven bastards and we need to be able to wander across their farms to keep an eye on them, is the gist of Guy Shrubsole's short chapter, 'Stewardship', in the Right to Roam compendium, *Wild Service*. We've lost half our birds, the chapter notes, and 'once-common creatures like hedgehogs have seen a collapse in numbers'. It isn't made clear why your local farmer is responsible for the ruin of Britain's hedgehogs but what we need to do, it's explained, is to get out into farmers' fields, behind the 'barbed-wire fences' so we can 'bear witness' to all their wrongdoings, and then 'blow the whistle' on their 'crimes'.

There is no doubt that some farmers, while producing food for the nation, do things they shouldn't. They are up against it and most of them have to farm in a way that keeps their often-struggling businesses afloat, but do the public at large really have the knowledge to call them out? Are we going to start flagging situations where spring barley would have been better for linnets than winter barley because of the stubble; are we going to start kicking off when people get an early cut of silage in, or when we believe that red polls might have resulted in a better sward than Simmentals? It's a nice idea but it seems unlikely.

At the same time, the extent to which access can be hugely detrimental to farming businesses is often little understood. The pig farming industry, for example, has huge concerns around biosecurity; sheep are frequently killed by wayward dogs, and most years, a number of people are killed or at least seriously injured by cattle, which quite reasonably leads to lengthy, costly, and deeply stressful court cases. It would make a lot of sense if farmers said that they didn't want anybody on their land at all. After all, farms are places of work. As well as bullocks that might trample you, on a working farm, there could be dangerous machinery, deep reservoirs, and hazardous chemicals. But, in spite of that, farmers are often welcoming. In a report published in 2021, on enhancing access opportunities in Kent, 44 per cent of 116 farmers, landowners, and land managers polled said that they would 'possibly' consider providing more 'permissive access'. Nineteen per cent said they 'definitely' would and just 7.8 per cent said they wouldn't. Equally, of 115 respondents, surveyed as part of the same report, just 2.6 per cent said they wouldn't consider enhancing 'existing access'.

Clearly, very few farmers are going to welcome a go-wherever-you-like free-for-all and they're probably not going to want you around if you're intending to interfere with conservation projects, or if you're planning to take pictures of a hedge that's just been coppiced to post on social media, in the hope of whipping up a storm. Ultimately, access campaigners who make a habit of unreasonably criticising farming inevitably contribute to a culture where the public becomes less welcome on farmland.

*

Gladys was four years old and she had a calf due to be born, when two dogs killed her. 'Two Labradors', Cameron Farquharson tells me, as we walk towards the gate to his Dorset farm. They chased her, he explains, to the edge of the rise some 150 yards ahead of us and she tumbled to her death. 'As a farming family',

Cameron says, while he climbs the stile, 'it put us in a really dark place.' Cameron, who is originally from Melrose, in the Scottish Borders, has one of the largest folds of Highland cattle in the South West but the loss, financially as well as emotionally, was considerable. 'We just all felt', he tells me, referring to his wife and his grown up children, 'that no farming family should feel like we did.'

The sky above Eggardon Hill, which was once a hill fort that was captured by the Romans, is bright autumn blue, with thin cloud swept across it, and among the tussocky grass, wax caps are coming up. Cameron is a big man. He wears waterproof trousers, boots, and his fleece and hat are embroidered with a picture of a Highland cow.

After Gladys died, Cameron put a post out on social media about the threat that dogs pose to livestock and the response was extraordinary. He hadn't appreciated, until that point, quite how large the global Highland cattle community is. There were Germans sending their condolences, he says, shaking his head in disbelief, and people from America. There was even a local farmer who offered to give Cameron a replacement heifer and calf. At first, he wondered what the catch was but the old boy said it was simply that he was selling up and he'd spent his life, as well as farming, working in mental health, and it would mean a lot more to him to give a few of his Highlands to Cameron than to get money for them all – the generosity of it brought Cameron to tears.

As we get up onto the first plateau, where Cameron's calves are grazing with their mothers, a few of them no more than three weeks old, he tells me that although it was Gladys that made the news, dogs attacking his livestock is nothing new. The statistics are so shocking that I almost find them hard to believe – the previous year he lost 10 per cent of his sheep to dogs and the worst day he ever had was when he lost 11 pregnant ewes. 'It was absolute carnage', he tells me, and when he called up the insurer he found himself apologising to them. 'It's what we're here for', they replied. Calls like Cameron's aren't rare.

Cameron is a tenant on just 250 acres split across two sites and the grazing at Eggardon Hill is owned by the National Trust. The trouble, as he sees it, is that the Trust is frankly more interested in the public, whom they make money out of, than the farmers who, in his words, 'do their job for them', by looking after the land. Dotted around the farm there are red National Trust signs that read: 'Even your dog can harm livestock, keep it on a lead', but Cameron tells me that the Trust previously gave the public the impression on their website that one of the joys of visiting their land is that you could let your dog roam free. 'It was like I've just lost a cow here', he says despondently, 'and they were saying to Joe Public, you can let your dog off the lead.'

The land on our left falls away and in the distance, beyond a patchwork of fields, the sea is cast silver beneath a bright band of cloud. It's very similar, Cameron thinks, to parts of the west coast of Scotland and even when it's hot in the summer a cold wind still almost always blows in. 'Right through from the Bay of Biscay', he tells me with pride. We stop for a moment and then he edges slowly towards a small calf, just a few weeks old, which is standing by its mother. It looks as though it has just been washed and dried, and you almost can't see its eyes among the orange fuzz on its face. The mother had another, he says in a whisper, as the calf looks down at Cameron's shadow stretching across the grass, but it died and the little boy is her second. When he's within ten yards of it, it turns to look at its mother, then it kicks its feet out behind it and bolts.

In the months that followed Gladys's death, Cameron started to realise that other people had experienced far worse attacks. At one point he was receiving about ten dog-related emails a week and the one that sticks with him was from a farmer in the North West who lost 42 pregnant ewes that were set upon by alsatians. They didn't kill them directly, he explains, but in their fright, the ewes all huddled together in a bid to stay safe and suffocated.

The law around dogs and livestock is, Cameron thinks, a grey area. It's commonly believed that farmers can shoot dogs if they are on the rampage but he's never, he says, shot a dog yet, and he doesn't plan to. The idea that he will always be up on the hill, with his rifle, just in case is clearly ridiculous and even then, if you do get a shot off he thinks that unless you had 'a hundred per cent evidence', you'd probably lose your firearms licence. 'The law kind of goes against you.' Cameron reckoned that a better thing to do was to start, after the death of Gladys, campaigning for stricter laws around dogs chasing livestock. Under the proposed changes, which had the support of Victoria Prentis, the then-Attorney General, dog walkers will face criminal prosecution if their dog chases livestock to the point of causing harm, including miscarriage. It is often the case that a ewe might seem fine but that her lambs have died. Part of the problem, Cameron tells me, as we get up to the top, where Eggardon Hill flattens out, is that he thinks most people's dogs are far less well-trained than they often think. The idea that somebody can walk with their dog at heel, and that they can call that dog back to them if it's too far out, might seem simple, and it's something a lot of dog owners think they can do but farmers with livestock will tell you otherwise. In practice, Cameron thinks it's just common sense that if you have a dog with you – for your own safety too, as cattle some-times attack people with dogs – it's sensible to stay off land with stock on it.

Eggardon Hill in the eighteenth century was owned by Isaac Gulliver, a prolific tea smuggler, and it's said that he planted pine trees on the top of the hill so that his ships had a naviga-tion point when pulling into Dorset in the dead of night but it's treeless now and the rough grazing is perfect for magic mushrooms, which are popular with the locals from Bridport. There was a boy up here the other day, Cameron tells me, wandering about for hours. When I ask him if he chases them off he laughs and says they aren't doing any harm.

Cameron's view is that although the legislation he would like to see enacted would make a difference, he doesn't believe you're ever really going to beat the public, particularly if you're a tenant farmer whose landlord puts access first. What you can do, though, 'is try to educate them'. What it is, is that he recognises he has the ability to show people the countryside. He realised this, he explains, just at the start of lockdown when he was hedge-laying. 'I was having my piece and this cow came up.' He gestures at his right shoulder to indicate how close she was. 'I thought oh God', he continues, 'I'll move on.' But when he did, she wandered after him and when he stopped for his lunch, he gave her a biscuit and 'we had', he says, 'a wee conversation and the rest is kind of history'.

Highland cattle are not generally thought to be particularly easy to handle but word soon got round, during lockdown, and Cameron started to get calls from people to ask if he would show them his cows. People would just come up 'with a flask of tea or maybe a beer and sit with the cows'. He thinks in retrospect, it was maybe people who were finding lockdown difficult, and had a 'few issues going on', but he didn't really ever ask. From there, the whole thing grew and he now does tours to show people the cattle and to explain how the farm works. They even, he says, get 'wee nursery guys' and he holds his hand out at waist height to show me how small they are.

One of the oddest things, Cameron thinks, over all the years that he's been farming Eggardon, is that the people who are most difficult don't seem to be the young. 'That's the worrying thing.' His children are between 20 and 25 now but when they were still at school they'd be up on the hill helping him and over the years, when asking people to put their dogs on leads and to accommodate whatever it was they were doing with the livestock, they've been 'spat on', 'sworn at', and one of them was even 'smacked with a walking stick'. One of the most aggressive people was a man who was apparently illegally collecting orchids and who refused to get his dog, which was marauding around while he had his head in the flowers, under control. 'It was dogs back on the lead or I'll call the police', Cameron says, in a stern re-enactment of the incident.

At the edge of the hill, below where the fort's ramparts once stood, the land falls away beneath us and on the other side of the deep gully there is an oak wood and a band of chalk. 'It starts there', Cameron says, looking across at the chalk, 'and it runs all the way to Moscow.' He pauses and then adds that he supposes the Russians might say it starts in Moscow and runs all the way to Eggardon. I ask him if he thinks about the history of the hill when he's out with the cattle. He nods. 'Yes, with my feet on the ground.' Can you imagine, he asks me, coming from the Mediterranean as part of the Roman army and being up here in January. He laughs then says that he wonders in 150 years time if people will say, 'There was a Scottish chap up here who once had Highland cows.' In the distance, in the bay at Poole Harbour, a bright haze has moved in across the sea. I ask Cameron if he thinks the situation with his animals will get better. 'It will. I hope it will', he replies, 'I'd rather have my cow back but we're bringing people up here now.'

*

In the context of access, livestock being chased, injured, and not infrequently killed by dogs is the most talked-about point of tension between the public and farmers. Over 30 per cent of households own a dog and there are now over 12 million of them in Britain, with the Labrador retriever being the most popular. There don't seem to be any figures in regards to how many walkers, ramblers, and wild campers tend to have dogs with them but I will always remember my primary school teacher telling us to be wary of any men wandering alone in the local park without one. Not absolutely, categorically a paedophile, they admitted, but walking without a dog, they suggested, was 'a red flag'.

Land access campaigners tend to concede that dogs are a problem – most trespasses are preceded by an email asking people to leave their dogs at home and in the spring of 2024, the Right to Roam campaign put out a press release suggesting that the next government should introduce measures to control dogs, alongside introducing a 'Right to Roam'. There are, though, other issues in the context of access and agriculture that don't bare their teeth in quite such an obvious way.

One hot spring morning, in Norfolk, I got up early to go and see an award-winning cheesemaker. Some years ago, it became clear that the future for mid-sized dairy farms was not particularly bright. The milk price was falling and units were getting bigger and bigger in order to survive. The other option was to diversify. They looked around and realised that nobody in Norfolk made good cheese. Twenty years later, the company is a major part of the county's food scene.

We walked around the dairy, where three men were hard at work, then we went to have a look at the cattle. What I hadn't realised fully is quite how difficult it is to make cheese safely. At every turn, strict food hygiene processes have to be in place and every cheesemaker's greatest fear is harmful bacteria getting into the product. One further difficulty happens when the cattle are stressed. There is a type of *E. coli* that lives quite harmlessly in the teat but when dogs worry the cattle or people appear in vast numbers, the stress causes the bacteria to be released.

Another dairy farmer, based up in Scotland, explained that his great worry with dogs is that when the opportunity presents itself, they eat the placenta of cattle infected with the parasite, neospora. Due to the 2003 Land Reform Act, walkers with infected dogs are able to walk across his fields. The neospora, in egg form, can be present in the dog's faeces and is snaffled up by cattle when they're grazing. The eggs hatch and kill calves while they're developing in the womb. There is no vaccine for neospora and an outbreak can be costly. Tackling it is also made challenging by dogs rarely exhibiting symptoms.

In sheep, sarcocystis, which is in the same family of viruses as neospora, can cause muscular cysts and in some cases, miscarriage too. It is spread from dogs to sheep through the contamination of grazing ground. It also causes lambs to develop slowly, which inevitably reduces the price that farmers get for them.

After going to see the cheesemaker, I drove to Little Snoring to see an egg farmer called David Perowne. David is a thoughtful man who has been around long enough to see the village he lives in change markedly. His family have been tenants on the same farm for over 150 years and as we sat there beneath his walnut tree he explained that 'the saddest thing' about the way rural life is evolving is that because of more and more second home owners, he no longer knows everybody in the village. When I told him I was writing about land access he laughed. There's a footpath, he explained, that comes right up to his yard. David thinks it was probably there originally to be used by workers coming to the farm but he now wants to see it closed because there's a risk that walkers might bring bird flu with them on their boots. The financial consequences, for David, who is a big player in the poultry business, could be immense.

David is hugely knowledgeable about local history. He knows the names of old men who would have lived in the local work-house in the winter and worked as labourers in the summer months. He can tell you who ran the bakery and when it closed, when cottages in the village were knocked together to create second homes, and he can tell you about farming families that sold up and left the area over a century ago. David is a man who has spent fifty years talking and listening. The thing about these paths, he explained, is that they were there originally to allow workers to get to chalk pits, or threshers to get to the yard, or to allow the vicar to get from Great Snoring to Little Snoring. It might make us sad that paths are being lost but they were created for people doing things that people, sometimes for the better, have long ceased to do. The way we use the countryside has evolved and the paths across it are bound to change too. It is about paths that work for the public and for farmers now, rather than insisting that the countryside be set in aspic.

On Boxing Day 2024, over eight months after I visited David, the Government announced that a proposed cut-off date for recording historic rights of way will now be removed. It was billed cutely as Labour saving the traditional 'Boxing Day walk' but farmers were keen to point out that when the dust settles scrapping the deadline has the potential to prolong uncertainty. Many of Britain's countless unrecorded paths haven't been used for forty or fifty years. The scrapping of the cut-off, which was set to be 2031, has the potential to dampen much-needed impetus to focus on what should be mapped, what should be improved and maintained, and what can be given back to nature.

*

Not infrequently, while driving through rural England, the smell of shit hits you. In autumn or spring, it's often manure being spread on the fields and there's a pastoral sweetness to it but when it's acrid, it's probably pigs. Pig farming is changing across Britain. Farms are getting bigger, the total number of pigs kept is decreasing, and outdoor units (as opposed to pigs that are farmed in sheds) are on the rise.

As farming goes, 'big pork' isn't particularly pretty. Sows

sometimes eat their young, run-off from dung pollutes rivers, and a lot of dead pig is imported from countries that farm in a way that is pretty horrifying. In China, for example, they have pig units that can be twenty storeys high and are often in pretty remote locations. It's not because Chinese pig farmers are shy about the brutal efficiency of their process. It's because whenever a person wanders past a pig unit or drives by one, they pose a very real risk to a country's pig farming sector. The risk is so acute that there are parts of the world where workers on pig farms, who have travelled to get there, must quarantine for days on end, in situ, before they're allowed to have contact with the animals. On British farms things are less extreme but in a road-side café in Suffolk, Ed Barker, a farmer's son and now the Head of Policy at the Agricultural Industries Confederation, explained to me that one of the great difficulties with taking young farmers on educational visits to pig units is that they have to have spent a couple of days at least away from pigs and they then have to fill out a two-page questionnaire. 'You have to give your life history pretty much', he told me, over a plate of eggs and a cup of coffee. The trouble is that if a visitor has been in contact with animals that have something like African Swine Fever, which is very common in wild boar in Europe, it could run through Britain's pig population like wildfire resulting in the whole sector, possibly right across the country, having to go into lockdown. Unable to sell their animals, pig farming businesses, which are often very marginal anyway, would go bang. If you can't sell any pigs you can't afford to buy grain to feed them and you can't pay your men. Pork exports, according to Ed, are worth more to Britain than the export of Scotch whisky – a line that no doubt get trotted out with great regularity by 'big pig'.

While official farm visitors can be controlled and managed, those who feel they're 'entitled' as Ed put it, to wander where they like, could be a disaster. 'It only takes', he told me earnestly – while the Beatles 'I wanna hold your hand' played over the tinny café speakers – 'one discarded ham sandwich.' The risk is that the ham could be infected by swine fever, which is a growing issue because of illegal undeclared meat imports, and that ham could eventually find its way into an outdoor pig enclosure where it might be eaten.

The irony, Ed pointed out, is that people tend not to like indoor pig units as they think they are cruel but if we are to have more access across the countryside, indoor pig units would be considered, by lots of farmers, to be a necessity. It is a fine example of where we, as humans, feel that our right to wander matters more than a farmer's right to a biosecure farm and by extension, a pig's right to a healthy, albeit short, life.

There are things farmers do such as siting their units away from paths and roads but it's not easy. One of the issues, Ed acknowledged, is that in an increasingly globalised world, people can be bringing all sorts of 'zoonotic nasties' back with them from a holiday abroad and he also thinks that the rise of the British staycation has the potential to be problematic. A nice weekend at a farmhouse B&B in Devon, where they keep a few Tamworths out back, followed by a little trespass the following weekend in somewhere like Norfolk, where there are a lot of outdoor pig units, could be the cause of the short-term ruin of part of our agricultural sector.

Ed laughed when I asked about the idea that the public might provide some service in terms of monitoring how responsibly and sustainably pig farmers are operating. 'Because the public are experts', he replied with a smile before calling for another coffee.

Some weeks after having breakfast with Ed, I spoke to Lizzie Wilson, who spent 19 years working as a pig farmer before becoming Chief Executive of the National Pig Association. Lizzie, like lots of people at the helm of British farming, sees all sides. She wants the countryside to be open to all and she uses footpaths, in East Anglia, almost every day but the public, she recognises, for pig farmers, chicken farmers, and those who keep cattle, can be a problem.* As well as endless diseases, a lot of them, she thinks, are concerned about animal rights activists. Not every farmer, she recognises, 'is a good farmer' but there is a misheld belief that pig farming is cruel. 'So the idea that the public need to be able to monitor what farmers are doing, I'd be careful with that one.'

Lizzie pointed out to me, as though it was entirely obvious, that the way farming is depicted on television, both in terms of supermarket advertising and on twee programmes like *This Farming Life*, is often very different from how farmers have to operate to make a profit. The issue is that what's being depicted in the media is more like farming as was, thirty or forty years ago, rather than farming as it is now. The problem this creates is that those who are setting out see a disconnect between what is held up as good and what is necessary to make a profit. 'Profit', Lizzie was keen to point out, shouldn't be a dirty word. It is entirely necessary to pay workers proper wages and to grow a farming business. Her father, she told me, himself a lifelong farmer, is always 'farming other people's land' from the car when they're driving down country lanes but you never really know what's going on, on somebody else's farm, so the idea that the public will be able to usefully critique agricultural practice is one that, like Ed, Lizzie is clearly dubious about. That idea also, Lizzie cautions, suggests that it is 'black and white', that farming is 'good or bad', which simply isn't, she thinks, the case. Like most things in life, 'farming has about 50,000 shades of grey'. Is it, for example, better that pigs are farmed inside where their dung doesn't runoff onto the land or outside, where the pollution risk is greater but they can feel the sun on their backs?

It isn't simply disease, Lizzie added. The number of times, when she was farming, that they had the public take piglets home because they couldn't see the mother anywhere and then

---

* Bovine tuberculosis can be spread on clothing and boots.

they'd ring the farm up to tell them about the 'orphaned piglet', was apparently quite staggering. In general when the sows are farrowing, they don't like to be disturbed. Pig farmers always ask shooting parties to avoid pig units when farrowing is going on because beaters moving through the unit can cause sows to panic and then crush their piglets. The trouble, according to Lizzie, is that shoots pay more rent on land than tenant pig farmers, so their sport takes priority over the piglets. It is often, in land access narratives, imagined that anybody on the land, be it a pig farmer or a shooting party, actually owns the land but this is very often not the case.

What interested me most about talking to Ed and Lizzie was the picture they painted of farmers as a group that feel the public is against them. They are, the narrative runs, destroying the planet and keeping us all out while they do so. As that boy at one of the many Right to Roam meetings I attended put it, we aren't the ones destroying nature, they are. Every time activists call on the public to monitor them, those activists inspire division.

*

Miles Partridge, who is sitting across from me, in his farmhouse kitchen on Dartmoor, asks me again how I found his phone number. I don't really have the heart to tell him that I got it from a whole load of details posted online by the Devon Hunt Saboteurs Association, so people could call the hunt supporters up and harass them.

I had no interest in anonymously abusing him and his family over the phone; what I wanted to know about is what it's like to be a commoner now and whether access is a problem. With all that's said about the commons being stolen from us and the need to 're-common' the countryside, it's easy to imagine that commoners have gone the way of the wolf but they are still out there, trying hard to make their farming businesses work. They have the supermarkets to contend with, they have their landlords to contend with, and Natural England, Miles explains, as he sips his Nescafé, are making their lives difficult.

Miles is a tall, wiry man, with grey stubble and crooked teeth. 'That's Dartmoor', he says, pointing out of the small window behind us, 'and it's nearly all fucked, every common.' The issue, as Miles sees it, is that the commons are now chronically under-grazed and as a result, bracken, molinia grass, and scrub are spreading out across the land.

In the 1980s, in order to encourage farmers to produce more food, 'headage payments' were introduced which resulted in the number of cattle and sheep on the commons being increased to a level that almost everybody admits was ecologically damaging. But currently, commoners like Miles feel that the pendulum has swung too far the other way and the balance has tipped. As a result, due to undergrazing, the commons are, according to Miles, in 'a hell of a mess'.

Farming on Dartmoor, as with a lot of beef and sheep farming across the UK, is a pretty marginal activity and Miles believes that things could be on the cusp of going from marginal to totally impossible. The commoners are all waiting for a new review to be published on the management of protected sites on Dartmoor. In recent years, Miles explains, Natural England has made it known that they would like to see stocking densi-ties reduced dramatically in order to allow plant life to flourish. Back in June, at the village hall, Miles tells me that they were talking about a 90 per cent reduction, which would mean the end of his life as a farmer.

His cattle, he says, as he puts the kettle on for another cup of coffee, are 'leared' to the land. When he puts them out on the commons again each spring, they head for the same crab-apple trees.* 'Ancestral knowledge', he says while spooning out

---

* Learing, like 'hefting' are the terms used to describe the settling of a flock of sheep to a particular part of a common. It is a very local word.

more coffee, 'but men are leared to the hill too.' When I ask Miles if he thinks of the commons as being his, given he doesn't own them, he shrugs and tells me he doesn't think it really matters much whether you own the land or whether you're a commoner, it's more about what you do with it. 'We are all', he says as he sits back down, 'just specks, you see. We're just passing through.' This is a really important point in that there is a strange obsession in Britain with who owns the land, when often the way it's farmed and managed has relatively little to do with its ownership and a great deal to do with who occupies it.

What really got to Miles after the meeting in the village hall was that the representatives from Natural England promised they would come to see the common. He wanted to show them what sort of state it's in and they had promised they'd come. 'They promised the moon and the stars', but a month later they told him they just weren't going to be able to find the time.

It's odd really that the commons have become such an integral part of the messaging around access when the actual commoners like Miles are, for the most part, ignored. The Countryside and Rights of Way Act (2000) and the Law of Property Act (1925), for those on horseback, give the public the right to access most common land. Miles tells me he absolutely wouldn't want to see the public kept off entirely but he certainly doesn't see the commons as being a place that's 'for the public' – it's a place for farming and the public are welcome if they behave. 'Have you been up to Birmingham?' he asks. It's a bit oblique but what he seems to be saying is that being able to get out into the countryside, for people in urban places, is important. At the same time, though, he says that wildlife on Dartmoor flourished during Covid. They burned some scrub at the top of the farm and then in autumn, 'because of Boris's restrictions' and the consequent serenity, lack of footfall, and lack of dogs, there were curlew there. Yet, Miles himself is potentially, as a commoner, having his access to the land for his animals restricted. Freedom to camp on the commons is talked about a lot but those who are 'leared to the land' being free to live as commoners doesn't get much airtime at all.

What's happened, Miles thinks, is that the commoners have been slowly squeezed out and their management of the commons and access to the commons has been restricted. As he clears our cups away I realise that there is a thread that runs through all of this. Everybody believes, whether rightly or wrongly, that their relationship with the land is limited and controlled by somebody else. The campaign for more access claims to be locked out by the rich, while also admitting that they use the press and public outrage to strong-arm landowners into falling into line; landowners like Alexander Darwall feel that their freedoms are being restricted; and commoners feel that detached civil servants don't understand. Britain, for all of us, is 'their' country, rather than ever truly being a place of our own.

We head out into the yard and get into Miles's truck. The sky, across the valley, is milky grey and the weak sun, having not long come up, is already starting to go down. ABBA comes on, on the radio, and we head down the drive to cross the river. He does wonder, he tells me, as we head up the other side whether people these days have a bit too much leisure time. He wouldn't, he says again, want the public kept off the commons but it sometimes feels like there's a group of mountain bikers everywhere he turns in the summer months.

As he drives he tells me a bit about the local area and all that's changed over the years. There was, he says when we get out onto the main road, an 'old sage' who used to walk back home from the pub 'every dinner time'; he'd drop a match whenever he came across a bit of ground in the winter that he thought was overgrown. Burning, Miles explains, always used to be par for the course on Dartmoor. When there was a bit of ground that had got away from the beasts and was going rank, they'd just set light to it and in time, new growth would come. But currently a form needs to be filled out and Natural England has to be consulted and often, by the time the commoners get a response, the seasonal window for burning has passed.

We turn right past a church with stained-glass depictions of the Crusades and Miles tells me that the trouble is four-fold: the overgrown meadows aren't much good for the stock to eat, he doesn't think they are good for birdlife, they make the commons inaccessible for walkers and cyclists, and they present a fire risk. If stocking densities really are limited as much as he fears, the commons, he believes will 'look worse than they do now and there'll be a bloody great forest'. He points ahead of us at the overgrown hillside and tells me to just imagine if that went up in April or May with all the birds nesting and all the insects. 'Bloody lot would be gone', he says, shaking his head.

The gate to the field is tied up with a piece of rope and I stand aside after opening it so Miles can drive through quickly enough to get on up the slope. The field is both steep and damp and the other side of the stone wall, the commons begin, mostly thorn, bramble, and rhododendron. 'Just look at that', Miles says, when I get back into the truck and we drive past it, 'and it gets more and more encroached every year.' The hill below us runs down into the valley and on the other side a commercial forestry plantation marches across what would once have been grazing land. In some ways, Miles admits, plantations make sense. Commercial forestry operations are lucrative whereas grazing isn't. For over twenty years now, Miles has been farming Galloway cattle and he tells me that in the South West of Scotland lots of hill ground has been ploughed up and planted with Sitka spruce. 'Cold, hard, horrible places.' Everybody, Miles accepts, needs to make money but putting 'paying bills aside', what we're really talking about, he says, as we walk to the edge of the field 'is community'. The previous week he was at a funeral for an old local farmer and the place was packed out.

In decades to come though, if the commons have gone, a Dartmoor funeral will be a very different thing.

*

To Katie Squirrel, who is sitting in a tractor cab somewhere out in the fields beyond the farmhouse, her dad telling her down the phone how to turn on 'auto-steer' doubtless just sounds like her dad but to me, sitting on the other side of the kitchen table, it's that funny paternal mix of mock exasperation and muted pride. He tells her to press the little button on the right armrest until it turns green. 'The button where?' I hear her reply before he tells her again that it's on the right armrest. 'Sorted?' he asks her. 'Yeah', she replies, as though she hardly really needed to ask at all anyway. 'Sometimes a bit fickle, these things', Jeremy says as he puts his phone down on the table in front of him.

The Squirrels have been farming at Wattisham, in Suffolk, for four generations and Jeremy reckons they've always been somewhere nearby. 'We haven't come far really, he tells me, leaning back in his chair.

It sounds very grand to say that Jeremy lives in a moated house that has existed, at least in part, on the same site since the late medieval period but it isn't quite like that. Wattisham Hall, at one point, was given to one of the king's favourite cooks but a lot has changed since then and much has been taken down and rebuilt on a more modest scale, not least because at the end of the Second World War a fighter plane that had been improperly repaired crashed into the farmhouse, killing a cousin of Jeremy's grandmother and an Italian prisoner of war who had been sent to the farm to help out. His grandparents avoided being killed because they were at market that day. 'Grandma', he tells me, 'was heavily pregnant with mum at the time.'

The hall is long, two storeys high, and the timber frame, once exposed, has been covered over with plaster. It is the principal house on a 365-acre arable farm, which supports quite a number of Jeremy's extended family. There are people in the village, Jeremy notes, not least his near neighbours, who seem to have a great 'chip on their shoulder' about how much land he owns and its value on paper, but he really doesn't care, he tells me, if a Suffolk acre is worth £20,000 or £2,000. They have no interest in selling and frankly, he thinks that if land prices were lower and if land was less of a tax-efficient store of wealth for 'external money' – he nods towards the door, presumably in the theoretical direction of London – it would be easier for people to get into farming. Young, would-be farmers, he thinks, don't have a hope.

Jeremy is deep in arable country. Suffolk was once made wealthy by the wool trade but barley, wheat, oilseed rape, and vegetables are what most East Anglian farmers are now interested in. Jeremy seems to be a very reasonable man. Access for people in the village matters to him. After all the public are the farmer's customers and you need, he tells me, to keep customers on side but Caroline Lucas, when she introduced the debate in Parliament on the Right to Roam, went down in his estimation. He says with a very genuine sense of regret and then adds that 'sometimes she seems to talk a lot of sense', but not then. He really doesn't understand why anybody would want to walk through his arable fields, which look much 'the same from one corner to the next'.

Some years ago, Jeremy went to Parliament with one of Ed Barker's brothers to lobby MPs including Richard Benyon, then the parliamentary undersecretary for Defra, when funding was withdrawn for creating and maintaining linear access on farmland. A number of farmers had spent considerable amounts of money installing paths and they felt it was unfair that the grants were suddenly withdrawn. Jeremy is a little evasive when I tell him that some people would be pretty horrified about the idea of landowners being paid to allow people to explore the countryside but he suggests that really, for some, the payment makes access a focus when it otherwise wouldn't be. There is, he thinks, often an incentive for large estates, which can monetise footfall through cafés and small businesses, but for farmers on a few hundred acres, there has to be some sort of motivation to allow people to wander across, 'their factory floor'.

Farming, in Jeremy's lifetime, has changed immensely. When he started out farmers used all sorts of 'hideous' chemicals that are now banned but they still rely on pyrethroid-based insecticides and glyphosate to spray the fields off. Some of the things they are using, which are commonplace, would kill 'God knows how many people', he tells me, nodding thoughtfully, if you poured a litre into a water source. His point is that modern farming, rightly or wrongly, often sees people using products that are harmful to humans and farmers are required to inform the public when a footpath passes through fields that have been sprayed. Quite how that would work though, Jeremy wonders, if they could wander everywhere, he doesn't really know.

For the first time in Jeremy's life, back in spring, he was standing outside at dawn and he heard a nightingale singing. 'First time round here.' He is not, I think, the sort of man who would take to Instagram that day to post a long thread about how blessed he was to have heard it but it clearly meant something to him. Jeremy thinks that simply to look at farming as farming no longer makes much sense. Many of them, in part because they're given grant money to do it and in part because they've realised how much wildlife has been lost, are now starting to create margins for wildlife and to restore long-forgotten ponds. It's all possible and Jeremy clearly enjoys being part of it but it impacts the way he thinks about access. If he was just farming wheat right the way up to every hedge, he wouldn't, he admits, have any problem with people walking around the edge of the crop but there are things there 'for wildlife and biodiversity and that's a game changer'. You can't really, he adds, just have people roaming about, jeopardising your results. After all, it is a little counterintuitive that farmers will be paid public money to create space for wild-life and the public will then come and ruin that space on sunny afternoons with their spaniels.

They recently, with the help of Suffolk Wildlife Trust, dug a pond out in a small wood that was previously an unproductive field. The Trust is apparently very clear that they must fence the pond in to stop dogs going swimming. Anti-flea treatment and dog shampoo can be very harmful to aquatic life. But Jeremy has been wondering whether they should go further and just fence the whole wood in. It would result, quite quickly, in a thick, thorny, tranquil habitat, which would be perfect for that nightingale he heard but they'd also end up with complaints from people in the village and there's every chance Jeremy might get targeted by the wider access campaign.

There are, Jeremy says, picking up his phone to google the details, some new payments that have just come in to compensate farmers for creating access. 'Here we go', he says, scrolling with his index finger, 'options for 2024.' The payments aren't huge: £92 a hectare, £77 per 100 metres of footpath, and £158 per hundred metres of cycle path or bridleway. 'But it does add up over the years', he says, putting his phone back down on the table.

Just like David Perowne, that Norfolk egg farmer, one of Jeremy's main observations, and it's something he thinks the new 'options' could help to change, is that lots of old paths lead to places that no longer exist. 'They don't actually go anywhere and that could be improved by connecting them with permissive rights of way.' Farmers, however, would only really get on side he believes if it was clear that new paths were permissive, as opposed to them creating one and subsequently finding they'd relinquished control forever.

*

In the field to our left, a pair of foxes' ears are sticking up out of the late spring grass. Flavian Obiero, who came to Britain from Kenya at the age of 15, and who now farms pigs on 61 acres in Hampshire, leans across me to get a better look at the animal out of the window of his truck. He shakes his head and smiles. 'So cocky', he says, admiring its audacity, 'so relaxed.' Flavian tells me he doesn't mind the foxes until they start to take his piglets.

Flavian's farm, which is owned by Hampshire County Council, sits between a scrap metal yard and the M27, running between Southampton and Portsmouth. It isn't beautiful country anymore but there is something charming about the seven-acre wood, which was actively coppiced not all that long ago, and the hawthorn-lined track that separates the small fields. Flavian wasn't really looking for a farm when it came up. He had a vague notion that he wanted his own place at some point but a friend of his mentioned the holding and he decided to have a look. The biggest challenge, he tells me, for young people wanting to get into farming is finding the land to get you going. The rental cost is often not all that prohibitive. It's simply a case of a lack of availability.

We drive on and Flavian tells me to watch out for a thorn bush that's hanging over the track. It got him, he says, when he was on his rounds some days ago. There is an immense sense of energy about Flavian – some of his relatives, back in Kenya, grow vegetables though he is not, he explains from a farming family but farming is something that he always wanted to do.

In Britain, 61 acres is considered very small for a farm. There are people on the west coast of Scotland who have crofts that are almost as big but Flavian looks at things from a Kenyan perspective. 'In Kenya you've got someone with like one acre – got goats on that acre, maybe one or two dairy cows. You've got chickens.' He steers the Hilux round a rut on the track then adds, thoughtfully, 'You'd be growing some veg in one corner.' Flavian isn't farming quite as eclectically as that but he does have a butchery unit back in the yard where he makes charcuterie, he cooks whole pigs for parties, and he stops to tell me about his goats, which 'are somewhere' and which like to browse the thick hedge across the field to our right that separates the farm from the railway line. 'Screw that', he replies, when I ask if the goats are for milk. 'They go for meat', which is apparently always very popular, when he heads into town to do South London markets.

There is a big narrative that if you step off a country lane, anywhere across England, you'll be standing on land owned by a major aristocrat. It's true that a small number of people own large estates but it's also perfectly possible that if you jump a hedge in the Home Counties, you'll end up on land not owned by somebody like Flavian but that's worked by some-body like him. It's a charming idea that you'll be sticking it to a guy in a big house somewhere nearby but the farm might be council-owned like Flavian's or it might be owned by a guy in a big house, while being rented out to somebody who's only just making ends meet. The actual landowner quite possibly wouldn't really care that you're there and it's important to recognise that access to land is a struggle for would-be farmers, probably to a far greater extent than finding somewhere to wander is a struggle for would-be walkers. His butchery unit, he tells me, was bought from a friend of his who was a tenant farmer who got 'turfed out'. There was a death in his landlord's family and their holdings had to be split. It would be almost impossible, Flavian explains, for a young tenant farmer in the Home Counties to buy their own farm. Just an acre of arable land can sell for over £10,000 and many young farmers would be doing well to make twice that in a year. Flavian tells me he's not really sure where the land goes when private landowners or local councils sell it but he thinks it probably goes to prop-erty developers. After all, you're hardly going to make your money back by farming it.

For a while, before he was on his own place, Flavian worked

in Sussex in the South Downs National Park, on a farm that had sheep. There was the inevitable issue of people letting their dogs off the lead but there were also, he tells me, people who, in spite of very clear requests to shut gates, seemed unable to do so. When it comes to dogs, he admits he doesn't even trust his own. Just a couple of days previously, one of his collies chased one of his few sheep into the river. 'I don't know what got into its head', he says, but he thinks we need to teach people what dogs are. 'They came from a wolf. If it sees an animal running or an animal that looks like prey, it will chase it.'

Flavian points to the field on his right that was once full of horses. Part of the reason he took the land on, he explains, is because he felt that his pigs could regenerate the ground. Like most tenancies now, his only lasts for three years rather than being a generational tenancy, which means he feels he's really got to get on with things or he'll find that he's out before he's managed to create a viable business. Part of being a young tenant farmer nowadays, he says matter-of-factly, isn't just finding a farm but it's also having an exit strategy. With tenancies being so short you need to know what's going to happen next. Flavian's catering and charcuterie business are strands of his enterprise that will probably outlive his current farm setup.

A little like Cameron Farquharson, Flavian tells me that the public do need to respect rules in the countryside. As a pig farmer he knows that matters greatly, but how can we, he thinks, expect them to understand farming if they don't actually get to visit farms. They are, he says enthusiastically, our customers. We get out of the truck and he points to the formerly coppiced wood at the other end of the track. In time, he is hoping that the local agricultural college, at Sparsholt, will send students along so they can bring it back into active management. It's not something, he admits, that he knows very much about but he's hoping that he can learn along with them and that in time he can get a local nursery along to learn about woodland management too.

Behind us, in one of the paddocks, he has reseeded some rough ground that was once grazing and he tells me in order to explain how he sees the world that there's some wheat there too and even he, as a farmer – although he adds, 'okay not an arable farmer' – can't always tell the difference. Some weeks ago he had to pull it up 'to see what seed was underneath'. He doesn't want people jumping the fence and walking on it but if he can't tell the difference, how, he asks me, can we expect the public to be able to know where they can and can't walk. It perhaps wouldn't be all that surprising if his solution was just to keep people out, given the obvious complexities of knowing where you can and can't go but like Cameron Farquharson he doesn't think that's the answer. 'We can't sit back and say they need to learn.'

The pigs, when he climbs over the electrified wires, start jostling and grunting their way towards him. I reach down to one of the larger ones and he tells me to be careful. 'That big one', he says while walking among them, 'he can have a bit of an attitude.' Flavian tells me that because of the rate at which they mature and can therefore be sent off to the abattoir, they suit his enterprise. Cattle would simply be too slow-growing and arable on such a small scale would be difficult but he seems to totally reject the idea that landholdings need to get bigger and bigger. He is surrounded by tenant farmers and they all make it work through trying hard to find things that work for them. His neighbour, James, does farm arable and it works because Flavian buys it to feed his animals rather than James getting driven down on price by a big grain merchant.

Flavian has a curious ability to see things that others appear not to and his need for everything to pay – you can't afford for anything not to work, on this scale, he tells me twice – leads him to some interesting conclusions. One of the reasons he is keen on getting people onto the land to see his farm is because he thinks people don't value farming. We only spend, he says

205

to me while unloading straw from the back of the truck, 10 per cent of our annual income on food. Whereas, in somewhere like Kenya, it's as high as 50 per cent. There are socioeconomic reasons for that disparity but Flavian also thinks that if people understood farming, due to farming becoming more transparent, they would value what farmers actually do and would be prepared to spend more on good food.

He breaks off to tell me that the pig standing at his feet is his mate, 'Pablo', then he walks into the other paddock, where little piglets are arguing among themselves, and starts bedding up. Flavian's son is only seven months old but he hopes that in time he'll take to farming. He supposes, he says to me, that at some point he'll have to say to him, 'You might only be half as black as I am. But you're black. You need to know that. That's how you're going to be treated.' He wonders, he says to me, as he goes to the back of the pickup again for more straw, if he's become immune to people staring at him but he supposes, he says resignedly, that 'it's life. So yeah. You get on with it.'

*

There was nothing extraordinary about what Jeremy Squirrel had to say. He's the sort of farmer you'll meet in every village in every Suffolk town, a rich man on paper, but a hard worker, who is motivated by trying to create a business to hand on to the next generation, the little Squirrels. He could, it was very clear, go one of two ways. If access works for him and for wildlife, he isn't opposed to it at all but if it's used as a stick to beat him with and if there is nothing in it for him, he will shut up shop. In short, the latest iteration of the land access movement has created concerns for Jeremy Squirrel when he would consider himself to be pretty pro-access. Where there was relative harmony, there is now discord.

Cameron Farquharson is interesting. Access has become part of his business but more than that, he has recognised that providing education is essential if he is going to have a viable business at all. In every instance, I realised that farmers are up against it because of the public and that often the challenges they face, particularly in terms of biosecurity, are too complex to be understood by most of us. Farmers ought to be listened to, rather than castigated.

Flavian Obiero, whose resolve and grit are inspiring is a great example of the many forms that access takes. When we think of farmers, we shouldn't immediately think of them as a bunch of rich white men who are trying to keep us off the land – we should realise that some of them desperately need more access. Flavian has achieved so much but others like him, would-be farmers without an acre to their name, can't get a start. Sometimes those who we think are robbing us of access are busy fighting for it too.

7

Scotland

How well does land access actually work in Scotland where there is, sort of, a 'Right to Roam'?

After the Sea Anglers' had closed, we walked up into Stornoway and stood on the corner, listening to two boys playing the accordion while we ate a pizza from Prontos. She was a student nurse, about my age, and she told me that she wouldn't be staying in Stornoway, not after she qualified. 'Glasgow', she replied, as though to say, 'where the fuck else', when I asked her where she'd go. People were dancing, arm in arm, stomping their feet on the pavement in time to the jig. Each time the accordion players stopped, a shout would go up and they'd start again.

We wandered down Point Street to the taxi rank and sat on the wall talking for a while. When one eventually came, I got in and the girl spoke to the driver for a bit in Gaelic through the window. They chatted and they laughed, and she looked at me and they laughed again and he looked at me in the rearview mirror and they laughed some more and then we set off for Grimersta, on the other side of the island. I asked, on our way out of town, past the Thai cafe that has since burned down, about what she'd been saying. 'This and that', the driver shrugged, 'nothing much.' For a while we drove in silence then the driver asked if we'd had much of a week on the Grimersta.

'Not really', I replied, 'two salmon in total and I had a small trout.' He looked round at me and nodded. 'We've all fished Grimersta.' There was a van in front of us, doing forty, and he overtook it then knocked the lights up into full beam. He didn't, he told me, poach anymore, in fact he wasn't sure anybody still did. 'Thing of the past now.'

The Isle of Lewis rises up out of the Atlantic, 126 miles from the Scottish mainland, almost on the same line of latitude as southern Greenland. With its flat windswept expanses and the complete absence of trees, it isn't beautiful in the way that lots of the West Coast of Scotland is. The local accent is soft and on the side of the road, in summer, men cut peat. It isn't an obvious holiday destination either but it draws people back. In spite of the hold that religion had on the island until very recently (the ferry only started sailing on Sundays in 2009) there's a sense of independence about Lewis, a sense that no matter who thinks they might own it, it's an island that belongs to the islanders.

If you knock around with land access campaigners in England for much more than five minutes, you'll be told by somebody, often somebody who has been to Scotland all of three times, that land access works brilliantly north of the border. It would be wrong to dismiss that entirely but Scotland is a large and varied place with a fraction of the population of England. In England there are 434 people per square kilometre, whereas in Scotland there are just 70. And while England has a population of over 55 million, Scotland has just 5 million. To suggest that all is well, beyond those blue '*Failte gu Alba*' signs, betrays a deep lack of understanding. Much like in England and Wales, there are places where things do work but, as is the case in England, there are also huge problems.

*

The rain, between Crianlarich and Tyndrum, is coming down so hard that I don't see the two hitchhikers, on the side of the road, until they're just in front of me. I stop forty yards on and reverse back towards them. They are soaked through and like me, they are also heading north to Fort William. I help them push their rucksacks into the gaps between Jessie's cage and they climb onto the back seats. They'd been standing there, they tell me, for quite some time. 'Sometimes it's like that, man', the young guy, who must be in his early twenties says, 'you can wait for like an hour. Even when it's raining.'

They introduce themselves as Cat and Josh. Cat is from Bath. Josh is from Lancashire and they've had a difficult week, working their way up Loch Lomond, sleeping in laybys and under piers. 'We thought', Josh tells me, 'that Scotland was this promised land, where you could just sleep wherever, 'cos that's what we're into, but all up Loch Lomond there were these no camping signs.' I tell them that I think it's a sort of camping management zone where you need a permit. 'Exactly, man', Josh replies, 'exactly.'

Cat asks me where it is I'm headed and I tell her I'm not really all that sure. I'm going up to Harris to talk to some crofters and maybe some poachers about how they understand land ownership and access for a book I'm writing. Cat tells me she writes, 'Journals mostly. Broad brush-stroke stuff', about all the places she goes, and Josh tells me he really 'digs' my life and asks if I've heard of Jack Kerouac. 'Yes', I reply, 'I sometimes think of him when I'm at a service station or at a Costa coffee machine. I'm keen to get off the road.' Josh laughs and tells me he really 'digs' Kerouac.

Their week heading up Loch Lomond hadn't been what they'd hoped, Cat says resignedly, but they did find a little boat. 'Like totally abandoned', Josh adds, and they found some oars and they took it up the loch. Cat tells me that she doesn't think it was actually 'completely' abandoned. 'Like, it was pretty new and I was kind of shitting it because I thought somebody might be waiting when we got back, like a shepherd or something.'

They are heading, in a roundabout way, for a festival called 'End of the Road', and then Cat is going on to Colombia alone to travel there for a bit. Josh strokes Jessie through her cage, then tells me been thinking about where he'll go next.

When we get to Fort William, they ask if I'd mind dropping them up behind the houses. There's some forestry there that they've seen on a map, where they plan to sleep for the night. 'We'll have gone on before anybody's up and about.' They don't really know where they'll be going on to, they tell me as I help them put their rucksacks on, they just want to get as far north as they can in the time they've got.

In the winter there are often as many crew on the ferries to the Hebrides as there are passengers, but in the summer months they are almost always at capacity and bookings have to be made a long while in advance. Residents, on the islands, complain that if something sudden happens in July or August, like a relative dying on the mainland, they seldom make the funeral.

The only ferry to Harris that still had space when I tried to book, five weeks in advance, in late May, was the 6 a.m. sailing from Uig on Skye. I would have stayed on Skye if there was anywhere with a room but the island is one of Scotland's most popular tourist destinations and your chance of finding anywhere, if you leave it last minute, is pretty slim. Instead I stay in Fort William and set off the following morning at 3 a.m.

It's still dark by the time I cross the bridge to Skye and drive north to Uig. On the side of the road, stags are illuminated in the beam of my headlights and every couple of hundred yards, there are boards that read 'teepees', 'camping', and 'pods', most of them with signs stuck over them reading 'no vacancies'. There is a lot more money to be made from putting cyclists up for the night on your croft, than having three sheep and a cow.

It takes me just over an hour to drive the length of Skye and by the time I get to Uig, dawn is starting to break. Nobody on the ferry is having a good time – the sea is rough, a toddler is screaming, and after a sausage sandwich, I lie on the floor and sleep.

In 2003, the Scottish Land Reform Act granted the right to access, 'responsibly', most land and waterways in Scotland, including moorland, woods and forest, grassland, field margins, coasts, rivers, and lochs. Hunting, shooting, and fishing are excluded as are places that charge for entry, such as the gardens of historic houses. Farmland where crops are grown is also excluded. Conservation is something of a blind spot. It is important to note that many Scots object to the idea that they have a 'right to roam', what they have, they'll tell you, is 'a right of responsible access'. It is an interesting point of difference, too, that unlike England and Wales, very few 'rights of way' have legal protections. There is a path network of some 11,000 miles, as designated in 2003, under the Land Reform Act. It is sometimes noted that because you can, in theory, wander where you like in Scotland, the path network can be pretty lacking in places. I remember my mother, while she was recovering from being in hospital for a long time and was trying to walk as much as she could, telling me she had no interest in scrambling through the heather. She just wanted some good paths in Dumfries and Galloway. In England, on the other hand, she noted after a trip to Sussex, 'There are paths everywhere.'

The islands of Lewis and Harris, which are one land mass, have a complicated history. Lewis was held initially by Clan Macleod but in 1598, King James VI of Scotland, later to become James I of England, granted Lewis to a group of 'noble' colonists from

Fife who sought and essentially failed to 'civilise' the inhabitants. From the outset, Neil and Murdoch Macleod, the sons of the clan chief, launched attacks on the settlers and forced them to head back south. The King then gave the Mackenzies of Kintail permission to take the island and they hunted down Neil Macleod. The Mackenzies held Lewis until 1844 when it was bought for over half a million pounds by James Matheson, the co-founder of the Hong Kong-based trading house, Jardine Matheson. Matheson, in turn, sold the island in 1898 to the Mancunian industrialist, Lord Leverhulme, who established what became Unilever, and who was known, by the islanders as *Bodach an t-Siabainn*, 'the soap man'.

Leverhulme's grand plans for Lewis and for Harris, which he bought the following year, and for the 30,000 people who lived there, all failed and the crumbling remains of the whaling station stand as a memorial to his 'fancy dreams' as the Lewismen put it. When I visit the whaling station, on my way round the island, there is an eagle sitting atop the red-brick chimney stack by what was once the blubber boiler.

In 1919 Leverhulme, at a meeting, told the men of Lewis he wanted to build them new homes to replace their 'hovels' but was told by them that 'poor though these homes may be, you will find more real human happiness in them than you will find in your castles throughout the land.' On realising, in the early 1920s, that his business plans would come to nothing, in part because of the resistance of the islanders, Leverhulme decided to go south. Some of the land, like the farm at Grimersta, was sold in parcels to wealthy fishermen but 64,000 acres around Stornoway, including the castle, was given to the people, effectively becoming Scotland's first community land ownership project.

On the night I talked about poaching to that taxi driver, I also met Boydie, a local prawn fisherman, whose band, Peat and Diesel, has shot to pretty substantial fame with songs like 'My

Island', which incidentally, was being by those in the queue while I was waiting for my pizza. There is a strong musical tradition on Lewis and Harris and many of those involved don't take Peat and Diesel seriously but the sentiment in that song is a very real one. It is their island and they'll go where they want and they'll fish where they like. Poaching has long been a scene on Lewis and I wanted to understand what it's really about. At one point there was money to be made by selling the salmon door to door but it was never, it seems, just about money. It was an act that said these are our fish and these are our rivers.

In the morning, down at the pier, by the cottage I'm staying in, there are two fishermen boxing up large brown crabs. Jessie runs round and round, then crouches in front of them, as though to pounce, before she turns and runs away. 'If you're very quick', the older man says, when I ask if I can buy a couple. The younger man, whom I take to be his son, is friendlier. 'Just give us ten and take whichever ones'. I take one of the bigger ones and a smaller crab then I pass the boy two fives, which he folds up and zips away in his jacket pocket.

When the older man walks up the pier to reverse his truck down the boy asks if I'm on holiday. 'Not really', I tell him, 'I'm just here for a couple of days because I'm writing a book about the land and crofting and poaching.' They load the van, six white boxes, two stacks of three, and then they nod at me politely as they drive off into the drizzle, past the castle and away up the hill towards Tarbert.

All morning I make notes and then at lunch, I take Jessie out for a run on the hill. She works the peat hags, her nose down, quartering back and forth and every hundred yards or so, a Jack snipe gets up and flies into the wind. Down below, on the rocky beach, the carcass of a fishing boat, painted red and blue, is rotting away in the bladderwrack.

When we get to a fence, we head down to the road and Jessie stops to watch the sheep, which are grazing some four hundred yards away, among the reeds. I tell her not to look at them and she looks at me doubtfully before turning back to stare at them intently. On the road, a Land Rover passes and the driver, a man in his sixties with a severe face and high cheekbones waves at me haughtily.

About ten minutes later, he comes back the other way, and pulls up into the layby. He nods at me and I tell him I'm out with the dog to see if she's steady around sheep. 'Wise thing to do', he replies. He tells me he's just going to be putting some sheep in the fank in front of us, which has been built out of breeze block, and we chat a little. His father, he says, was a gamekeeper at the castle when he was a boy, and the poaching used to be a big thing but it's historic now. He moves slowly and deliberately, like a horse when you're speaking to it. 'We own it now', he says, gesturing to the land. He tells me he's the chairman of the North Harris Community Trust. 'You'll have to come by and see me.' I ask when would be good, when's a good time. 'Never a good time,' he replies.

That afternoon, I drive to Balallan, on Lewis, a small grey village that has a charity shop and a post office with a red corrugated iron roof. Set back from the cottages on the main road are a number of ruined crofts, where the land has run to ferns and reeds and the buildings, most of them with their windows smashed in, look as though nobody's lived in them for 40 years. It's widely acknowledged that some of the newer houses in Balallan were built with money made from salmon poaching and a local gamekeeper, whose wife is from the village, tells me he's never felt particularly welcome there.

But in decades past, animosity between poachers and those who were tasked with stopping them was greater than it is now. Just before Christmas in 1994, a former gamekeeper on the 8,000-acre Aline Estate, which sits on the boundary between

Lewis and Harris, had his oil tank hacksawed through and the windscreen of his van smashed. The incident followed on from the Aline Estate having one of their boats cut in half. Eight years later, in an incident thought to be related to the police attempting to crack down on poaching, three men broke into the police station at Balallan and burned out the police officer's car. Two years after that, in a move that the Scottish press referred to as leaving the land to the poachers, after endless 'intimidation and violence', the police shut the one-man station.

Poaching in the Lochs, the parish that rises into the hills around Balallan, has a long, rich, and complicated history. On 23 November 1897, in the *Glasgow Herald*, it was reported that the authorities tried unsuccessfully to dissuade a large group of 'squatters' and crofters from raiding the deer forest on the Pairc peninsula. The land there, which the people had once farmed, had been turned into a sporting preserve under James Matheson and was tenanted out to Joseph Platt. The deer were getting fat while the people were going hungry.

The raid started at daybreak during a period of reportedly 'beautiful weather'. The men gathered with guns and flags and 'the Balallan people had a piper at the head'. The watchers, who were employed to keep the poachers out of the forest, were powerless and some 1,100 people spent three days killing some 200 beasts. Some men used knives while others, it's said, used muskets which hadn't been fired since 'the 45' at Culloden. The camp, on the banks of Loch Seaforth, was reportedly a sort of utopia where Gaelic songs were sung, venison was boiled over peat fires, and a royal stag, with twelve points on its antlers, was suspended as a totem. It's recorded that one of the raiders, sitting among the smoke said, 'our forefathers selected Park [sic] as the spot above all others in the Lochs where God intended that we should dwell. But now we are slaves, while the land that is ours by right is consecrated to deer.'

In the months that followed, the *North British Daily Mail*, which later become the *Daily Record*, sent a reporter up to Balallan – the story, which highlighted the plight of the raiders and the families, led to donations pouring in from across the British Isles and far beyond. The Lewisian diaspora, driven away by hunger to the Canadian lumberyards and the Australian bush, gave generously. The impact of protest is often hard to measure but on Lewis people will tell you that crofters' rights in the Highlands, when they did come, came to a great extent because of the actions of men from Balallan and Pairc.

I once asked a gamekeeper who lives in Stornoway whether the boys from Balallan, as they are still known, poach because of some sort of connection to their relatives who poached then. He shrugged and told me there's maybe a bit of that but they do it, he reckons, mostly for the thrill and for the drug money.

It's quite possible – in a world where most salmon are put back by anglers and the stuff you buy in the shops is farmed – that it's those on the Western Isles, who know somebody, who are eating the very best salmon around.

*

The tea room is open and I sit down with a bowl of soup and the local Historical Society newsletter, *Dioghlum*, which means 'to gather'. Their emblem is a leaping salmon and on the front page is a picture of three men who boarded the SS Metagama in 1923 to emigrate to America. Two of the men, it's revealed inside ('turn to page three to find out what happened to them') returned home to marry local girls but the third, Donald Ferguson, was never heard from again. On the fourth page, there's a song, written in Gaelic but translated.

> *There are many mothers who are sorrowsome,*
> *And lovers that are heartsick,*
> *Since the Metagama sailed,*
> *With the boys from home.*

Many nights we cannot sleep,
And by the fire, when I am alone,
I hear the sounds of your footsteps coming home,
And your beautiful voice.

I never believed it,
yet you told me –
You stretched out your hand to me,
And said, 'Here, mother, goodbye.'

I order another cup of coffee and then I walk down through the village, and turn left at the garage, where improbably well-kept cars are shining out on the forecourt. The rain has stopped and down over the water to my left, the flies are out, catching the light. A little way on, there's a boy sitting on a small bike and he looks at me, as though he doesn't often see people walking up the lane, and then his father appears. He is dismantling an old shed next to a new one. 'New shed?' I ask him. 'Aye', he nods, 'taking the old one down.' We stand for a bit and we talk about the new shed and what a fine shed it is, then I ask him if they ever have many people walking past the croft at all. He tells me that they don't really. 'Not out here. On Skye it would be different right enough', but he tells me that lockdown was different. The trouble, he explains, is that his sheep just graze out on the hill and they don't like people much so when crowds started descending on Lewis they took off. 'Days we spent walking the hill trying to find the sheep. They'd go quite some way. Didn't they?' The father looks down at the little boy and the boy nods back at his dad in shy agreement.

When I arrive back at Amhuinnsuidhe, the ghillies from the castle are by the larder, standing around a pickup truck. Their day, one of them tells me – a young guy who is just there for the summer – has been a difficult one. They were out with Americans, who are staying for a week of stalking, but all the way up the hill the deer just seemed to be dispersing and then when they got up onto a plateau they saw a group of three walkers at the top. 'Germans or fucking Austrians or something like that', Adam, the headkeeper tells me. In the end they did get a beast, but it was quite by chance – they had cut their losses and were heading back to the castle when they came across 'a group of reds with a nice stag in among them'. The beast, they tell me, is hanging up inside the larder – usually, what they do is they butcher them up and leave an honesty box, and passing tourists stop off on seeing the 'venison for sale' sign. Adam, who at 26 years old is missing most of his front teeth, tells me that it is 'fucking difficult'. They have a job to do, in keeping the deer in check and taking paying clients out to stalk them, but at the same time he can't begrudge those who get in their way. After all, they are all up there for the same reason. 'It's fucking beautiful, man.'

That night, the boys invite me up their bothy and we sit around drinking cans of Tennent's and smoking roll-ups – the floor is sticky, there are gralloching knives on the table, and there are boxes of shotgun cartridges by the microwave. Most of the boys are just seasonal workers but Adam stays the whole year round and does maintenance work in the winter – there is always a fence needing fixed or digger work to be done. 'What's that like?' I ask him. He is leaning out the window smoking a roll-up. 'Grinds on you. You look out the window, it's three o'clock and it's dark.' I ask him, before I go, about the poacher I want to see. 'You'll not find him', he replies, 'he's in the jail.'

*

In a hut, up on the hill, out on the West of Lewis there is a man who lives a lonely life in a bothy among the heather. He was a poacher once, with a rod and a line rather than a net, but he watches the rivers now, in return for a bit of legal fishing.

There is smoke rising from the chimney when I go to see him and he is bent over his peats, stacking them by the stove. His bed is a mattress on wooden pallets and he has a small Border Terrier, grey at the muzzle.

'That's your peat', I ask him. 'That's the peat, boy, good and black.' He holds up a chunk of it for me to look at before he puts it in the stove. 'The dark stuff burns well', he says as he prods at the fire, 'and that's a lovely smell comes off it. Takes you back in time.' He stands and looks at his little dog who is sitting expectantly by its bowl. 'So you've not lifted any salmon nets this year?' He shakes his head. 'Is that because the main man's in jail?' He smiles and tells me that boy's not poaching anymore, 'he's finished anyway. His best days are behind him.' He trails off then says, without giving me any reason at all, that he – the main man – will just find it hard now. The game has apparently changed. He stokes the fire once more then tells me that good weather is on the way so he'll move bothy – there's one out on an island, in the loch, built when the poaching was at its worst and the watchers feared for their safety. He's got, he continues, a few jobs to do there and there's a stove there too, for the peats.

I'm told that the man in the bothy used to run with the poachers but then from time to time, the estates would start receiving the odd anonymous text message telling them that the boys had a net out on the hill and were planning to set it that night. The split came, apparently, because the boys insisted on using gill nets, which allowed them to catch whole pods of fish, whereas the man who turned gamekeeper wanted to fish with rod and line. There simply aren't any longer, he reckoned, enough fish to carry on in the way they were and for him it wasn't, I'm told, ever about great quantities of fish. It was just about being out on the water, on a river owned by somebody else.

Later that evening, after asking around in Tarbert, I pull up outside the chairman of the North Harris Community Trust's house. He is standing at the sink, peeling potatoes. I knock twice at the door but he doesn't come so I knock a third time. Still he doesn't come so I knock at the window. He looks down fiercely at the potatoes in the bowl. It seems it's not a good time and I'm about to turn and go when he looks up and gestures towards the door. When he opens it he is pretty cold but he tells me to come in. It isn't, he confirms, a good time but nonetheless, he invites me through and we sit in his conservatory. The house is hot and very clean and light rain has just started falling on the windows.

Calum sits, indicates for me to sit too, then leans back in his chair, knits his fingers together and holds his hand to his mouth. The castle was owned, he tells me, along with the estate, by the Bulmer family originally. 'Cider . . . they were the ones who owned it last.' But in 2003, it came up for sale, the Scar-Hall family bought the castle and the fishing along with 350 acres, and a trust was established to buy the 50,000-acre estate on behalf of the community. The Scottish Land Fund, Calum tells me, put up a lot of the money, the local enterprise company contributed, and the local people raised a lot themselves too.

He looks out through the large windows, peering into the distance, as he tells me about the buyout, as though he's suddenly struck by the enormity of it all. There is something awkward but regal about him and if you were a tourist, you could be forgiven for thinking that Calum is the laird. What it has given them, he tells me, is 'a sense of responsibility to actually manage the land'. Since time began really, he says with a shrug, the community has had no control but they now know it will never be sold again against their collective wishes.

It's hard to say, he admits, how it would have gone if another wealthy family had bought the place because it's impossible to know what sort of plans they would have had and how much control or access they would have given people. Half the time, when people have estates in the Hebrides, Calum thinks you never really see them. They might show up just for two weeks of the year and the rest of the time it's just their staff that are left behind: stalkers, factors, and watchers to keep the poachers away.

One of the things that the Trust is committed to is providing unrestricted access to the land – in Scotland people can obviously wander where they like but on Trust land they like to go further. They employ rangers to encourage access, they allow locals to stalk the deer, and they help people, as he puts it, to enjoy the place.

Calum is keen to tell me that generally it is all going very well. The only great concern they have is the declining population – the population has halved in the past fifty years across the whole of Harris. Part of the reason for that is because property is so expensive. Local people are being priced out by wealthy incomers but it's also because building houses is about 30 per cent more expensive than building on the mainland, due to the cost of getting materials over as well as a lack of labour. In Stornoway, the following day, at the Italian restaurant I meet a plasterer from Glasgow who commutes up each week and stays in a hotel. 'Just silly money what you can charge up here', he tells me, while we're eating our pasta.

Another issue that they face in the Western Isles is people inheriting crofts who then do nothing with them. Calum points out of the window behind me. That, he tells me, was a croft that was inherited by an Englishman who never actually visited and in the end, much to his approval, the man was 'dispossessed' by the Crofting Commission and the croft was reallocated. They always try, as a Trust, Calum explains, to give vacant crofts to young people but there isn't much demand.

The revenue streams for the Trust, he says vaguely, are varied but if you ask around, locals will tell you that none of them are all that lucrative. Calum sits back in his chair and tells me he'd like to see more ground across Scotland in community ownership, because it allows people to engage with the land

and with the culture, but that what it takes is those who are actually committed. Harris needs more people. He's quite sure about that, but not the sort of oddballs who move up to escape the world and shut themselves away.

One of the cultural shifts that the Trust buyout has created is that the deer now belong to the people. When the ghillies at the castle are taking guests out, they can't ask walkers to go another way because it is not their boss's land. It's important too, given the history of Lewis and Harris, to note that the castle is in effect buying deer back from the people. The shift has also made the creation of a community stalking scheme possible, whereby locals get to shoot the deer as part of a management programme.

It's hard to say really, quite how successful or otherwise the community buyout has been because it's hard to know what the alternative was – in Stornoway, a man who works on neigh-bouring land says to me, 'off the record' that the word is that the Trust is struggling financially. In truth a lot of Highland estates run at a loss but they are often propped up by the cash rich. The Trust, I'm told, pulled out of the island-wide deer management group because they couldn't afford the annual fee of a couple of hundred pounds. The impression that the man on the neighbouring ground told me most people have is that community-owned estates are well-intentioned and function well initially, when subsidised but when it comes down to 'long-term running costs it gets tough for them'. There has been a lot of talk, apparently, of 'plans to improve housing for young people' but they have struggled to realise them due to a lack of funds. With the very best will in the world, as my contact put it, 'housing is driven by the market and demand and prices (especially in some areas of Harris) are just too high for locals' and he can't see what the Trust can do about that.

With nothing much else to do and with plenty of light left, I drive north to Lewis to see the Callanish Stones. The roads are almost empty and the sky is a wash of warm grey. Summer comes late on the island but the heather, up on the hill, already looks as though it's starting to go over.

Some 5,000 years ago, in 'the heathenish times' – as they were called locally in nineteenth-century Lewis – people whom we know very little about built stone circles on the island from slabs of Lewisian gneiss. We do know that they were places of religious activity but we know no more than that. Some archaeologists believe they were built as places to watch the moon, others believe that they align with mountains, and it was thought, long ago, that they were petrified giants who refused to become Christians.

All we can really assume is that they were places of some sort of worship. They provided a way of connecting then and to go to them now and to touch those lichen-covered stones is to connect with something both spiritual and forgotten. To touch those stones is to connect with the spirit of something five thousand years old and to be denied access to them, as has happened on similar sites, on other islands, would be a denial of something immense.

The rain starts coming on more heavily and I walk back down to the road and on crossing the ditch, I see a child's shoe and some used fistfuls of soggy toilet paper. It is the chief complaint of Donny Whiteford, a gamekeeper who lives not far from the stones. The tourists come in their campervans, he tells me, they fill up on fuel and on groceries in Inverness, and all they leave is their rubbish and the contents of their chemical toilets in the ditches.

*

Three months or so before I went up to Lewis, a young guy who had been camping walked into a small shop some 26 miles west of Inverness and told them he'd knocked over his camping stove. He reportedly asked the lady behind the till if she would come to the door so he could show her what was wrong. The problem was apparently fairly obvious. The hill was on fire.

Over the coming days, under the hot spring sun, firefighters – many of them local volunteers: shepherds, crofters, and gamekeepers – fought the blaze, and on the following Friday I drove through the night to get there. At that point, much of the hill was still smouldering and people had fled their homes. It was, according to some, the biggest wildfire that's ever been recorded in Britain.

When I got to the fire station, with Iain Hepburn, a local volunteer, most of the lads were out but the Chief, a wiry man in his late fifties, with short white hair, put the kettle on. It was only mid-morning but it was already 22 degrees and outside the open-fronted temporary station, small boys with sunburned arms were cycling round and round, seemingly excited by all the trucks and the helicopter circling in the smoke.

There was a sense that they had the fire under control but everybody seemed to accept that as soon as the job was done, there would almost certainly be another one. Climate change, Iain told me, has changed everything, 'the land is like a tinderbox', and every day in high summer he thinks there must be 'a hundred close calls' caused by campers and walkers, be it cigarette ends, stoves, or campfires.

But people, according to the Chief, often don't appreciate the consequences of their behaviour. Men like his are now getting attacked by people when they ask them to put their fires out. 'It is', he said, slurping at his tea 'the nature of things.' But it isn't, he admitted, always the case – some years ago, he had a memorable situation where a man wandered out of his tent in the night to go to the toilet and thought that the best thing to do, in the spirit of keeping the hill clean, was to drop a match on the toilet paper, at which point the dry heather lit up. He was, the Fire Chief recalls, hugely apologetic.

It would be useful, the Chief thinks, to start trying to educate people when they are young, right from their earliest years at school, about how to be responsible in rural places, but in reality he feels that the information is already there for people to see. It's just that some don't bother to read the signs and others read them but don't care. Of course, the Chief added, it's why Loch Lomond has a no drink policy. It's not about the drink, but it's about how reckless people become 'when they're *pished*'.

On the wall, on a whiteboard, one of the men had drawn up a list of priorities: crew safety, public safety, and the recovery of an ATV were listed. Two of the crew, while fighting the blaze, had rolled a vehicle and had been taken to hospital.

The grass and the trees, surrounding a track that had been dug into the hill, were all starting to look thirsty. Since April there had been almost no rain, and Iain's Land Rover threw up a cloud of hot dust. Halfway up the hill, on a plot of land that hadn't burned, there was a house where a woman had left her husband behind with a hose to try to keep the flames at bay. She had taken their children and had gone in search of safety. Further on, beyond the frontier of green, the land was all charred heather and the occasional blackened trunk of a rowan tree.

Where the road ended, we parked up and then stood by a boathouse at the edge of the loch. Trout rose in front of us, their mouths emerging and then disappearing so quickly you could hardly say if you really saw them at all. Iain has been fighting fire all his life and he told me, while looking at the blackened hill to our right, that whenever he's out and about he imagines the land ablaze and he thinks about how best you would put it out. What they usually do is they 'back burn', which is essentially setting a smaller fire which burns towards the advancing fire. When they connect, the smaller of the two has already used up all of the fuel and they both go out. 'Fire', Ian told me, with hard-earned respect, 'is a greedy thing.' We stood in silence for a bit, watching the helicopter come sweeping across the loch before descending to fill a large orange bucket. 'All the adders on the hill', Iain said, as he watched it, 'they'll be cooked and all the nesting birds.' The helicopter rose at a 75-degree angle, hauling the bucket of water towards the trees. It turned once, in a large circle, then the bucket swung out from beneath it and a great column of water fell.

Down in the village the café was full of tourists and the lady making the coffee was struggling to keep up. 'Are you a reporter', she asked, when I got to the front. I nodded and told her I'm interested in how well land access works in Scotland because there's lots of people who say we should have the same thing in England on account of how successful it is. She smiled and shrugged. All her life, she told me, she's lived in the Highlands and she's never seen anything like it. 'The boy initially said it was a stove', she told me as she poured my coffee, 'but they're now saying it was an open fire he was having.' She stopped for a moment to re-tie the cord around her apron. 'We're literally building the paths for people to come through here and make fires but at the same time, the area does need tourism. We do need it though.'

*

The following morning, on Harris, after boiling the crabs and eating as much as I can, I'm sitting out the front, writing up notes, when the factor walks past. He is a large man, always in a rush, and always looking at your shoes when he talks to you. 'So it is', he tells me, when I ask him about the stalking being disrupted by walkers, but there's really nothing, he thinks, that can be done about it. 'Maybe', he tells me, as Jessie runs around at his feet, 'maybe we need a wee app, for the phone, where people could look and see where we'll be out stalking. You can't keep people out.' He looks out to sea where the fishermen are coming in, in a small metal boat, and I ask him if he knows where I'd find Steve Dilworth, an artist over on East Harris. He shakes his head. He's not, he tells me, heard of Dilworth.

The east side of Harris is different. The land is softer. There are ponds full of trout and lilies and beyond a van without any wheels, red paint scorched by the salt and the sun, five old men are standing together at a sheep fank built of breeze blocks. They stop talking when I pull up and one of them walks down the path towards me. His directions, when I ask where the artist Steve Dilworth lives, are both vague and definite. 'Back to the fish farm. Then there on the left.'

I arrive ten minutes later, coinciding with the postman. We stand next to each other on the step up to the cottage and he knocks. Steve Dilworth comes to the door, takes his letters and looks at me. I tell him I've come separately. I have nothing to do with the postman but I read something about *Cillein*, his 'deep time' sculpture and I want to know how I can get to it. He pauses for a moment and then asks if I'd like a cup of tea.

His cottage, which was, he tells me, a total wreck when he bought it forty years ago, smells faintly of hash and on the stove there is a pig's trotter, trotter end up, in a pan. Steve is between hip replacements and he lumbers about, putting the kettle on before walking, heavily, over to the fridge. 'I was going to come initially', I explain to him, 'to speak to some guys about salmon poaching and why they do it but they're proving hard to find.' He brings me my tea, and sits down with his at the opposite end of the table.

'Harris', he says, pushing his glasses up his face, 'has become a bit strange really.' When he first moved to the island, there were almost no tourists at all and now they are in an odd

situation where almost every second house is a holiday home
and there were, apparently, just two children born on the island
the previous year. The room, Steve's kitchen-cum-sitting room,
is simple and chic, and it feels much more Scandinavian than
Hebridean. There are books, house plants, the large wooden
table, and up above the cabinets, there is a vast array of obscure
spirits. Steve, as well as making grotesque sculptures out of
human bone and animal flesh, sacrifices for, as he puts it, 'a
lost tribe', seemingly likes making cocktails.

He tells me he's vaguely aware of the access stuff going on
down in the South West of England but he wonders if where
we've gone wrong is that we're now too keen to ask. Harris, he
says fondly, used to be a place where people just did things
without permission. When he first moved there men would
come in vans, totally drunk and leaning out the back, to sell
fish that they'd poached. The draw of the place was its beauty
and how cheaply he could live there but he also seems enam-
oured with the wildness of it. 'Don't ask', he tells me as though
not asking is a noble thing.

In spite of his crumbling hips, he looks strong and when he
leans across the table to get his iPad he does it like a labourer
rather than like an old artist. He is hard to pin down – Iain
Sinclair once wrote that Dilworth 'has the sense to avoid talking
about his art', and there is an awkwardness when I ask him if
he can still work without being able to get out onto the land
to find the sort of objects he usually works with, often once-
living materials. He shrugs and scrolls, then he says that his
work doesn't engage with local culture but it's inspired by a sort
of energy that exists underground. It is about connecting with
timelessness.

Cillein, he tells me is far, two hours walk into the middle of
Harris and two hours back. 'No signposts.' It's not that I don't
have time. It's only just gone midday but even he seems to be
slightly unsure of where it actually is or was. But there's another

work, a work that's just down the road. He tells me it's easy enough, just a mile or so down the road and then you turn left up 'the corpse road' and you keep going until you hit a plateau. It's just above there.

He puts the hob on, to bring the pig's trotter to the boil and then he shows me his workshop, telling me as we head through that he always takes the opportunity of his wife being away to eat things like pig's trotters. His workshop is a place full of ropes and power tools. There are vials labelled 'storm water' and jars of formaldehyde, as well as bird wrecks and cast antlers. We talk about eating woodcock (there is a woodcock skull on a table) and he talks not like a gourmet but as though he's an artist talking about eating his subject as if it gives him some sort of greater understanding of their being.

That evening, I set off up the corpse road. In the west there is a double rainbow and the light is starting to go. Some half an hour later, up above me, I see a ridge that looks vaguely like the one Steve described. It's steeper than it appeared to be at the bottom and by the time I'm halfway up, I'm grabbing at tussocks and digging my knees into the moss. There is no art at the top, just a thin lochan. By the time I get back down onto the corpse road, it's dark.

*

The Saturday is my last day on the island, and conscious that I haven't achieved all that much, I drive back to Balallan. 'I think that's right', a road mender had told me, when I asked him some days previously. 'He's in the jail but I'll tell you where he lives, just in case.'

I pull in some way beyond the village beside a low grey harled house. It looks completely shut up – there is a boxing bag hanging in the hall, weights on the floor, and a dog kennel out the back with no dog in it. I knock three times but nobody comes so I leave a note and my number. 'Wanted to talk to you about the poaching. Speak some time maybe.' Then I head to the bar at the Tarbert hotel to write up more notes.

That afternoon as I'm heading back to pack, Adam comes out of the bothy in his jeans with a bottle of Buckfast. 'We've got a proposal.' The proposal is that they have all drunk too much to drive so they were wondering if I'll drive them into Stornoway for the night and one of them will run me back in the morning in my car in time for the ferry.

On our way back through Balallan, heading to Stornoway, Adam points out a croft that his granny left him. The house, he realised, was going to be too expensive to renovate so he sold it and now it's running to ruin.

It's seven o'clock when we get into town and we park by the docks and then we walk to the Lewis Bar. 'I fucking told you he's in the jail', Adam says, when we're standing outside, having a cigarette. What I should have done though, he adds, is spoken to the poacher's cousin. Adam apparently caught him a while back out on one of the Castle's lochs. 'It can't be him', the factor had said, when Adam called to tell him. 'He was in an accident and his leg's in a cast.' Adam insisted it was. 'I was saying to the factor, I'm looking at him now.' The boy was apparently aggressive at first, telling Adam he'd break his jaw but in the end he changed tack and said they could maybe just have a beer and when he finally got out the boat, he came across the heather, hopping on one leg, his other in the cast. There was part of him, Adam admits, that thought it's sort of fair enough really, travelling across the island and heading out over the peat on one leg, just for a salmon.

I leave Lewis without having made any inroads among any of the poachers at all. Then, over the months that follow it becomes a sort of craziness – I try every lead I can think of and occasionally, somebody does get back to me. But usually, it's just to tell me to 'get fucked'.

*

In the *Los Angeles Times*, in the spring of 1987, the then-travel editor, Jerry Hulse, wrote a frank piece about a hotel he'd visited at the western end of Loch Earn. 'Ewen Cameron's hotel', he writes, couldn't be described 'as elegant or castle-like or charming'. During his brief stay, Hulse banged his head on a very low bedroom ceiling, and found it all in all to be a place that was 'remarkably undistinguished'. Except that Ewen Cameron himself, a huge Orson Welles-like figure, was a seemingly memorable host. He had been British caber-tossing champion, he held European records for the hammer throw, and every night – unless he'd invited Gaelic singers along to perform – he'd prop up the bar, drinking Scotch while spinning tales about his time in the navy.

His son, Big Gus, sits across from me, blowing on a bowl of soup that looks comically small. His hands are twice the size of mine and at 60 years old, he has a thick head of hair. As he eats he mumbles away about how much Lochearnhead has changed. The hotel that his father ran was originally built as a staging post for the British Army on their way north to Culloden. The Camerons, ironically, ended up on the wrong side, fighting with the Jacobites, and many of them lost everything. Gus tells me that the Camerons have lived in the Highlands for time eternal but after Culloden, many of them set sail for America where they now number almost two million.

Gus ran the hotel for 18 years but gave it up in the end because it was simply too much work. It wasn't hard graft apparently but the hours were long. He'd often be in at dawn and he wouldn't get away again until the early hours of the following morning but he's stayed involved in tourism and hospitality all his life. He's run holiday cottages, chalets, and a watersports centre down on the loch. Gus gives the impression of being somebody who is deeply embedded in the community. He is very involved in running the local Highland Games, he's long been a volunteer with the mountain rescue, and on his drive he has a red phone box, which his wife, Ollie, tells me serves as a bar when they're hosting parties.

Tourism is the lifeblood of Lochearnhead but it's also caused huge problems and all the way down the loch, camping, other than in designated sites, and drinking are now banned. One of the great things about the loch is that it's easily accessible from Stirling and Glasgow by train and bus but that accessibility has been problematic. Gus admits that it's probably not a problem in much of Scotland but where they are, young guys often get the bus out, with carrier bags of booze and cheap tents, and then have fights when the sun goes down with other campers, sometimes due to sectarianism.

There are lots of wonderful people who come to visit the loch, Gus tells me, but there's a crowd that he certainly wouldn't confront about littering on his land. In 2013, a 21-year-old who had been on a fishing trip stabbed a neighbouring camper to death after a drunken disagreement.

Then, just three years ago, he called the police when he saw somebody down by the water with a crossbow. To give them their due, he says as he goes to put the kettle on, they arrived almost immediately in riot gear and dispersed everybody. That same summer, 21 people were charged with 'irresponsible camping', including somebody who torched a large pine tree just along from their campsite where they were flying a Union Jack. Over the following days, Gus was out clearing up bottles and human shit.

It was only in 2017 that unauthorised camping was banned at Lochearnhead. Gus tells me that the locals got on to the National Park Authority about their concerns and they took up their cause, which he thinks is amazing really because they are normally very 'pro camping'. There wasn't, he thinks, all that much opposition to the legislation except for a couple of hill-walking groups who he thinks generally misunderstood the point. In his experience of working with the mountain rescue, proper campers arrive late and head off the following morning not long after first light. Whereas fly campers are a problem.

In reality, Gus doesn't think that land access legislation in Scotland has really changed things all that much in terms of where people actually go – it hasn't led to people spreading out, finding new areas, or falling in love with nature. Those who liked to climb Munros still climb Munros and those who descend on Lochearnhead with a carload of Buckfast, still do.

One of the frustrations, however, as a small-scale landowner is that he is relied on to facilitate access in accordance with the wishes of third parties. He is currently, for instance, battling it out with the National Park who want him to upgrade the stiles and bridges on a six-mile walk he created on his farm before land access legislation came in. They are insisting he insure himself and he tells me that he doesn't want to take on any liability. After all, he can't see that there's much in it for him.

When he talks about all the people who used to come to the hotel, all of 'the characters', many of them not even taking those low-ceilinged rooms and just sleeping rough, he smiles. During 'the Glasgow fortnight', when factories in Scotland's industrial city closed, hundreds of workers and their families would come up. 'They'd sleep under trees. There'd be a plastic tarpaulin in every tree and there'd be five or six people underneath it.' His father didn't mind because they'd drink in his pub and when there were so many of them that they ran out of trees, Ewen would charge them a few pennies to sleep on the squash court. It's been some years now since anyone like that came and longer still, Gus tells me, since the tinkers came. 'I always remember old Dokie playing the pipes on the road. He hadn't had a bath in twenty years.' Dokie's wife, Ollie adds, sold white heather to all the tourists and she'd curse you if you refused to buy any. 'Glasgow fortnight does still happen', Gus says, as he tops up my tea with the last of the pot, 'but I suppose they all go to Torremolinos now.'

*

Willie Fraser is in full flow about Dr Johnson's eighteenth-century travelogue, *A Journey to the Western Islands of Scotland*, when we hit a patch of ice on the road heading west along the River Beauly. Time slows, the trailer on the back shunts us towards the silver birches, and Willie countersteers hard. When we come to a stop, Nicola Willamson, who is sitting in the passenger seat, laughs nervously. Willie shakes his head and we continue at a steadier pace.

The place names when Johnson was travelling through the Highlands in 1773 were different, Willie continues, but it gives you an extraordinary sense of the time. In a bit he's just read, Johnson and Boswell stop in Portree and there's a boat there set to take families to America. After the Battle of Culloden in 1745, landowners on the Jacobite side had lost a great deal and rents had been hiked, but in America, Willie says, glancing back at me, 'they'd have their own land and people could keep what they grew'. Nicola nods and tells me that 'the 45' changed everything.

Down to our left, the Beauly is iced up at the shallows and just off the road, a black grouse cock sits in spindly hoarfrost-covered branches. Willie slows the Land Rover to get a better look at it and it takes flight. He grew up in Applecross, in the 1970s, where he was the son of a crofter and like most boys of his generation, he was often out after fish and game in places he shouldn't have been in but poaching, he tells me, commercial poaching anyway, doesn't happen much these days. When he first started managing deer, for the National Trust for Scotland, over 30 years ago, poaching was big business and it was pretty cut-throat but people don't seem to bother much anymore.

There is something understated about Willie and he tells me there's nothing political about his understanding of the world but he is uniquely well placed to have a view on land access. He grew up on a peninsula that was almost bought out by the community, he's been at the sharp end of culling deer in busy hillwalking country for much of his life, and he's currently the property manager at Kintail and West Affric, one of the National Trust for Scotland's great estates. He's been around long enough to say it how it is and every third or fourth story, all of them delivered with a smile and enthusiastic gesticulation, is 'a story that's not for the book'.

The Land Rover is full of boots and ropes, and beside me Willie and Nicola's rifles rest against the window in their slips. Willie has been taking Nicola out to shoot deer for some time. She first became interested, she tells me, through doing land surveys for her day job. So often she'd report that there were too many deer on the ground that were destroying the trees but she came to appreciate that bringing their numbers down isn't all that easy. 'Conservationists in warm offices will just say get it done. It's your problem.' But she feels they often show a real lack of respect for the people actually doing it, a lack of respect for the deer, and a lack of understanding that it takes a lot of time and skill. From there, she decided she wanted to get involved.

At forty, it seems as though Nicola has lived five lives. She's lived in Borneo and Canada and Shetland and almost everything she's wanted, she's gone out and got. It's not that easy, she tells me, for a working-class woman from suburban Fife to get into deer management but she fancied it so she made it happen and when she's out on the hill, she feels like it's exactly where she's meant to be.

When Nicola first started out she was a ranger in the Trossachs. She is hugely pro-access and is generally opposed to individuals owning large swathes of Scotland but due to its proximity to Glasgow and Stirling, Loch Lomond on a sunny summer weekend could be hellish. It was, she explains, easily accessible to about two million people, which is great in theory but in reality they'd end up with crowds all the way up the loch. Some of them were fine but others were pretty hard to deal with and wouldn't be told that hacking green branches off trees to make a fire wasn't such a good idea. 'Places like Balloch get trashed', Willie chips in, they have parties and 'get *pished*'. It's not the sort of thing, Willie continues, that you ever really see up in somewhere like Affric, but then we've still got a good 45 minutes to go until we get to where we're stalking, so it's probably not all that much of a surprise. He pauses as he searches for the right words. 'We don't have that people pressure, so in some ways you're comparing apples and pears.'

The fog on our right hangs low over Loch Affric and the tops of the hills up behind are covered in thin icy snow. Willie looks out and says it's no good really. When the sun shines on the tops, the hinds will move up into the warmth and we don't have all that much daylight to get to them. Usually, when he's going for numbers, he sleeps out in one of the bothies and heads out as soon as dawn breaks.

There's no doubt in Willie's mind that there are access honey-pots north of the border and he'd be interested in a tourist tax being imposed but ironically, the right to roam in Scotland – which he reminds me must be seen as a right to responsible access – resulted in less disturbance on National Trust ground. The trouble, during the stag stalking season anyway, which runs from July through to 21 October, was that sporting estates would restrict access, resulting in more people visiting Trust ground. The Trust, just like other landowners, needed to shoot a certain number of stags, for the benefit of woodland, during the stag season but they never excluded people from any of their sites so they ended up with everybody who fancied a walk in the late autumn weather. The Trust's land access policy is informed by the Unna Principles, as laid out in 1937. Percy Unna, the then-chairman of the Scottish Mountaineering

Council, who died after his heart gave out on Beinn Eunaich, in the Grampian Mountains, was a wealthy Eton and Cambridge-educated engineer who gave the Trust the funds to purchase mountains for the nation. 'We'd never say "you fucked up my stalk" or anything like that', Willie shrugs. 'But you might say "you can go where you want but would you mind if we went in front of you?"' The funny thing, Willie continues, is that the very same people who managed deer, including himself, were often involved in the local mountain rescue but when they were out with rifles they'd get called 'fucking toffs', whereas when they were out with stretchers they were 'heroes'.

Nicola, who has been sitting eating her breakfast, turns round and scratches Jessie under the chin. She has been perched restlessly at my feet. 'Will you bring her up the hill?' Nicola asks. 'Probably not. If it's warm enough in the bothy, I might just leave her there.' Willie says he'll try to get the fire going for her – the temperature gauge on the dashboard reads minus eleven.

Nicola thinks that those estates that try to actually engage with the public and have designated car parks and plenty of signs have much less trouble than those that try to keep people out. 'It's not just responsible access. You've got to have responsible land ownership.' If it cuts both ways, she thinks it creates a culture of respect, which is fundamental. In her experience, if walkers feel that they're welcome on Highland estates, they are much more likely to take a different route if their presence gets in the way of deer management.

At the end of the track there is a ford through a burn and just beyond it an Argocat is parked undercover beside an empty building that would have once been a croft. The Land Rover won't be much good if we have to extract a hind carcass from up on the scree. While Willie loads up the rifles, Nicola tells me that not all landowners are bad people, she thinks that some of them truly think they are doing their best both for the community and for the wildlife on their ground, but she thinks we can do better. 'Can we not have more agency over our lives?' In part she feels like we're still living in the shadow of 'the 45' and that we don't really have the confidence to go it alone and would rather have the security of being supported by a wealthy landowner. To her, access isn't just about walking or sleeping out on the hill, it's about being able to manage the land and having the ability to be part of devising a plan for its future. There are people, she tells me, who don't live here and can't vote here who have more of an ability to dictate what happens to Scotland than she will ever have but it's not just foreign landowners. There are plenty of absentee Scottish landlords, she adds, who spend most of their time in Edinburgh or London. Nicola pulls a hat on, then lays her red plait against her shoulder, where it comes halfway down her olive-coloured deerstalker's smock.

Willie starts the Argo and the ice around the exhaust pipe begins to thaw. 'The thing is', Nicola tells me as we climb in, her in the front with Willie and me and Jessie in the back, 'I wouldn't want to be a landowner. It would be really stressful but I'd maybe want to be part of a community that owned land.' Willie pulls his gloves on and the black tyres spin on the icy wooden bridge. 'That', he shouts, over the grunt of the diesel engine, is the side of it that people don't see. It's almost impossible, he admits, to run a Highland estate profitably and the trouble with relying on grants is that 'they can dry up tomorrow'. Jessie climbs up onto my lap and I wrap her inside my jacket, then a couple of hundred metres on, Willie stops the Argo to blow some warmth into his gloves. The wind is coming straight over the bonnet and he can no longer feel the brakes in his hands.

Twenty minutes further into the Glen, we pull up beside a small bothy where a shepherd would have once eked out a meagre existence. There is plyboard across the windows, corrugated sheets have been bolted onto the old stone walls and the lock is frozen hard. During the winter months it only tends to be used by deerstalkers but over the course of the summer, well over a thousand people spend the night there, while they are out walking in the hills, often for two or three days. Willie stands at the door trying to find a lighter that he apparently had some days ago. He then goes to the truck, gets his flask and tries to throw his tea over the lock. 'Missed completely', he says as it runs down the door and starts to freeze. We stand around for a bit and then with the admission that it's probably pissing in the wind, I tear a page out of my notebook, roll it up, and start blowing hot air into the lock. Nicola looks on and says, in a tone that suggests we'd be better off trying to send Jessie over the hill to the nearest Tesco to bring us back a box of matches, that 'it might work'. But a moment later, Willie tries the key again and it turns. We make coffee and then Nicola and I sit on two maroon leatherette chairs while Willie sets the stove, muttering as he goes about one of the other stalkers leaving 'the place a mess'.

The thing about owning land, Nicola says, as we sit drinking our quickly cooling Nescafé is that you can't really own it. It was here long before us and it'll be here for millions of years after. 'It's just a construct.' What she does accept, though, is that where you've got one owner, things tend to happen, for better or for worse, more quickly. Whereas, where you've got lots of owners, and the land is held by the community, you end up with great stalemates, where half the community wants to do one thing and the other half wants to do another. 'Is this going to happen or is that happening. Too many fallings out.' She takes her hat off and runs her fingers through her hair then says that what she thinks works best is when a community gets professionals in to help them to devise a management plan, and then the community implements it. Like most of her thinking, it all comes back in a roundabout way to people, no matter who they are, having agency over the land around them. In another context, it might feel idealistic but coming from an ecologist with windburned cheeks, a gralloching knife on her belt and a .270 rifle by the door, it makes a lot of sense.

With just three and a half hours of daylight left and Jessie tucked up in blankets by the fire, we head out through the Glen on an old drover's road that runs alongside the burn. As we go, Willie talks about the impact that deer are having on the hills – there's no doubt, in his mind, that they are destroying forestry but he doesn't believe, as is often suggested by rewilding zealots, that without deer and sheep, the landscape around us would be covered in trees. He points at some spindly oaks up above us and tells me that they have been protected by fencing for decades but they are hardly thriving – the land in Glen Affric is poor and even if the hills were once covered in trees, our climate has changed considerably. Their intentions might be good, Willie and Nicola agree, but the problem is that the detached but well-connected often set the agenda without engaging with those on the ground.

There are three stags up above us, and behind them where the frozen heather becomes rocky scree, a group of hinds are grazing but there is almost no wind and there is no easy way into them. If the stags run, they'll go too. We get out and lean on the Argo, while passing Willie's binoculars between us. Nicola is currently trying to create a local economy for venison. There's plenty of it but getting it onto people's plates can be difficult – Nicola tells me it just gets shipped out the country or Tesco buys it for £10 a kilo. Surely, Nicola says, the venison from the local area should be there for local people. The point, in her mind, wouldn't only be about making good food available at a reasonable price but it's about giving people more of an under-standing of the deer and ultimately the land. She wonders though if people even know how to cook it anymore. The community in the villages around the Glen would have once lived on local venison and lamb, but they are now disconnected from those creatures, totems of a lost culture. Willie shrugs and says that to be honest, as the son of a crofter, he's eaten enough mutton not to bother with sheep ever again.

We climb into the Argo and head back the way we came, back down the glen and on past the bothy to the bottom of a track that runs over the hill. Nicola and Willie sling their rifles over their backs, push rounds into their clips, and then they walk on ahead, Willie at the front and Nicola in the middle. To our left water is tumbling down a gully and above us a raven drifts. Not long ago, walkers would often call estates to ask whether there was any deer management going on but it seemingly happens less now. Nicola isn't totally sure why but she suspects it's probably the case that in some areas there are just too many people to do that and that over time people have become disconnected from land management. But the extent to which walkers actually disrupt stalking is a bit of a moot point. Willie reckons that, with the exception of Trust land during the stag season, there probably aren't many more stalks ruined by walkers now than there were before access was opened up.

On our right about three hundred yards away, just to the left of where the sun is shining down on the snow, a group of hinds are grazing. Every time we stop they look up and when we walk on again, their heads go down. We head further up the path, to gain some height and then, when we're out of view of them, we cut across the face of the hill, stooping in single file, one behind the other. Willie picks his way through the snow and rock, with the lightness of somebody who's done this countless times, and Nicola and I step in his footsteps. 'Willie', I whisper to him, 'will they actually be able to hear us from here?' He turns and smiles. 'Well, if we get there and they're gone, you'll know.' And then we continue until we get to a large mossy boulder where we crouch with our backs to the beasts.

Nicola and Willie load up, then Willie stands and peers over the top of the rock before ducking down again. He shifts his head from side to side. 'We're kind of hemmed in. If we go up that way they'll spook and head for the ridge.' We lie in the snow for a bit. Down in the glen, smoke rises from the chimney of the bothy into the cloudless sky. On the hill opposite us, in the distance, two walkers appear as small black shapes against the white. 'Thing is', Willie says, 'about spoiled stalks. It's often just that "us and them" mentality.' He shrugs, stands again to have a look at the hinds, then tells us there's an eagle landed behind them.

After she's managed to get more venison onto people's plates locally, Nicola wants to then work with policymakers and landowners to try to bring about change in terms of who actually 'has access to the deer'. Even if people live in the Highlands, she tells me, sitting with her back against the rock, they often think that deer stalking is just for 'hoity-toity people in tweed'. That perception doesn't really ring true but she admits that it's hardly easy for anybody and everybody to get into it, largely because the land the deer are on tends to be owned by wealthy individuals and that comes with the stalking rights. 'I think', she says in a half whisper, 'that the law should change so deer are held in common.' She isn't sure exactly how it would then work but there could be some sort of syndicate or scheme that local people throughout the country could sign up to.

Willie who has been nodding along in vague agreement gets up again to have another look at the deer, then he passes me the binoculars. It takes me a moment to find them and when I do, three of them, three of about twelve, are staring at me, their ears twitching, with the eagle behind them still perched on a rock. All we can do, Willie says to Nicola, is try to get beneath them. They load up then Willie gestures to me to wait then they drop back a little and then start to descend, bodies flat against the ground, both of them holding their rifles up to keep their barrels out of the snow. Below me, where the tops of the rusty heather are coming through, they disappear from view and then, after what feels like quite some time, the first shot goes off. There are two more in quick succession and a moment later, a fourth. To my left, the hinds appear, mature animals and calves, running hard into the wind, and away over the crest of the hill.

The mid-afternoon sky in the west has turned pink and Nicola is ahead of us, leaning back with a rope between her hands and two gralloched beasts below her, tumbling and sliding over the snowy scree. Willie looks up to watch her for a moment. 'She's strong', he says with a nod and then he continues on. They thought, he tells me, that they were just about on top of the deer in Affric but a recent count showed that they are some way off. There's no reason that they couldn't have the local community involved with the stalking, Willie thinks, but all the way up here in Affric it would be hard. Getting the beasts out is never easy and equipment is required but it's something they are starting to think about more and more at the National Trust for Scotland and it would work further south. After all, if National Trust land is held for the nation, surely the deer are ours too?

*

In late September, when lapwings are gathering in the fields and the last of the swallows have almost gone, I drive north to Scots Dyke for a gathering. Built in 1552, the dyke marks the division of the debatable lands. Campaigners from the English side and campaigners from the Scots side are going to come together to share wisdom, hope, a bottle of Newcastle Brown Ale and some whisky.

We meet in a farmyard where Jessie digs for voles by a patch of nettles. There are probably ten or twelve of us on the English side. There are some young people from Manchester, a handful of old hillwalkers, and a few land access campaign heavyweights like Andy Wightman who has come by Tesla and Nick Kempe who has sat on almost every access-related committee in Scotland in recent years. I chat briefly to Nick about Scotland's national parks and Loch Earn. Shaking his head, he tells me that the whole situation, in terms of national parks anyway, has been terrible but we shouldn't, he doesn't think, focus on Scotland's bad news.

After twenty minutes or so we realise that there are another five people round the corner, including a man in his forties in a tweed cap and his two teenagers. We all head down to a rocky ford to cross the river. Jessie runs back and forth through the water and I'm told to put her on a lead. It was, one of the organisers tells me, a 'no dogs' trespass.

On the other side, we sit in the long grass to put our boots back on. Next to me, the man who joined us in the farmyard is speaking to his children in Gaelic. It was, he tells me in a Glasgow accent when we set off again, his grandmother's language and he promised her on her deathbed that he would bring it back into the family. The British, he adds, were trying to erase his people's ethnicity from the map, here in his own country.

For a while, we wander round and round, trying to connect with the campaigners on the other side and eventually we see their red banners among the trees. We shake hands, people hug and we collect together. There were, it seems, slightly more who started out from Canonbie in Dumfriesshire, two miles north of the border, and we number about fifty all in all. Nadia Shaikh, who works with Right to Roam, stands beneath an ivy-covered tree in front of a large banner and invites the gaelic-speaking father of the two teenagers to make an offering. He demurs at first, theatrically, saying he couldn't possibly, he's only just met us all, then he takes a step forward, raises his left hand and starts to sing. His children look on awkwardly as he sings beautifully, placing his hand against his heart and then when he's finished he translates for us from the Gaelic.

*May you have raven power, may you have eagle power,
may you have the power of our heroes at your back.*

*May you have the power of the storm, may you have the power
of the moon, may you have the power of the sun, and once
again may the taste of honey be upon your lips until you've said
everything you need to say, until you've spoken the contents of
your heart and know that we are at your shoulder.*

When he's finished the translation he holds his fist up in solidarity and cries out as though he's going into battle. A lady with a blonde fringe, standing across from me in a blue down jacket, joins in. When there is quiet again, Nadia says there will be one more offering and then we'll head back to the river. Andy Wightman comes to the front and presents the Land Reform Bill to a child who has come from the English side. We walk back the way we came, as one, and a group of girls with banners covered in thistles start to sing 'Freedom, freedom, the right to roam.'

At the river, a bagpiper is standing on a hummock, keeping time with his foot. The Gaelic singer and Nadia stand next to each other on stepping stones that cross the water, to mark the end of the ceremony, Nadia and the Gaelic speaker stand next to each other. Taking a hip flask of whisky from his pocket, the man toasts first, taking a hip flask of whisky from his pocket. He toasts to the ancestors, to everyone present, to the river, and lifting his index finger to his eye, he toasts to 'the good people on the other side'. When he drinks, Nadia drinks too, lifting a bottle of Newcastle Brown Ale to her lips. Then they stoop down and pour their whisky and beer into the river where it breaks against the rocks. Nadia offers a last word. 'There's that land', she says, gesturing back to the woods, 'and then there's this land. Somehow the birds can't see those borders and somehow the roots of the trees grow on both sides so while there is a border there's also not a border. What does that mean for us?' The Gaelic dad nods and Nadia looks down at a bit of slack water in front of her. 'I think it means we have to understand the borders within us.'

It's a sweet idea but it's not much more than that. A cock robin will kill another male that strays into its territory and crows kill other crows. Rabbits fear raptors and raptors fear foxes. It's only humans that feel we deserve to be able to walk uncontested across the land. And what does that mean for non-human life? It means fire, it means disease, and it means endangered species becoming even more endangered.

It would be a little unfair to say that for most access campaigners, Scotland is a faraway land of which they know nothing but it wouldn't be totally wide of the mark. Every time somebody in walking boots in the Home Counties says look how well 'Right to Roam' works in Scotland, I feel pretty uncomfortable. Evidently, a number of those who access land in Scotland are not all that responsible. I once spent a week in a caravan with a German man, on Skye, who was working as a ranger. His stories were both amusing and depressing – some days before I arrived he'd been sent single-handed to deal with a bunch of campers who were threatening people after spending a weekend binging on ecstasy. It was just five months after I'd met that gamekeeper in Speyside who spends much of his time trying to persuade local mountain-biking groups not to tear through capercaillie leks because they are contributing to their near-extinction.

The narrative, as regards to wild camping and caravanning in Scotland, in nice English weekend papers, is that it's a joy and every digital nomad should head up there without delay. But the tabloids often present a truer picture or at least an overlooked reality – the *Scottish Sun*'s 'locals brand area the "Wild West" after "feral" campers destroy beauty spot', and locals 'so sad and angry' over damage in Glencoe, are just two of many. Hardly a week passes without a tale of mindless destruction. And yet, we are endlessly told that if only we could access the land in England, we would respect it.

It is also inescapable that Scotland is roughly two-thirds the size of England but has a population of just over 5 million as opposed to a population of just over 55 million. There is a reason that in remote places, such as Harris, access in the summer doesn't cause all that many problems, although it would be wrong to say there are none at all.

The role that Scotland should play is not one of being pointed at from Surrey as an example of how marvellous access is. Scotland should be looked at as an example of both the benefits and the harm that more access can bring, and a big part of that is listening to those on the ground about their lives. I recently spoke to Nicola Williamson who told me that her venison for the community project is progressing. The power of that shouldn't be underestimated. It is the creation of a very visceral connection with the land and she is just the sort of person the countryside needs.

*

At first it was all very sporadic and it took a long time but eventually some of the boys on Lewis did talk. They wanted to know what I knew and who I knew, and they wanted to know why I was interested at all. They were incensed to learn that people on the island had told me poaching no longer goes on and in the end they wanted to tell me everything and they wanted to show me the pictures to prove it all too.

They do it mainly, one of them admitted, 'for a bit money'. Before the season starts they take orders and then when the spring fish (which they reckon are the best) run up the rivers, they catch them and drop them off after dark. None of the poachers, they told me, really eat the fish: 'Never eaten salmon in my life', one of them said, but added, quite seriously, that he should probably try it before the fish stocks go extinct. As for who buys them, their biggest customers are apparently retired gamekeepers, 'retired keepers and the old timers'. But it's not, they were keen for me to understand, only about the money – 'All I want to do', one of them said, 'is to be able to go fishing in places. I'd like to go fishing on places, even if it's just with the fly and we want to keep a certain amount of fish, even just one or two.'

For some time we talked about whether I should use any of their pictures in my book – they seemed somewhat disappointed when I told them it wasn't that sort of book really but I appreciated it all the same. And then they asked me again, as though they had told me too much, who I knew? I told them I didn't really know anybody on the island particularly well but I tried a few names. They hated everybody and had stories about run-ins with them all, except for one of them. The last keeper I mentioned had seemingly caught them poaching one night and had given them 'a go with his salmon rod'. He even once took them out in his boat and they spoke about it as though it had been the best of times. 'Him, he's brand new.'

8

Ritual and Transgression

*The spiritual importance of access, and the land
as a place to transgress together*

It was quite a while ago now but I distinctly remember her climbing naked into the small hire car I was driving and slamming the door hard. Mo must have been in her mid-fifties at least but she looked good for her age. Her skin was totally unwrinkled and like most naturists, so I came to discover, her pubic hair was neatly trimmed.

The club, except for Mo, her husband, and a few old stalwarts, was pretty empty. It was late autumn and quite a few of the members had gone to Europe in search of sun but there were just about enough people around to speak to and on the first night we had a few beers in the clubhouse. All of us sitting there naked on plastic chairs.

Mo explained to me as we drank that there had been some discussion about whether or not to let me in. A couple of years previously, a local tabloid had burned them with a cheap article that compared the Yorkshire Sun Society to a swingers' club – all they wanted me to do in my piece for *The Yorkshire Post,* her husband explained, was to really capture the society as it is, not as it's imagined to be by 'textiles' beyond the gate.

That night, I lay beneath a blanket in the designated visitor's caravan drifting in and out of sleep. The people on the pitch next door were sitting round a fire with some naturists from Switzerland. I could hear them explaining to the Swiss visitors that things are different here – the public don't like naturists.

The following morning I had breakfast alone. Cold fog had rolled in across the heavy Yorkshire fields and there was just one other person perched on a chair on the other side of the room, naked from the waist down but with a jumper and jacket on, and with a bowl of cereal resting on his milky white thigh. 'No clothes', he said to me eventually. 'Well, no', I replied. 'Mo said I could only come if I abided by your principles.' The man shook his head and nodded towards the door where drops of rain were starting to fall on the glass. 'We're naturists, son. We're not masochists.' We ate our cereal in silence after that. Then I went and found some trousers, returned for a cup of coffee, and looked at old photos pinned up on a board – there was a photo of a young woman cradling a dog, there was a grainy picture of a muscular man holding up a trophy, and there was a collage of pictures of work parties in the 1930s cutting down trees and levelling the ground on the 26-acre site.

After breakfast, I wandered through the cabins. Most of them were shut up and a few of them looked abandoned but next to an old caravan, on a corner plot, a man who must have been in his late seventies was bent over in a flower bed, working the ground with a garden fork. When I stopped to talk to him he told me, all the while carrying on digging, that he was planning to plant a wildflower meadow but he was also going to keep some of the ground as it was for vegetables. His wife liked gardening too, he explained but not as much as him and they had been members of the Sun Society for a long time. After a while he asked if I would like to see the whole site and he popped his head into the caravan to tell his wife who was sitting at the table that he was going to show the young lad about a bit but he wouldn't be long.

He walked ahead of me and told me as he went that the paths through the scrub took quite some maintenance but they all mucked in together. After fifteen minutes or so we emerged through a clearing onto the grassy western bank of the Holderness Drain. In 1926, George and Wendy, the club's founding members, had travelled, by boat, up the river in the hope of finding somewhere where they could live differently. The field across the water was being ploughed and a flock of gulls followed the tractor. As we stood there, the old man told me that he used to like to walk naked in the Pennines with his wife, 'loved it in fact'. But they don't do it anymore – in the age of the cameraphone he reckoned the chance of someone taking a photo and uploading it was too high. 'It's up online and then they all start saying you're a pervert.' He shook his head and told me it makes him a bit sad but it's just not a risk worth taking.

Naturism is a funny thing. I usually find, when I get sent to write about something, be it Crufts or Bully XL owners, that I come away feeling I understand the subject and have a degree of empathy with those involved in it but in all honesty, I can't really see the appeal of gardening naked. Most naturists when pressed aren't able to tell you what it's about but in a way that's not the point. The point is that it really matters to them, that it's part of their identity.

I might not fully understand it but it saddens me greatly that the old guy who was gardening doesn't feel as though he can confidently walk naked through the Pennines. Having access to those hills facilitates his act of transgression and his quiet contribution to the counterculture. If we deny him access, in this instance through the threat of moral condemnation, we limit his ability to express himself. Access isn't just about walking. It's about creating culture and connecting and a lack of access is to limit culture and in some instances, such as closing down free parties, or seeking to have long-running Gypsy horse fairs banned, it's an act of cultural destruction.

*

As London pubs go, the Charles Holden is pretty forgettable. In the corner there is a man in sports shorts, banging away on his laptop, two-finger typing; a restless golden retriever sits barking by the bar, and in the corner, next to the radiator, a thin man, dressed completely in black, and with small lively eyes, looks up at me. 'Ah', he says, 'and you look just like you do online. I was googling you.' His voice is grey, smooth, and pleasant.

I get a half of Guinness and then when I sit down Nick tells me he managed to find that *Yorkshire Post* piece online. 'I just wanted to say that I think you really got it. It was very well observed and you went beyond the cliches.' Nick Mayhew-Smith, now 54, is the Clubs Officer for British Naturism and has been going nude since one particularly memorable school exchange trip to Germany, when he was introduced to it by the family who were hosting him.

Like most writers he has had a patchwork career. It has some-times, he admits, been a bit 'threadbare' but he is one of the most significant British writers on naturism and he sits, creatively, at a fertile juncture between nudity and spirituality. Practising naturists will know *The World's Best Nude Beaches and Resorts*; *Bare Britain*; and the follow-up *Bare Beaches* but he also writes on sacred places in the landscape and Celtic spirituality.

Nick explains that naturism really exploded in 1920s interwar Germany during a time of great social upheaval. 'There were all sorts of movements', he tells me, finishing his beer, 'Nazism obvi-ously became the dominant one but there was a rambling and hiking movement too and it is very, very closely aligned to naturism.'

He leans towards me and tells me emphatically, 'that's your Right to Roam. In Germany rambling and hiking went hand in hand, and were virtually synonymous actually with naturism.' Nick tells me the common consensus is that these various movements were a backlash against rapid industrialisation, a backlash led by the urban proletariat. 'Of course we look back at it now through the lens of Nazism, but it was also a time of socialist and utopian ideas.'

We get two more beers and Nick explains that there is a sort of twin track running through the International Naturist Federation, a body he gets involved with from time to time. On one hand, they want to protect, promote, and build up naturist clubs and communities but they also want naturism to be accepted anywhere at any time. As he sees it, those are two quite different things, almost at odds with each other. There is a worry, apparently, among some that naturism in clubs is hiding, that naturists are building their Jerusalem behind gates and are creating a fenced utopia rather than spreading the naked word by getting out into the world.

Naturism is bigger in France and much bigger in Germany than it is here but Britain, in Nick's words 'quite bizarrely', is where the current iteration of the naked rambling movement is at its strongest. Nick tells me it's a small scene but it's worth getting in touch with them to see if they'll have me along. Those involved, he continues, almost all of whom are men, are deeply devoted. When I ask why it is they are all male he holds his hands out as though it's a dumb question. 'Our bodies are all equal, or so it goes, but that's not true if you're a naked woman on your own in the countryside.'

In 2016 at the University of Roehampton Nick completed a doctorate on 'nature rituals' in the early medieval church and he tells me it kind of relates to everything we're talking about. Nick's focus was the way that Christians like Cuthbert overwrote their own Christian narratives onto already deeply storied pagan places. 'This was', he says, in wonder, 'a demonic land. Britain was full of dark places that were difficult to get to. Nonhuman spaces in the landscape were forbidden. They were dangerous and profane.'

While he was writing, Nick kept coming across evidence that watery places, like rivers and lakes, were seen as 'capricious' and 'antagonistic' to human life. They were places where monsters lived. Nick, through swimming naked, feels that he is engaging with those storied landscapes, he's literally swimming through places that are 'the repositories of deep memories'. To be naked in the British countryside is to connect with the holy and the magical. It is as close as we can get to becoming part of that history and that magic. Naturism, he tells me, is important, but there is something beyond the nakedness. 'Do show them a bit of ankle', he says as he gets up to go to the toilet. 'Readers always like a bit of ankle but do look at the spiritual too.'

*

Nathan, who must be in his early thirties, stands twenty yards out from the rest of us, with the North Downs rolling away into the distance behind him. He has a white plastic Londis bag on the crook of his arm and he isn't posing for the photograph as such, he's just standing there, straight on. Two men, twice his age, are taking a photograph for him. 'That is nice', one of them says cheerfully. 'That is nice, Nathan.' The three of them, Nathan and the two men, then gather round the phone together to have a look. Nathan doesn't say anything but the two men agree all of the pictures are very nice.

We carry on back into the woods, about twenty of us, mostly older men, most of us with rucksacks on, and Jessie, my dog, walking at heel. At a stile, we pause, and a nice man who went into woodland conservation after a career in IT crouches down to speak to Jessie. It is a long way for a small dog and she sits there panting and looking at him before lunging at his crotch. 'Oh dear', he says in embarrassment. He fends the dog off, stands back up, and we walk alongside each other, chatting about nightingales, coppicers, and the history of the Sussex Weald. We are about halfway up the group. In front of us, there is a Frenchman in a small red hat whom I sat next to at lunch. 'You do not do the naturist stuff', he asked me. 'I don't', I replied. 'Not usually.' Luc, who lived in Norwich for some years, told me that England is a great place for naturism. In France, in spite of what people think about Europe's liberalism, it is actually illegal to be naked in public.

The woods in front of us are thick with bluebells and Keith, a retired schoolteacher, draws alongside me. He is a gentle man and he has been a naturist for a long time but only when he retired did he actually 'come out'. He always worried, he tells me, that parents or those in the common room would find out and would think he was some sort of degenerate but that day, when he had finally retired, and he could be in the group photograph, which seems to be a customary part of every naked ramble, was one of the happiest days of his life. In a hushed tone, he tells me he thinks it's maybe easier to come out in Britain as gay than is it to come out as a naturist.

Up ahead of us, a jay squawks, and as we draw nearer, it dips across the ride and disappears behind an ash tree. When Keith was young, he used to sometimes walk naked by himself but he no longer has the appetite for it these days. In part, he likes the company but he admits that he also worries about the possible consequences of solo nudity. Unpleasant incidents, with walkers calling naturists perverts and paedophiles, aren't a regular occurrence but they do happen, and not so long ago a man in their extended network ended up in court, defending himself from what the judge ruled was a spurious allegation about indecent exposure. The five pounds that I paid to join British Naturism, I paid in part, Peter explained as we took our trousers off in the car park that morning, meaning that I was covered in case a claim was made.

The British Naturist Ramblers all seem to be very aggrieved that they struggle to attract female members. There is one apparently, called Janice, and Keith tells me that he was delighted to hear that of all the many walking groups she's a member of, she thinks the conversations that she has with the Naturist Ramblers are of the best quality. 'The trouble though', an old guy from behind me adds, 'is that ladies aren't made to feel comfortable in the nude, and they can be sensitive. One nasty incident and that's it.' Keith thinks that one of the most frustrating things about the lack of female members is that a group of naked men aren't as readily accepted in the countryside as a mixed group might be. 'It would sort of lend us legitimacy.' For all that, though, he does wonder if naturist ramblers need to be a little less apologetic. For some time, Keith has been involved in organising walks on RSPB land. But they apparently don't really like the idea of twitchers having to share footpaths with men in nothing but their boots. They tend to suggest, Keith explains, that the naturists can have access when there is nobody else around but that, to most of the group, defeats the point of trying to normalise nakedness.

In the middle of a hazel plantation, we stop for a break, and I lie back next to Jessie beside a rotten oak stump. Some of the group are talking about statins and I half listen while watching a red kite drifting above me. When I wake, fifteen minutes later, almost everybody else is asleep, naked bodies sprawled out across the ground, rucksacks for pillows. The kite has gone and the sun is going down.

For the last few miles, I walk with Bob, a small man with a blue track top tied around his shoulders. What it's all about, he explains, is 'rampant nature worship'. Naturism, he believes, is essentially pagan. The trouble, Bob continues after a bit, is that in the past when only aristocrats had access to the land, the nature spirits were off-limits to the common man. What he tells me I need to do is think about 'recreation'. He rolls the word around his mouth. 'Recreate.' He says it slowly, sounding every syllable. 'Recreate yourselves.'

That evening, we go to the pub and various members ask me, enthusiastically, if I'll come back. I tell them that I won't, that I'm sort of done with naturism, but I'll spread the good word. I promise to tell anyone who'll listen that it is a sort of pagan thing, and that they are kind people and not perverts.

*

It had been some years since I'd last seen my friend, George. At school we were close but he got kicked out a couple of weeks before our final term ended for fighting with one of the science teachers. When I got in touch with him he told me he didn't really know all that much about the free party scene. It was sort of on the periphery of the stuff that he's into but he could probably, he thought, point me in the right direction.

When I get to the bar, George is standing there on the phone having an animated conversation about a party in Germany. He is trying, he explains when he hangs up, to get a float to Berlin for 'Love Parade' but the paperwork is proving difficult.

We order chicken and he fills me in on Save Our Scene, a movement he set up during the Covid years, in response to the Government not allowing nightclubs to reopen as the situation eased. After the pandemic ended, his focus shifted to highlighting the plight of clubs and dance culture more generally. 'We've gone from like 3,000 nightclubs to 860', he tells me, breaking off to check his phone, 'and the rate of closure is spiralling out of control.'

Our food comes and George explains that what we're seeing as a result of all these clubs being closed is a huge rise in illegal raves in the woods and fields and squat parties. 'It's only gonna become more and more of a problem and the Government will wake up one day and realise, "Oh my God. We've got this huge issue on our hands again."'

In the 1990s, after the Criminal Justice Act effectively banned raves, the authorities started to feel like they had control. The Act gave the police the ability to remove 'persons on land in the open air', listening to music 'played during the night' which is 'wholly or predominantly characterised by the emission of a succession of repetitive beats'. Although free parties never went away, the police, as a result of the Act, gained far greater powers to stop parties like the Castlemorton Free Festival, which happened in late May 1992 and which was attended by some 40,000.

The thing about *the party*, according to George is that it's an almost organic thing that can't be killed and nor does it just disappear when venues go. What you end up with is a kind of strange fragmented scene that gets driven underground. Part of that is that DJs don't make any money but he also reckons that squat parties, which are one of the consequences of losing venues, can be pretty dangerous. Free parties in the countryside, he adds vaguely, are pretty safe but 'in London in the squat party scene you got a lot of grooming going on. Like child prostitution and really dark horrible stuff. Kids find these places, these parties, and they get exposed to these worlds.'

After lunch, we lie outside on sun loungers, and George tells me there is one guy he knows of who has links to the free party scene, a guy called DJ Fu.

It takes me a while to track Fu down – for much of the summer, he says, when I finally do get him – he was in Africa, DJing out in the desert. He says he'll speak because I'm a mate of 'Georgie boy' but at the same time, he'd rather not because as it happens, there are five books he's thinking of writing himself and he doesn't want to give away all his stories. What he's sitting on, he tells me, is 'bestseller stuff', and what he's after is 'a major publishing deal'.

In the 2000s he was in a gang that raided 19 cannabis factories. 'Listen brother', he tells me twice, 'it's not fiction.' Some years after that he flew to Cyprus where they took over a radio station. 'That story', he assures me, 'would sell like wildfire.'

He won't disclose what the third and fourth book would be about but the fifth, he tells me, would be about the free party scene. In a strange way, Fu thinks the scene's current appeal is partly due to free parties being a source of excitement in a world where excitement is hard to find. The way it works, he explains, is that beyond the people bringing the sound systems, nobody really knows where they're going. You just get given a vague part of the country and a number to call on the day that will give you a meeting point. Generally those organising free parties use a burner phone with a pre-recorded voicemail message. 'Got to be a bit smart, brother. Party line, not on Facebook, not on socials.'

When I ask Fu if farmers or landowners ever turn up and whether they mind, he says, 'Course they turn up, geezer.' But again, he reminds me that kids need to be 'a little bit smart'. The ideal scenario is that everyone keeps the phone number to themselves, gets in there when it's dark, and by the time the police turn up the following morning, everyone's done. 'Bish bosh, we're drinking tea, munching on our bacon sandwiches.' Fu tells me that some parts of the UK have always been free party hotspots, such as the South West and East Anglia, whereas there are other parts, such as Essex, where it's not worth trying. I ask him why and he says it just is what it is. 'They just won't have it. Free parties in Essex, forget about it.'

In recent years, Fu thinks they've really been clamping down hard on the scene. He doesn't tell me why except that he thinks those involved are perceived as outlaws. 'Basically, we don't consent, yeah. We don't pay tax, we don't live by the rules. Unless you're kind of in it, it's really hard to explain.' Fu seems to think that although the police know they are unlikely to see parties that are 20,000 or 30,000 strong, like in the 1990s, they still fear illegal mass gatherings and they try their hardest to nip them in the bud. Only the previous week, he was at a gathering of just 15 down towards Stonehenge and the police sent a drone and a helicopter. The whole thing was tiny but Fu explains that with the advent of social media, after the party has been established, word can get out and people pour in.

What Fu thinks the authorities fail to see is that free parties in remote places are as safe as it comes. 'We look after each other. Everyone knows everyone and if anyone bad comes in the circle, they get dealt with.' He points to Frenchtek, a huge annual party, which happened in 2023 on 70 hectares near the usually-quiet hamlet of Fouillereau, right in the middle of France. There were 30,000 people, 40 sound systems, and the party ran from Thursday to Sunday. Seven people ended up in hospital including a man who fell asleep under the wheels of a car and was subsequently run over, and later the Red Cross were deployed. But Fu insists that the ravers create their own culture of safety. There were, Fu tells me, two men who assaulted a girl and justice was served. The wheels were taken off their car, they were 'slapped up' in front of everyone, and were then marched out with everyone chanting '*violeur*'. It sounds a little odd but the landowner reportedly felt that those partying behaved so well, including turning off the music for two hours each day to tidy up, that he decided not to bother pressing charges.

When I ask Fu who he can put me in touch with, he tells me he can't put me in touch with anyone. 'I don't know you', and if I hadn't come through 'Georgie boy', he continues, he wouldn't have spoken to me at all. But he tells me too that if I really want to understand, I've got to go to the parties. 'Follow your nose, brother. Read between the lines.'

Throughout the summer, I do my best to find a way in. I contact Fortune Audio, Tree Hugging Crew, Descendant Audio, Croaktek, Rotten Noise, and a whole host of other people running rigs, but none of them give me so much as a crumb. The general consensus is that the police don't care much about arresting people who go to illegal raves but they will always try to confiscate rigs because without them, there's no party. Consequently, the crews that build them and drive them across the country are cautious. A number of individuals, just people devoted to the scene, do come back to me and most of them say much the same thing: free parties are beautiful and empowering and I'll only ever understand them by going but they can't give me any party lines. One young guy is apologetic but says that they don't just pass them around because when 'dickheads' get hold of 'the loco', and turn up, nights 'go west'. By early August the closest I've got is being added to a Telegram group run by somebody in the West Country who is shifting industrial quantities of ketamine and then just as summer is starting to run out, I hear back from a filmmaker called Elliot. He is trying to get a documentary made that compares the squat rave scene with the free party scene. He tells me at length about his understanding of how and why the two scenes differ. At squat parties, he thinks there's always a chance that you're going to get stabbed but the further you go into the wild, the more the mood changes. He can only recall one or two occasions when things, at a free party, have soured. 'I think about the reasons they differ quite a bit and I think it's just something about being out in the nature and stuff. There's something so pure about it.' He also thinks, although he tells me lots of people would disagree, that being outside in the open, rather than being enclosed in a warehouse, inspires a sort of tranquillity. On the legality of free parties, Elliot says he's not too clued up really. He guesses that somebody must own the land they party on, and sometimes farmers turn up but he doesn't think it matters too much because most ravers are committed to 'leaving no trace'. The principle, Elliot tells me, is totally fundamental to the movement.

By the time we've finished talking, he's texted a number through. It's the line for 'a massive two-day party', with multiple crews, which is due to happen the following weekend some-where in the South West. 'Obviously', he says again before he rings off, 'don't give it to anyone else, and no socials', but more than anything he wants me to speak afterwards. He wants me to tell him what I thought. He talks about it all as though he's sending me on a trip to see something that will make me realise things I couldn't have possibly known before.

We are buying beer at the petrol station just before the Hammersmith Flyover, heading west out of London, when the first location drops. The person reading the note sounds oddly like a small child: *'Hello ravers and welcome to the South West bank holiday free party hotline. Start getting down to the Bristol-Gloucester area. Please call back after six o'clock for directions to the main convoy meeting point, which you'll need to be at by nine p.m.'* The message rounds off by saying that the party location is sheltered but outdoors and adds, before breaking off into a jungle track, that anybody coming down should be prepared to stick it out for two nights.

Jack, who is sitting next to me in the passenger seat, opens a can of beer and then pulls a map up on his phone and prods at the cracked screen with his index finger. It's not, we both agree, very much to go on. 'Whitminster, Dursley, Tetbury.' Jack runs through various places on the map in between Bristol and Gloucester. 'I guess we'll be there for a bit', he continues, looking at the clock on the dashboard, which at an hour fast, is reading 1.30 p.m. We decide, eventually, that Stroud would be a good place to find a pub to sit in for a bit, while we wait for the second location to be announced, and we head off down the M4, sitting in the slow lane while heavy drops of rain start to fall.

Until Monday of the previous week, Jack had been living

and working, as a sculptor, at a large warehouse in Kings Cross, surrounded on all sides by fish storage units. His mornings would start at around 4 a.m. when workers would turn up in lorries to load up with fish to be sold at Billingsgate. He thinks that on reflection, it was clear that something was amiss. The landlady had been uncontactable for some time and more and more letters in brown envelopes were dropping through the door. One evening, he pressed the answer machine button on a landline that nobody used and found endless messages from a debt collection agency. Jack rolls a cigarette, lights it, opens the window, and cold rain starts to blow in.

He was in the midst of creating a flock of lapwings out of plaster, for an art installation we were working on together, and he was too immersed to give the oddness of the situation much thought. Then, one morning at 5 a.m., a group of men, all in black, started hammering on the warehouse door. He could hear them talking to each other. 'Someone's put that up as a curtain', 'there'll be people living in here.' Jack climbed out of bed and went to see what was happening. 'Shitting myself', he admits. They had come to repossess the building. It transpired that the landlady, in renting cheap living space to Jack, three jobless girls, and a Belgian who made leather fetish wear, had been acting illegally. The property was commercial and that aside, the landlady hadn't been paying any rent to the owner of the building. 'But to be fair', Jack tells me, as we pass Heathrow, 'if you're a young artist in London, you just take what you can get.'

By the time we get to Cirencester, the weather has cleared and because we've got so much time to kill we go to the Roman amphitheatre where we pick brambles, then sit at the top of one of the slopes, eating them and drinking beer in the sun. 'It says here', Jack tells me, reading off his phone, 'that after the Roman Empire collapsed, the amphitheatre became a rabbit warren then a place for bull baiting.' A small black plane above us is flying sharply upwards, casting a white plume out behind it against the bright blue. It sweeps round, creating a circle, and then turns sharply inwards to add large eyes and a smiling mouth.

We head on to Stroud where we spend two hours in an almost-empty pub garden, sitting under a wisteria, while waiting for the next message on the party line. When it drops, it's late, and it seems we should have gone much further west. 'Get to the Asda in Swansea by nine p.m. – convoy will be leaving there at ten p.m. so don't be late to guarantee vehicle entry to the party. Park sensibly and do not attract attention.'

After an hour on the road, we stop at the Severn Bridge services to get coffee. There are families gathered round grubby tables at Burger King, and tired salesmen eat sad sandwiches but there are young people too, shaven-headed girls with neck tattoos, New Age Travellers piling out of old vans, and bright-eyed kids in hatchbacks full of duvets. At an M48 motorway service station that in 2019 was voted Britain's grimmest, there is a sense of anxiety and magic.

The tide is right out beneath the Severn Bridge and the mud is black. Cars tear past us, girls in bright pink fur and topless boys. By the time we get to Port Talbot, the last of the sun has gone down over the Atlantic and fumes from the steelworks are lit up purple and blue, drifting into the low clouds. At the Asda in Swansea the car park is alive. Women in fishnets are doing laughing gas and people are sitting together on plastic camping chairs. I go inside and queue up for cigarettes. The lady at the till, pointing towards the aisles, asks the guy in front of me what we're all doing. She has never, she says cheerfully, 'seen anything quite like it'. He tells her, as though he has no idea what she's talking about at all, that none of us are together. He's just staying at the Travelodge across the car park 'to visit family'.

By 9.45 three police cars roll into the car park, lights flashing.

'So what happens now', I ask a toothless Bristolian in a Hawaiian shirt, who's been telling me about keeping chickens in Portugal before his wife left him and took their dog. 'We wait', he replies, 'then we scramble.' I head back to the car and the three police patrol cars drive round and round for 20 minutes while everyone hangs tight. The car park is still filling up and a red VW, with sun-bleached paint, pulls up next to us. 'It's the young ones', the driver explains to Jack. 'It's the kids. They draw attention. They can't help themselves.' At 10 p.m., the party line hasn't been updated but horns start going and people start pinging past us. We follow and end up one car park over, next to the petrol station. 'We just spread out', a young northern guy tells us, 'we spread right out and then we go.' He's come all the way from Carlisle and he seems delighted that I've never been before. 'There's gonna be three thousand people', he says over and over. 'There's fuck all the police can do, but this party is the one. This is the right one to come to.' The police roll round in front of us and the officer in the passenger seat takes a picture of everyone's licence plate.

The mood, by half eleven, starts to hollow out, and it feels like people are drifting off. We ask three boys, who can't be much older than 17, whether it matters that the police have come. 'Nah, bro', one replies. 'It'll happen brother. Trust me. This has happened so many times.' At 11.45 the party line is updated but all it says is that everybody should hang tight. They are going to rush the sound systems up onto the mountain and then they're going to drop the final location. Ten minutes later the coordinates are released and a girl standing next to me, in a puffy camouflage dress, throws her joint onto the ground, jumps into the driver's seat, and drives away. We fall in behind, the lights of the convoy stretch on ahead of us as far as we can see and the rain starts coming down hard. It has just gone Sunday and we are all heading for Rhigos Mountain.

On the way there, five patrol cars pass, sirens wailing,

seemingly trying to get ahead of us, and 40 minutes later when we get to the mountain road, heading up into the Cynon Valley, it seems as though it's over. They have all pulled across the entrance to the firetrack into the forest and there is a helicopter sweeping across the sky, a searchlight moving back and forth beneath it over the tops of the trees. 'I don't give a fuck', a boy behind us says in a Bristol accent, 'we'll leave the cars and walk if we have to. We'll have a fucking riot. We've come to party.' Jack and I get out and stand on the side of the road looking down into the forest. All around us, teenagers are talking about abandoning their cars to head into the trees on foot in search of the rigs. We head back to the car and sit there with the heater on. The night feels autumnal and hopeless. One car ahead of us, the girl in the camouflage dress who had been smoking the joint squats downs and pees on the road. She stands, then climbs up on the passenger seat and leans on the roof for a while, looking up towards the mountain. Some moments later, she notices liquid on the run, running out beneath her car, and she gets down on her hands and knees to try to work out what's leaking. Then horns start beeping and before we've worked out what's happening everybody behind us seems to be turning and driving flat out back down the hill. There are three cars across the road in places, driving inches apart and the helicopter drifts above us. Somebody has found a firegate in the trees and has managed to smash the lock off and roll away the boulders on the other side. The police can't get up the mountain fast enough and within ten minutes all we can see of them is a cluster of flashing lights growing fainter, down in the valley.

It's a steep half-hour drive up the mountain and when we get to the top, the helicopter is hanging low in the rainy sky, hovering above a clearing in the pines where three crews are still setting up their rigs. It's 2 a.m. and it seems like some of the crusties have been in situ for a while – a half-clothed girl is lying on a camp bed in a caravan, blowing plumes of smoke into the air and two women, who must be in their fifties and who look as though they've been on the road for some years, are slicing up limes for a cocktail they're making. 'It almost didn't happen', one of the guys building the biggest of the rigs tells me when I pass, 'but those are always the best parties.' The crews themselves spend thousands on putting parties on – they have to buy the kit, maintain it, get it all there, run the generators and they make nothing at all. Some people suggest that they should be paid for all of their efforts, but any money changing hands would undermine the whole philosophy of the movement. Illegal raves high in the mountains, complete with no car-parking charges, are one of the only truly free ways to enjoy rural Britain.

By 3 a.m. the lights and projectors are going and Jack and I stand in front of a hypnotic video of a detached eyeball, with a large dilated pupil, rolling round and round with pink octopus tentacles meshing and unmeshing behind it. We watch for a couple of minutes, then we walk back to the car to get more beers. When we get there, some guy who has been locked in his van, gets out and starts shouting at his girlfriend then vomits. He tells her he was in there for an hour and she replies, through tears, that it was only ten minutes at the most and that she didn't mean to lock him in there. He starts saying 'you did', over and over and moves towards her as though he might hit her then he vomits again, bent double in the mud, retching. 'I'm not fucking doing this', she cries, crouching with her face in her hands.

Back at the party, some New Age Travellers have got a hot water urn going and fifteen of us, including a man with a dog, stand there in the rain drinking coffee. He tells me that the dog is two years old and that it hasn't been to many parties but that he's been partying 'forever'. He explains that what the police will do is just try to contain the whole thing – they won't let anybody else in and they'll try and get the sound systems on the way out. The man turns away then picks up a bit of wood and throws it into the blackness with his dog running after it.

At 4 a.m., all of the sound systems are going, all carefully positioned so that they don't drown each other out. Jack and I stand among the crowd in front of a stack of speakers playing a jungle mashup of the Prodigy. Raindrops, as they pour through blue and green beams, catch the fluorescence, and speckle the night. A man comes and stands next to us and asks if we have any 2CB. 'I'm sorry', I reply, 'we don't.' He smiles and says 'That is a pity', because nor does he. He talks for some time about Russia. 'Does anybody ever tell you that you look Russian?' He stares at me hard, then puts his arm around Jack. After a bit his sister appears and asks where we're from. I tell her we've come from London and then I tell her we actually only came because I'm a writer. She smiles at me. 'Nobody gives a fuck why you're here. We're all just here.' A couple of minutes later, for no particularly obvious reason, the man takes against us and leaning right into Jack tells him he'll run a piece of glass across his face. His sister tells Jack to 'ignore the silly cunt', then offers him some ketamine by way of an apology.

Back at the hot water urn, two young topless guys with mullets and a girl in a black crop top are holding unlit fire sticks. 'But do you think people will actually like it?' the girl asks. 'Yes', a lady with a feather sticking out of a dreadlocked bun replies. 'They'll love it.' She says it like an encouraging mother and the girl nods before walking off through the mud. The fire, when they light the sticks, illuminates the soggy, churned-up ground and a crowd gathers. The boys start spinning their arms, creating flaming wheels in the night while the girl juggles above her head, staring up into the flames. We all huddle together, cheering and whistling, and a man standing next to me, with no teeth, tells me that he hasn't been to a party like it in years but that he split up with his wife a couple of months ago and he found the scene again. When the performers finish, at half five, a huge roar goes up and everybody drifts towards the biggest sound system. Ten minutes later, the rain stops and light starts to seep into the sky, revealing heavy grey rain clouds, together with all the bodies and nitrous oxide canisters strewn across the mud. Jack and I pick our way through and stand where the ground drops away to forest. There must be ten or fifteen of us looking across into the low-lying cloud. In the night it was impossible to see where we were in the blackness but at first light, the land starts to take shape. 'It was a colliery', a boy to my left, who seems to be by himself, tells me. I ask him who owns the land now and he looks at me with big black pupils and tells me thoughtfully that nobody knows. Nobody seems to know and nobody seems to care. In the moment, the mountain belonged to us. We had made it ours, a place that had been mined and then planted up with commercial forestry.

We sleep for a couple of hours and then it takes a long while to get back down the mountain and we don't say very much to each other. We're going to get out of Wales and we're going to get coffee. We drive past the broken gate and out on to the road and then at the bottom of the hill we see the flashing lights. A police van and two patrol cars, as we were told would happen, have the road completely blocked off. I spin round and go back the other way. We drive right over the mountain and then when it looks like we're away we start talking again, I put the radio on, and Jack rolls a cigarette then we round a corner and drive straight into an almost identical roadblock.

The officer walks slowly towards the car and then stoops so his head is almost inside the window. 'Where've you come from then, boys?' I tell him that we came from that party, the one they failed to close down last night but I tell him I'm just a writer and Jack's just a sculptor. I was only there, I explain, because I'm writing a book on land access. He looks at Jack and then looks back at me. 'Very interesting, boys.' I try to get ahead of him. 'It took me ages to get that party line.' The officer cuts me off – 'Well, it didn't take us very long at all.' He looks to his colleague with the van and then looks back at us. 'Do you think', I ask, 'that policing free parties is a bit like policing fox hunting?' He nods thoughtfully. 'In a way it is. Some people love it and some people hate it but if they're away up there, doing their thing, personally I've not got much of a problem with it.' He walks away and says something into his radio and then returns. 'You tell me this, boys, they say that they're going to party till Wednesday. What do you reckon?' Jack and I look at each other, then tell him it would be some going and it seems unlikely. It rained all night and there can't be more than a thousand people up there. The officer looks at us, taps the roof of my car, then signals to his colleague who reverses the van and we drive east to Merthyr Tydfil. That evening, I read that there were five arrests and one of the sound systems was impounded.

*

The young kennel huntsman winds the truck window down, sucks hard at the butt of his rolled-up cigarette, then flicks it out onto the street. It's November but the drains in the little town are clogged up with leaves, the gutters are spilling over, and the wind is winter cold. 'Hopefully', the boy says, with childlike enthusiasm, 'hopefully we'll be meeting here on Boxing Day but I don't actually know where we're at with that this year. We did always used to, apparently.' The old Nokia in the cupholder rings and the boy puts it on loudspeaker then tells the huntsman that we're on our way. 'Good lad', he shouts back.

'Trouble is', the boy says as we pull out of the town, 'nowadays there's all sorts of trouble.' He pauses for a moment as though that's all he's got to say on the matter, then he tells me that the biggest problem is that people move to the countryside 'and they don't get it. They just don't understand.' He looks round at me, seemingly waiting for some sort of affirmation, then adds that obviously you also give hunt saboteurs a pretty easy place to find you, if you meet outside the same pub on the same high street at mid-morning, every year on 26 December. He sips at his flask of coffee then says that it is a funny thing because in the past, even when he was a young child, the local hunt was a big part of village life 'but villages are quieter now'. We pull off the road onto a farm track and the boy says that in some ways he thinks hunting made a mistake when it started to hide away in the hope that if they just quietly got on with it, people would leave them alone. 'I'd say that people forgot what hunting was about but we didn't remind them because we were scared.' There are, the boy tells me, all of these bad stories, stories about how awful hunting is but he supposes that hunting doesn't do anything to tell its story. 'Yes we kill foxes', but it's not, as he sees it, all about the killing. It's about the hounds and the horses and the people.

In the yard, there are followers of all ages. 'You got the posh ones', the kennel huntsman tells me, 'and you got the not posh ones. Him there, he's a lawyer.' He points to a surly looking man who is tightening the girth on a fine grey horse.

I open the back of the truck and Jessie leaps out, squats down for a pee, then runs round and round, sniffing at the sheep shit on the concrete, and creeping nervously past the horse's hooves. All around the yard there are sheds with mossy corrugated roofs and a magpie perches on a stack of old tyres by a silage clamp. The Masters talk about the day, about where we can and can't go, two middle-aged ladies drink a bottle of champagne, and the terriermen sitting on their quad bikes ask each other quietly who I am: who the guy with the little green notepad is.

At half ten, the kennel huntsman unloads a large bay horse and takes it to the back of the lorry. It stands for a moment while the boy takes its rugs off. Gathering up the reins in his left hand, the huntsman swings his boot over, sits back in the saddle, then waits. The hounds grow louder and louder and when the boy opens the tailgate of the lorry, they pour out across the yard, grizzling in anticipation and scenting the air.

After twenty minutes or so, the huntsman turns his horse in a tight circle, blows his horn, then kicks on, heading off down the lane with the hounds at his horse's feet. The two whippers-in, both of them on dark geldings, trot along behind the pack and the kennel huntsman and I ride thirty yards back on a quad. The rain is coming down hard, rushing through the leaves of the oak trees and after half an hour, I'm soaked through.

At the end of the lane, just before a thatched cottage with a scarecrow in the garden we turn left through a gateway onto a field of winter stubble where pigeons are feeding on the last of the grain. The mounted field, 25 or 30 of them, come through behind us and stand together. The huntsman gathers up the hounds, tells one of his whippers-in to canter on to the end of the wood, then he trots away amongst the trees, casting the pack in front of him. There is a moment of pregnant quiet but the field soon starts talking, cigarette smoke and steam rising from the horses, hanging in the cold fog. 'Trouble we've got', the Master tells me, 'is this bloody "it's mine" attitude. Doesn't matter if somebody buys a big estate or a farm. It's that sort of attitude of "it's mine".' He smiles and says the words again sardonically. In the wood somewhere below us the hounds are speaking and the Master listens before continuing. 'They do come around sometimes and they stop being so bloody precious about it but it's difficult.' His horse, which he later tells me he got for a pound, is grazing away and he runs his hand across its neck. 'Fucking cold', he says bitterly before telling me that of course the other difficulty is shooting. 'It's a nightmare. Where there are big commercial shoots we often can't get on at all.'

One of the whippers-in trots out of the wood and tells the kennel huntsman to head halfway down. The hounds are marking an earth and we need to be there to head-off the fox if he bolts. We tear down the ride and the kennel huntsman rolls a cigarette beneath his jacket. For twenty minutes we sit and wait. A roe deer appears ahead of us and from time to time we hear the hounds but there's no sign of the fox. In the end it does bolt but it slips out of the other side of the wood, under a gate and onto a farm that the hunt isn't permitted to cross. Half the trouble, the kennel huntsman tells me as we head on to the next covert is that the hunt used to know everybody. They'd collect all the deadstock for the hounds and most of the farmers hunted but often, nowadays, the farms get bought up by those who just see land as an investment and have no interest in hunting.

For a couple of hours we tear through blocks of woodland with the huntsman ringing from time to time to ask if 'we've seen him on' or to tell us to get right out to the end because that's where he ran last time and that's where he will surely run again, but by two o'clock they still haven't found. Hunt staff don't text each other and there is a complete ban on videos – if the police do come, the kennel huntsman tells me, they are very welcome to their phones because there'll never be anything on them. The rain doesn't let up all afternoon and the woods, except for the odd jay that comes screeching out of the firs, are cold and quiet.

When we meet up with the field to head on to another part of the estate about a third of the followers have gone home. 'They'll be on the gin by now', a lady with a scar across her cheek tells me before jumping a ditch and heading up a steep track. The kennel huntsman and I go the long way round on the lane. One of the hounds has cut its pad and it sits across my lap, steam rising from its oily coat. The boy tells me he often thinks the field doesn't realise how much time goes into organising a day's hunting. For the hunt staff it isn't just about keeping the hounds fit, they spend most of the summer visiting landowners and trying to keep the country open. If it wasn't for the hunt, the followers wouldn't be able to ride across the land. Most of this country, he says, would be off-limits.

At the bottom of the lane, we turn into a wood where the terriermen are waiting for the huntsman's call. On the front of their quads they have shovels in rifle racks and on the back they have steel boxes with air holes where you can just make out noses and little black eyes. Some of them have their children with them and they shrug when I ask why they're not in school. We chat for a little bit about all the things the terriermen used to do when they were young – things that all country children did but things that don't happen so much anymore, like snaring rabbits and poaching trout. 'Shot her first deer when she was nine', one of the terriemen tells me, gesturing to his daughter who nods shyly. The terrierman asks me if I've read Nick Hayes' *Book of Trespass*? 'Thing is', he continues, 'I don't suppose we'd get on if we met, Nick and I, but there's a lot of truth in that book.' He tells me it's pretty sad really that people can't go where they want to because as a proper country person you sort of just expect to be able to go where you like. 'That', he adds, gesturing towards where the field passed, 'is what it's about for them. It's about being able to access the countryside.' We sit for a bit, all of us with our hats pulled down and our arms folded, trying to stay warm and then the terrierman tells me that in fairness he's pretty sick of the 'private' signs popping up in the countryside, 'and now you've got the cameras as well'. The children on the quad look at their dad, as though they've heard it fifteen times before and then the kennel huntsman's phone rings. The hounds are on the other side of the wood and they're marking an earth.

When we get there, the huntsman has called the pack back to him and he sits with the Master fifty yards away beneath the trees. They laugh among themselves as they talk about how far away it is they're meant to be when the terrier boys start digging – far away enough anyway that if somebody is out with a camera they can claim the whole thing was nothing to do with them. The earth, it seems, is much bigger than anticipated and as soon as they've broken through into the first section of the pipe, the fox moves deeper. The hounds watch on, some of them whining and some of them standing with their paws on the back of other hounds to get a better look at the men with their shovels. They are all crowded round the earth, squatting on their haunches, heads cocked, listening to the terrier somewhere beneath their feet, backing the fox into a corner. One of them calls up to us, 'It's about to go. Any second now it'll go.'

On the way back to the kennels we stop to buy beer. The boy tells me they take turns to buy beers, him and the huntsman, but he always tries to buy them after they've had a bad day's hunting because he knows then that the huntsman will only have one. If it's been a good day he needs to buy three or four times as many because they end up drinking for hours and talking about it all.

It seems strange to be driving among commuters and the traffic is slow. The boy tells me that his life, recently, has been a bit of a mess and in some ways it still is. He doesn't speak to his stepdad, who was a farmer, or his real dad but the hunting keeps him going and he's happy now. He wants to become the best huntsman he can. 'You got to be smart', he tells me, 'and you got to work hard. I should end up on a horse next year.' The huntsman has been giving him lessons and his jumping, he thinks, is coming on. The old phone in the cupholder rings. 'Good old boy', I hear the huntsman say down the line, when the boy confirms he's got the beers.

It is almost dark by the time we get back to the kennels and we feed the dog hounds. Then we feed the bitches. They sweep hungrily about our feet. 'Do you think', I ask the boy, 'that you'll be able to carry on doing this? The Master was saying you're losing more and more country.' The boy nods and tells me he thinks so. He'll be hunting somewhere. He'll be hunting if he can. Just so long as they don't ban 'trail hunting' because then they probably will have to stop and then he'd maybe be back to farming. It would, though, 'be something to do with animals'. The hounds growl and whine, as they each find their place, then there's the sound of flesh being torn and bone being crushed. 'But I don't think', the boy says, 'that there's anything I can do on that front. Just got to enjoy it while I can.' Four hounds in front of me, beneath the faint glow of dirty lamps, are pulling at something big. 'Horse's neck', the boy replies when I ask. We both open a can of beer and the boy walks among the hounds, telling me their names, while running his hand down their backs. He speaks to them as though I'm not there and he seems to speak to them all. He tells the hounds they are good, that they are 'good boys and girls', then he says it didn't take him long to remember all of their names, because what you do is you remember things about them, little things, you remember how they hunt and how some of them come to you and how some of them won't and you remember how they look at you. He tells me about the best ones, the ones he likes the most, and he tells me about the hounds that are still very good even though they are old.

About six months later, at the launch of *Wild Service*, the compendium of essays by high-profile supporters of the Right to Roam campaign, I mention to a lady who lives on Dartmoor – and who is one of the campaign's inner circle – that it's a funny thing because fox hunters share lots of problems with land access campaigners. The trouble they have, I explain, is that the very rich buy a hundred acres or so and then say to them that they can no longer come across land they've hunted over for hundreds of years. 'Good', she replies. At first, I think she doesn't understand so I say it all again and then a third time. 'Yes', she replies, 'good.' It makes me angry. It makes me angry because the land access campaign consistently misrepresents what hunting is in order to present themselves as fighting the good fight. 'It's a power performance', Jon Moses claims, 'of exactly those freedoms its early participants so often denied others.' What Jon's observation really is, is a curious instance of fox hunting being presented as what he would like it to be. Landowners hunt, sure, but so too does a cross-section of rural society, right across the class spectrum. The Banwen Miners, for instance, a working man's hunt in South Wales, used to keep their hounds in the lamproom of the local colliery.* Isn't it interesting, Moses once said to me, that a certain sort of person supports fox hunting but not hare coursing, which he explained to me is a working-class pursuit and a pastime of Travellers and Romani Gypsies. I sent him a few old clips from the Waterloo Cup, Britain's premier hare-coursing event (now banned), which was run initially on land owned by the 2nd Earl of Sefton and was won variously by Sefton, some of his descendants, the Earl of Lonsdale, Baron Tweedsmuir, the Russian nobleman, Count Stroganov, and in 1891, Lady Turnbull, daughter of the 9th Earl of Stamford, as well as lots of ordinary people. 'That was the thing about the Waterloo Cup', a sheep farmer's son from Potters Bar told me when I sat down with him to hear about his experience of going. 'It was toffs and tinkers, mate.'

Hate hunting. Hate the foxes being killed and the hounds being shot when they're too old to hunt on, hate the tradition and the songs and the poetry, and all those middle-aged ladies who drink too much, and hate the sound of a pack in full cry

---

* The Banwen Miners, after hunting was banned, became a bloodhound pack. They, like lots of hunts, 'hunt the clean boot'. They send somebody out to lay a trail that they follow.

when they hit a line of scent on a bright October morning. Hate it all you want but it seems distasteful for a largely middle-class movement to fit up lots of rural working-class people like that kennel huntsman as being 'toffs', in a bid to bolster a cause built on dubious figures and generalities.

It's hard to express quite what hunting means to those involved, in the same way as it's hard to really understand what naturism means to naturists. And I think there was truth in that conversation I had at the roadblock in Wales with that policeman – the free party scene has a lot in common, spiritually, with hunting. They are both illegal, for the most part, and to some they mean everything. They are a way of keeping a community and a culture alive – they have their own songs and their own language. They are part of what makes the British countryside the British countryside and in a complex way they depend on space and access. They are also both limited by the political establishment, albeit generally by different sides of the House. It's about identity and a wish to suppress it.

Just as naturists find their Jerusalem in the woods, and just as we built a sort of Jerusalem on that Welsh mountain while the police helicopter circled overhead, there is something spiritual in the hunt kennels, a sort of faith.

In Wordsworth's poem, 'Simon Lee, the Old Huntsman', he writes of Lee being a poor old man who is almost unable to work anymore: *And he is lean, and he is sick, / His little body's half awry'*, but *'still there's something in the world / At which his heart rejoices; / For when the chiming hounds are out, / He dearly loves their voices!*

*

At one point, Andy's landlord kept chickens in a large run outside his cottage but a fox kept getting in and eventually he decided there was little point in replacing birds that were only going to end up dead a couple of weeks later. Decades ago there'd have been a gamekeeper to keep fox numbers in check but over time family funds diminished, land was sold to neighbouring farmers, and now almost nothing remains of a once-grand estate.

I stand on the stone steps at the cottage door and I knock. The rain stopped on my way west to Devon but the wind picked up and the night in the valley is wild. A curtain is pulled back and Andy appears, in his tracksuit bottoms, threadbare socks, and a T-shirt with a buffalo printed across it. He is a man who looks both young and old, with a round face and a white beard. He apologises for the mess, then picks up the cage with Jessie in it, places it down next to the fire, and goes to the kitchen to get me a drink.

Andy's wife, Jess, is sitting on the sofa across from me. They lived in town for some years, she tells me, when Andy is pouring my beer, and she was working as an artist but then she got chronic fatigue syndrome and combined with Andy's depression, life became hard. They realised, Andy says as he hands me the glass, that the right thing for them to do was to sell their flat and rent, which is how they ended up down in the valley in Devon, in the cottage next to the old chicken coop.

All around the room there are books on fungi, mythology, and fish and there are tubs of drying nettles. Andy lies on a beanbag on the floor, wipes his glasses on his T-shirt, and starts telling me about the first time he took mushrooms at a party long ago. 'I must have only been sort of late teens, and someone brewed this massive pot of mushroom tea.' Andy thinks that in fairness, it wasn't that clear what had gone into it and he'd also smoked a lot of cannabis but he ended up sitting in a room all by himself having a complete meltdown. His girlfriend at the time, he tells me, as he brings through my plate of rice and fish, was the most promiscuous person in the world and it made him paranoid.

It was only years later when Andy moved down to the cottage that he encountered mushrooms again. Along with a neighbour, he'd been getting into picking woodland fungi like ceps, chanterelles, and field mushrooms, and one afternoon she knocked on the door to tell him she thought she'd seen magic mushrooms in a field where some sheep were grazing on the other side of the valley. 'Jess was away and I just thought, why not?' At first, he remembers it just seemed really nice. He sat there alone, looking at the curtain, edging towards 'a trippy place', and then the following morning he felt happy and content. He felt a sharpness he hadn't felt in years.

Jessie is lying on her back with her tail beating up and down and Andy pushes his hand into her cage and runs a finger across her muzzle.

Andy was 11 when he first felt depression and it's been with him ever since. 'I guess it's just my brain not making serotonin, but a weekly dose of mushrooms just gives me such a boost, just complete clarity.' Ever since his neighbour knocked on his door, it's become a sort of ritual for him. When the mushrooms come again each year and he finds them, it's as though everything is in the right place. Like swallows coming back, he tells me, or bats hunting moths again in spring.

There is, Andy thinks, a hugely spiritual element to both picking and consuming magic mushrooms. His psychonaut friends, he tells me, will talk about taking a visit to the astral plane and Andy reckons that, even though we don't have any evidence, it's almost certain that the ancient Celts used magic mushrooms and fly agaric, he's noted – that red mushroom with wart-like white spots – features in a lot of Norse mythology.

Andy goes to get me another beer. 'Well, I think', Jess says, 'I think, I might go to bed. I probably won't see you in the morning. You'll be gone.' Jessie opens one eye and watches her out of the room as she leaves. When he returns, Andy lies on the sofa that Jess was sitting on, his ankles crossed over each other. It can't be a coincidence, he thinks, that *Samhain*, the ancient pagan festival, which marks the beginning of the darker half of the year, at the end of October, falls when the mush-rooms come up. *Samhain* is, in part, about the blurring of our world and the other world, the world inhabited by fairies. It's a festival of fire, slaughtering cattle, and entering the liminal interzone. 'If you think', Andy tells me, 'that they are like picking and eating these little mushrooms and then these people appear. You can't really believe . . .' He laughs and trails off, then says that it's sort of like time itself changes. 'It is about access. Your mind becomes a bit more open. All your life you've been told that "X" is "X", everything's straight and clear but then you take mushrooms and you really start to see.'

Andy makes me a bed on the floor of a little room where his wife has an old printing press and I lie there thinking back on that horse's neck and the hounds. Some years ago, I was driving beside the Thames with a poet who told me that the thing about hunting is that the fox dictates where the hounds go and ultimately where 'the field' goes. It's not just about being able to access the countryside, she said, as though she'd been thinking about it for years, but that where you go is dictated by something wild. In the pursuit, we become animal. You should write about hunting, she told me some months later, when I told her I was writing about access, space, and spirituality: 'You should', she insisted, 'but people will hate you for it.'

Those men and women out on their horses, jumping hedges with cigarettes in their mouths and their heels down, were worshipping in the same way that we collectively worshipped in the Brecon Beacons when the sun came up. It was, as Bob said to me when we were naked in the woods in Kent, 'a sort of paganism'. The fox was a sort of devil-god to be worshipped, revered, and slaughtered. It felt like a cultish religion.

Nakedness is man at his purest, hunting is man at his most brutal, and free parties are raw collectivism and joy. To bring in the dark half of the year and to step into the otherworld, the Celts needed hills and fire, and still some 2,500 years later, we need space to worship too. And Andy is right I think. In some sort of way mushrooms are about access. We need access to get to them and they provide access to a previously-unknown periphery.

The following morning, Andy doesn't get up until after eight and then we sit in a pool of sunlight streaming through the glass doors, eating black pudding rolls. For a long while, Andy used to set off across Devon looking for magic mushrooms. He just sort of drove the lanes in his old car, he explains, and then he'd zigzag across the fields, sometimes trespassing, and other times he'd use old footpaths, most of which were totally overgrown and forgotten. He'd always heard about fields in the Welsh mountains where people could pick three bin bags full of 'liberty caps', but in spite of putting the hours in, he never found anywhere quite like that. At best he would pick thirty or forty and then return home. Part of the trouble is that the mushrooms grow on unimproved pasture but so much of Devon, these days, is covered in lime and drained. 'You've got a network of mycelium under the soil and they are basically looking to feed on dead grass stems but it's the older pasture you want, basically the more ancient the better.' In his search for more mushrooms, Andy started to go further and further afield, and one evening, about two years ago, just before dusk, he found it. 'It was', he says, finishing his black pudding roll and stretching out, 'completely mental.' He must have picked, he reckons, literally thousands of them that evening and he only stopped because he ran out of plastic bags.

The cloudless sky at ten o'clock is an almost unworldly bright blue and there is no wind, but tree branches have been blown across the lanes and the land is sodden. As we drive up the steep switchbacks to head across the top, Andy points out his cottage in the valley below and the large house up behind it. His landlord, he tells me, owned all of it at one point, almost everything we can see, but his landlord's father partied too hard. 'He'd sell a few acres and then they'd party for days and then they'd sell some more and now there's just a couple of fields and a few cottages left.' He's not so bad, Andy says, as he winds the window down. 'If you get him on a good day anyway, he'll get the sherry out and you can be there for hours.'

Thin hedges run along both sides of the road across the top and on our left, a covey of partridges are huddled together, drying out in the warmth of the sun. Andy points out the strip lynchets* on the hill opposite, that run in a sort of terrace across the land. 'Basically in return for working for the landowner, you'd get one single strip to farm your own stuff.' He tells me it's odd really because for all that it's beautiful, it's completely man-made.

Last autumn, just a season after Andy first found his 'field of dreams', he returned again. He was completely oblivious to the world, picking away, when a Land Rover roared up. He wasn't, he doesn't think, all that far from the footpath but the landowner, at least he's pretty sure it was the landowner, went nuts. 'He just started shouting what the fuck do you think you're doing?' After a while he calmed down a bit but he told Andy that if he caught him again, he'd effectively be jeopardising everybody's right to access the land in any way at all and since then, a fence has gone up with barbed wire running along the top.

We park beneath an ivy-covered oak, which has a deflated pink balloon in its branches. Ever since the incident, Andy has parked up some way off just in case the landowner clocked his

---

* Strip lynchets were formed by ploughing and created flat terraces on slopes that could be cultivated.

car, first time round. It takes us ten minutes or so to get to the field and as we walk there, woodpigeons and starlings feeding on the rape stubble on the other side of the hedge take flight. Every ten or fifteen yards, we spot a liberty cap just over the fence and Andy stops from time to time to tell me about them. 'You can peel their skin off like cling film', he says, pointing down to a clump of three. 'That one there, that's not a liberty cap. That's an ink cap', and 'That one – that's an older one. You can tell because the colour is changing to purple.'

At the end of the track, where the fence stops, we cut onto the grass. Andy clasps his hands behind his back in a statesmanlike sort of way and starts zigzagging, while staring at the ground. Almost immediately, he finds one and then another next to it and then at least five behind them. 'It's amazing that nobody else seems to know this spot exists', he says with delight as he picks them, drops them into a plastic carrier bag, then puts that bag in a hessian pouch. It is, he explains, as he wanders, about getting to 'the astral plane' but it's also just about making winter bearable. Winter, for Andy, has always been a difficult time. Every so often, when he's picking elsewhere, Andy tells me he sees people who are very clearly at it. You're always, he thinks, pretty vulnerable because you inevitably get massively engrossed in it, almost drunk on just finding them, and you end up totally unaware of who might be approaching when you're trespassing with a big bag of class A drugs.

After twenty minutes or so, he's worked his way down the edge of the footpath and we move further into the field. He picks in silence and I watch him looking down at the ground, trying to read it, trying to work out where they'll be, then I notice two dogs coming through the gate and behind them a man on a smart bay horse carrying a whip. His horse walks steadily and he calls his two dogs back and tells them to sit and wait. Then he trots towards me. 'Can I ask what on earth you're doing?' I pull my notepad from my pocket. 'What it is, is that I'm writing a book on land access. Everything from Travellers to hunting to foraging.' The man leans back in the saddle and looks at me with some confusion. 'Do you have much of a problem with land access?' He turns around to see that his dogs have grown bored and are hunting voles in the hedge. 'Huge problems, endless problems', he replies, 'the main problem is people just not sticking to bridlepaths. I can't work my cattle as I want to. I find my sheep all huddled up in one corner. But what are you actually doing?' I reach up to stroke his horse's muzzle but he shies away. 'He won't let you do that', the man says, 'he's a nice horse but he won't let you touch his nose.'

I tell the farmer all about the free party and the naturists and the hunting. He stands in his stirrups to let the horse piss then he calls his dogs to him. 'You know', he says, 'I wouldn't know half the farmers I know if I didn't hunt and I wouldn't be able to access that ground on my horse because my fellow farmers are generous enough to let the hunt across.' He lets his horse's head loose, so it can get at the grass, then he starts telling me about how much the hunt has changed. 'Hardly any farmers out now at all.' He asks again what it is we're actually doing. 'Foraging', I reply. He nods thoughtfully, then turns and points into the valley with his whip. 'That's access land. That's access land there you see and I haven't seen anybody set a foot on it in the twenty years I've been farming here.' One of the two dogs, a vizsla comes and sniffs my ankles. 'I suppose', the farmer continues, 'that it's not actually all on a path. You have to trespass to get there, but people could ask.' He tells me about his cattle and the lapwings that come in spring and the Travellers that used to come too until they locked them out and then his dogs start whining and he says that he really must get back to checking his stock.

He walks his horse down to the gate then trots away along the field, glancing back at us as he goes. 'That was him', Andy says, when he's out of sight. 'That was the guy.' A minute or so later the farmer appears, down below us, cantering up a goyle. There are clouds starting to gather in the east and the dogs are running.

*

A strange evolution has happened. In the past, the call for more access really was about access. Whereas, currently, there is part of it that seems to be about dictating how people ought to use the land. The call for access has become a call for control. Hunting is out, beating on pheasant shoots is out, fishing never gets mentioned. I'm not sure where they'd stand on free parties; access campaigners, in the main, or the ones I've met anyway, aren't into psychedelics. Clearly there are problems with illegal raves. You wouldn't want to be a roosting tawny owl listening to the hiss of ten thousand nitrous oxide canisters being cracked, and yet the land should be about freedom to be who we are, to become, to connect with each other, and to connect with countless things past.

9

Strangers

Who feels welcome in the countryside or otherwise, and are British villages racist?

Ezekiel has 12 days to lose 5 kg. 'Easy', he says, while leaning against a red-brick wall in a South London boxing gym. 'I go for a piss, I go for shit, I get in the sauna.' He smiles, revealing a gap where he's seemingly lost one of his front teeth, then he tells me that his upcoming fight is for a super middleweight title, up to 76.2 kg.

Ezekiel wasn't always a boxer. Until not so long ago, he was in jail for being a midsize cog in a drug-dealing operation that went wrong. He was almost, he says, getting away from it all when he was arrested. Something, although he isn't very clear about what exactly, went wrong with a 'runner' who was working for him and he got caught when he was down on the coast, sorting things out with another gang.

What I want to know is how it is for a guy like him to move through London. He shakes his head when I ask and says, with a shrug, 'You know how it is.' Ezekiel has been out of the game for some time but there are still plenty of places he can't go to. 'Can't go Peckham, can't go Lewisham, can't go Brixton.' There are even parts of New Cross, where he grew up, that he can't go to. When he was just young, and starting out, it was fun.

'Like a little game.' Bobbing his head from side to side, as though he's in the ring, he says that if he went somewhere, 'someone might see me. I might see them. It's fun at the time, innit.' But the trouble is, he goes on, when you've been in the game, you can never really get out of it. 'It's not easy at all.' The police, he tells me, never forget your face, people who were 'on you' never forget your face, and 'people you've hurt, they don't forget'.

It is late summer and outside, through the small window, I can see the sun going down over the church spire by the green. The whole situation is pretty bleak. Clearly it's not the case for every young black guy growing up in London but Ezekiel tells me that if you hang about 'with certain groups', it makes going to other places pretty difficult.

It should follow that England beyond the city, beyond Peckham, Lewisham, and New Cross, is a sort of haven where postcodes don't matter but Ezekiel tells me I'd be surprised. Some of his dealing was running county lines networks and it means, Ezekiel has found, that some parts of the countryside, 'which should be sweet', are pretty hostile. 'Obviously there are parts of the countryside that's good', he tells me, but in other places you might be just 'doing your thing', when there's someone else up there from 'Brixton doing their drug thing' and they'll remember you or they'll ask you where you're from. Ezekiel looks at me as though trying to work out if I follow and then adds, 'if you're a black guy looking hood, you know what I'm saying?' The trouble, Ezekiel thinks, is that people always know if you've been in the game. It's the way you talk, it's the way you dress, 'it's even the way you walk'. He trails off and I tell him that I guess I can go anywhere. He sucks the air through his teeth and says, 'Of course, you're chill.'

He's hoping, he adds, as he starts to wrap his hands, to change everything. He's going to change the way he talks, the way he walks, the way he dresses. He's even, he tells me, been reading books. What he'd like to do is he'd like to get his vocabulary 'up', he pauses for a moment, then says, 'I'm going to change everything about myself.'

A fortnight later, Ezekiel travels down to the south coast for his fight. He makes weight and goes on to win. That week, I drop by the gym with a copy of Joyce Carol Oates' *On Boxing* and John Healey's North London memoir of destitution and fighting, *The Grass Arena.**

It might seem a little oblique to try to understand access in rural Britain by talking to a young former drug dealer in a boxing gym but to grapple with the potential that the countryside has for the most marginalised, you need to think about how access works in the city. It's pretty horrific to think that for a young guy who got involved in some bad stuff, London is now full of barriers. It is a city to Ezekiel of hostile villages and Britain beyond, county lines aside, should be an escape.

About three weeks after I go to see Ezekiel, a thousand or so people gather in Southwark Park, with their bikes. They are mostly young black guys, some girls, and kids from what remains of London's white working class. Up at the front there is a banner that reads 'Bikes up, knives down'. The event was founded in 2014 by Mac Ferrari, who grew up in the North London gang scene, but he left that all behind and decided he wanted to do something to save young lives. The mood is edgy. 'These youngers', says a guy in his mid-twenties, who tells me he'd like to stay anonymous, almost never come together apart from at BikeStormz. He's always tried to stay away from trouble, he explains, which means he can 'know' different groups but

---

* A couple of months later I hear that Ezekiel has had to stop fighting. He suffered a bleed on the brain and had to be put into an induced coma. The guy who tells me says it's terrible really because he was just starting to win some big competitions and his future, in the ring, was bright.

at the same time, he says, he'd rather those groups didn't know he hangs out with other groups in other areas.

A young guy next to me is having a go at four police officers. They are only there, he tells them, to ruin the day. 'We are only here', one female officer replies, 'to make sure everyone has a good time.'

The mood is charged. There are boys on e-bikes in balaclavas cutting through the crowd and as well as feeling like a celebration there is an inescapable undercurrent of the unpredictable. Then, at just after midday, up on the band stand, plumes of multicoloured smoke are released. They drift together into a thick purple haze, rising among the plane trees, and then over the music, the organisers start chanting 'Bikes up, knives down' into their megaphones. All around me young kids, some of them with their tops off, are chanting it too.

When they ride out, at this point maybe some 1,500 of them, I'm sitting on the wall across from the park entrance with a local guy with blackened teeth and a flat cap. 'It's just unbelievable', he tells me. There is a bit of a jam at the park gates and some of the young guys are shouting. I tell the guy I'm planning to write about it and he tells me that BikeStormz is the only time you see this many kids from different places and 'there's no trouble 'cos they are all together and they move. They keep moving.' There are boys pulling wheelies up the central partition and others spill along the pavement. One young guy, probably in his early twenties, rolls out past us on a purple 'cruiser', steering with his right hand while rolling a blunt with his left. We watch until they are almost gone and we can only just hear the music, someway up Jamaica Road, then the man turns to me and bumps his fist against mine. 'Anyway, my friend, good luck with the book.'

It is hard, if not impossible, to really understand the invisible boundaries that cut through our cities if you aren't a young person either involved in, or on the periphery of, postcode-related violence. It is moving to think about Bikestormz as being kids declaring the streets to be theirs, and kids taking space back from a scene that they might be part of but that they didn't create. They are just pebbles on a beach covered in blood. Ezekiel talked about getting into the game but it seemed as though the game found him and he is now fighting his way out. BikeStormz is quite literally making space neutral.

In Alice Russell's beautiful and bleak 2022 documentary, *If the Streets Were on Fire*, which explores BikeStormz as a form of expression, as well as digging down into some of the challenges the organisers face, there is a scene in which they go to some dirt jumps in the country when the leaves on the silver birch trees are turning. It is the closing segment in the documentary and as the kids are all riding the jumps, Mac, the founder of BikeStormz, says that when they get out of town everything changes. 'I swear down in the city they don't look like this. I've never seen their faces like this.' In the city, he adds, they are running from knives but out in the woods, they are free.

The idea of the countryside as an escape from the city is fascinating but as with everything there is nuance to it. Some parts of the countryside, as Ezekiel told me, 'are sweet' but seemingly quite often, the experience that black and minority ethnic people have in the countryside isn't so sweet at all.

*

There are four of us in the foyer at LUX cinema, on Highgate Hill, wet umbrellas and steamed-up glasses.* We flick through the books on the shelves and drink coffee out of polystyrene

---

* LUX, which has been running since the 1960s, was a cornerstone of countercultural London. It was once run out of a squat but it's now a charity that supports emerging filmmakers, as well as housing an extraordinary archive of work by visual artists dating back to the early twentieth century.

cups while we wait to be ushered through. The film I've come to see is about black visibility in rural England. Some weeks previously, I'd read a piece in the *Guardian* written by Dan Guthrie, a young filmmaker, who noted that the British countryside still feels off-limits to those who aren't white, a countryside, the piece begins erroneously, that is still 92 per cent privately owned. I wrote to Dan, who is mixed race, and he replied that it was nice to receive something positive among all the abuse.

It is a 'relaxed viewing' and the lady who was at the desk stands up at the front in a reflective vest to tell us that we can dip into the quiet room whenever we like and that help is at hand should we need it. The lights, she promises, will not be switched off completely at any point. The idea for *Black Strangers* came to Dan, some years ago, after seeing mention of the burial of 'a black stranger' in the Gloucestershire county archives, who he discovered was also called Daniel. In the film, Dan wanders among ivy-covered trees and he 'talks' to Daniel as he goes, 'two outsiders separated by 300 years'. 'I wonder if the birds sang the same for you', Dan asks, 'as they do for me.' Dan wonders if when Daniel walked they looked at him as Dan gets stared at now. 'I know how it feels to be seen as a black stranger around here. The outsider, the foreign body, the "not from round here, are you mate?" I get how it feels to be the dark cloud on the distant hilltop.'

In late April, some weeks after seeing his film, I head west to meet Dan Guthrie in Stroud. I want to talk to him about the experience of being black in rural Britain. I'm pretty sure I first came across Stroud, at the age of 13 or 14 maybe, when I read Laurie Lee's *Cider With Rosie*. Since 1959, when it was published, the childhood memoir has sold six million copies across the world. It's mistakenly thought that Lee's book is all about the beauty and sweetness that we lost at some vague point in the first half of the twentieth century. Except that isn't really the book he wrote at all. *Cider With Rosie* is a tale of murder, poverty, incest where the roads are bad, and the almost rape of a 'simpleton' girl in the woods. There is charm to it but we think of *Cider With Rosie* as painting a picture of a countryside that never really was.

Dan is waiting for me at the train station and when I arrive, we walk into town to get some breakfast. As he looks down the menu, he tells me that Stroud is changing. It feels busier than it's ever been and the demographics are evolving too. When he isn't writing or making films, he works in the library and a big part of it is registering people. 'There's definitely a trend for like unusual kids' names.' In part he thinks it's the direct train, just an hour and a half straight into London Paddington but there's also a big arts scene and Extinction Rebellion, he tells me, that was born in Stroud. It attracts a certain type.

Before he entered *Black Strangers* into LUX's Right of Way project, which was initially an open call for work by 'black, Asian, and ethnically diverse artists' that challenged 'the narrative of the rural idyll', Dan tells me he didn't know much about the land access debate. He had spent a lot of time wandering in the countryside around Stroud and had often felt uncomfortable, but the selection of his work led him to realise that his feelings were part of something much bigger.

We order two fish-finger sandwiches and Dan tells me that in the days that followed the publication of his piece in the *Guardian* he must have received at least twenty emails, from the mildly critical to the completely crazy. 'I guess the headline caused a lot of people to get a bit . . .' He doesn't finish his sentence but adds that obviously he didn't write the headline. 'It's about driving clicks I guess but I got it changed.' When I ask him what the original headline was, he takes his phone from the pocket of his long blue anorak and scrolls through his screenshots. 'So it was originally *The English countryside still feels like a white middle-class club. We can and will change this.*'

After the emails started landing, it was amended to *The English countryside can still feel off-limits to people of colour. We are working to change that.* Dan feels that what he wrote was pretty sensible. He wasn't suggesting that the countryside should only be for black or Asian people, as some of his critics assumed, perhaps based on the headline. He was only ever talking about increased representation. The message that stays with him most clearly was sent by somebody with the email address 'enoughisenough81.7%', which he assumes refers to the percentage of white people in the UK. The sender took the trouble of copying in most of the Conservative cabinet and called for Dan to be sanctioned for racism.

Dan's film, *Black Strangers*, all started with a 250-year-old clock that he's known about for as long as he can remember. It's fixed to the wall next to the primary school he went to and every hour, on the hour, a black tethered child, a little 'noble savage', just above the face, strikes a brass bell with a club. Three years ago, Dan wrote to Stroud District Council to suggest that a conversation should be had about relocating it to a museum. It is, Dan feels, 'an offensive relic from the transatlantic slave trade'. A panel made up of local councillors and community representatives was elected to discuss the clock's future. Dan tells me that everything was very considered and he spent a lot of time in the local archives trying to understand the history of the clock and the context in which it was made. He wanted to know if there were any black people around when the clock was being assembled and that's how, he tells me, he found out about Daniel. But there was very little about him. He was only 'a footnote'.

A consultation about the clock was opened and 1,600 responses were received, with an overwhelming majority supporting the proposal that it should be removed. As with Dan's piece in the *Guardian*, anonymous emails started to land in his inbox and almost at the same point that he got a team together to film *Black Strangers*, an anti-fascist group contacted him to say they'd discovered that Britain First was planning to come to Stroud to protest against the clock's removal. In the end, they didn't show but a cloud of anxiety hung over the filming. He only ever wanted the clock to be removed to make Stroud feel more welcoming but as the issue rolled on, and as it became a little battle in the extended universe of the culture war he started to feel less and less welcome in a town that had been his home since he was three.

As he eats, Dan tells me he can't remember really when he first felt uncomfortable when walking alone but he has recently inherited a dog after a relative died and he feels as though as a dog walker he's been legitimised. In part, he thinks, because there's an expectation that he's going to move on with this dog rather than being perceived as loitering. He thinks that when you're a child you feel free in your naivety but at some point that changes. 'I mean, you get to a certain point', he says, putting his sandwich down, 'and maybe someone just has a little talk with you about how the world sees you.' It was his mother who spoke to him. 'It wasn't meant as a negative thing or a warning. It's just like this is how it is.' We finish up and Dan suggests we go for a walk along the canal.

A moorhen paddles on the edge of the reeds and Dan tells me that a while back he came across a 1951 archive film on the British Film Institute's BFI Player called *West of England*. Scripted by Laurie Lee and voiced by the actor Stephen Murray, the film was commissioned to promote Gloucestershire's cloth trade. But Dan thinks that beyond cloth it also promotes a troubling notion of rural Britain. To him *West of England* represents the sort of monocultural countryside that he thinks people believe they need to defend from some imagined threat posed by those whose faces don't fit. 'I guess', he surmises, 'they feel like they're in a position where their place is being crushed.'

By the rail bridge that runs across the canal two shaven-head men with a dog sit watching their floats. They look up as we pass and I shout over asking if they've caught anything. They shake their heads, and I ask them what they're fishing for. 'Anything that swims mate', the younger one shouts back, 'anything that swims.'

As we head on up the hill, towards Rodborough Common, Dan tells me he thinks the situation is changing a bit. There are all sorts of groups emerging that promote black access. There is Flock Together, a birdwatching collective for people of colour, there is Black Girls Hike, which provides opportunities for black women to diversify the outdoors, and a rambling group in Yorkshire even inspired *Black Men Walking*, a play by Testament, a rapper and theatre-maker, that was put on at the Royal Court, in London, in 2018. But Dan thinks that in spite of all of that being positive, it requires you to head out together and to be part of a community. Access to him means feeling comfortable to go it alone. 'I guess in a way, it's knowing I can go somewhere without an agenda, to walk on my terms. It's hard to think about what it means. I just want to do it and not think about it. That would be freedom.' The train rushes by heading to London and a cheerful middle-aged man in tight nylon shorts shuffles down the track in front of us.

At the top of the hill, the path opens out onto a tarmac road and we cross over to carry on up the pavement for a bit. Dan tells me that you can see right across the valley and he wants to show me the view. 'I'm feeling a bit done with it', he replies, when I ask if he thinks he'll always live in Stroud. 'I spent a lot of time trying to make something happen and I've done as much as I can do.' The process that Dan initiated resulted in the council recommending that the clock be removed but it isn't simple. Sending it to a museum would cost about £35,000 and its removal could ultimately be vetoed by the Government.

We stand next to each other by a garden gate looking down over the valley. Dan, after a moment, says you can almost see his house but it's behind that clump of trees on the other side. The streets run the length of the hill and above them, on the right, there is what looks like a church. A window cleaner pulls up behind us, wishes us good morning, then starts unloading his van. 'It's not really a church', Dan tells me, 'you can't go to services there but there are these big arches on both sides. I think they were maybe for coffins to be carried through.' Dan pauses and then says that it was where he was taught to ride his bike as a child.

Dan didn't want to come to the blackboy clock. He didn't really tell me why, in any great detail, but he did say he doesn't want to end up like one of those people who gets pictured in a local newspaper, pointing at a set of broken traffic lights or an unusually large pothole. 'Makes sense', I said as we shook hands and I wished him all the best.

You could quite easily walk past 'Blackboy House', which is a large gothic building, without noticing the little figure but when you see it, it's pretty striking. The boy's lips are big and red, he wears a grass skirt, and there is a noose around his neck. Behind me four men with cans of beer walk by – we nod at each other, then they fall back to chatting. The clock was installed when the building was put up in 1844 but it was built 70 years earlier by a Stroud watchmaker, possibly to advertise tobacco. Somewhere nearby, sparrows are singing. It is ten past twelve and it'll be a 50-minute wait, which is too long to wait really, just to watch the tethered boy bang the bell.

*

That morning with Dan, and not just because it was a rainy day when the trees were bare, was pretty flat. There was something beat about him – as he put it, he'd done all he could to try and get the blackboy clock removed but nothing much seemed to be happening. It would have undoubtedly meant something to Dan but the tragedy of it is that even if it had been moved to a museum, it's hard to see that it would really have changed the lives of black people in Gloucestershire. It would have almost just been a sop to something immutable.

Some years ago, I walked into a Suffolk pub with a black friend. As we drank, glances were cast across the room. Some were curious, even friendly. Others, less so. There was a man leaning over the bar with bloody knuckles, and a butterfly stitch on the side of a bruised eye socket. He might have fallen but I'm pretty sure he'd been fighting. At the time, I thought I was possibly just imagining it. We weren't local after all but they were the very same looks that came our way six months previously, when I walked into a bar in South West Scotland with a Pakistani friend while we were waiting for a bus. The trouble, as Dan explained in his quiet way, is that looks are oppressive. The glances of others can situate us as an insider or otherwise but how do we change the way people look at others – how do we change the white rural gaze?

Fiona Williams, the author of *The House of Broken Bricks*, which explores the struggles of a biracial family in Somerset, was far more explicit than Dan when I spoke to her about rural racism. Fiona's parents came to Britain from Jamaica in the 1950s and she loves the countryside but her stories are pretty grim. Her young son was never invited to the birthday parties of his friends at primary school and children in her daughter's class would make monkey noises at her. The whole thing, she explained, made her daughter 'hate herself'. When I spoke to her, Fiona and her husband, Jo, had moved to Exeter from rural Somerset because they didn't want their children to be the only non-white kids at the local secondary school. In time, though, she hopes to move to Dartmoor.

Just before I spoke to Fiona she had been up in London giving a talk at a bookshop in Brixton. A lot of the audience were black women and about half of them told her they wouldn't go to the countryside again because they'd been and the experience had been 'awful'. What they mean, Fiona explained, is that they'd been 'stared at'. The trouble, though, Fiona continued, is that the people who had stared at them almost certainly wouldn't have felt they'd done anything wrong. 'We just had a look at them', she said, with a sympathetic shrug.

Fiona pointed out that the complexity of the black experience is that it is very different for men and women. If a young black woman walks into a pub, lots of men want to buy her a drink; if some black toddlers are there having lunch, people think they are cute and exotic, but people fear black men. 'Society is kind to beautiful people.'

Interestingly, like Dan, Fiona has had trouble with the media using her work to create sensationalist and divisive headlines. The *Guardian* taking balanced copy and turning its divisiveness up to gas mark seven is wholly irresponsible. Not only does it inevitably result in racist abuse, as happened to Dan, but it furthers the very division that a lot of media outlets purport to be fighting.

In a similar vein, one hot summer's day, I met a very grand director of a famous British museum at an English country house. It was a little strange to meet him in such a setting, and to find him so at ease, given he's been at the centre of a storm about English landscape paintings evoking 'dark nationalist feelings'.

My new acquaintance wouldn't, he told me, have this book going out with the title '*Their Country*'.* It would not be happening, 'on his watch'. He'd insist on '*Our Country*', in order to be less 'othering'. He didn't, of course, know anything

---

* *Their Country* was the working title of the book. The suggestion being that everybody feels that the way they get to enjoy the countryside is limited and shaped by somebody else, no matter who you are, but in the end *Uncommon Ground* was felt to be stronger.

about the book but that didn't seem to matter much in terms of being sure about how it should be framed; framing first, then let's worry about the actual content some way down the line.

The suggestion that the likes of Constable and Turner can inspire feelings of racial othering and darkness hit the headlines hard. The *Telegraph* got very upset about it and the *Guardian* ran with it for a while too. Perhaps that was the point – radical chic posturing, done right, is good at raising a museum's profile and the profile of the museum director too but it's also irresponsible. Farmers and farm workers are often what I suppose some would call 'othered', and suggesting that celebrated depictions of the places they work, have shaped and love are essentially racist, is not easy for them to take nor frankly to understand. Not because they are stupid but because the claim itself is opaque and fanciful.

A couple of years ago, I worked on a theatre project with a young artist who worked, by day, as a gallery technician at the Tate. He once told me that the security guards, many of whom were black, were always amused when the white management reframed the work or came up with messaging they felt was more inclusive. It meant, they told my friend, not one iota to them and yet it was sort of meant to be all about them. 'We're doing this for you, fellas.' And yet, it wasn't really about them at all. It was about the management luxuriating in righteousness. It's hard to imagine that anybody has wandered out into Suffolk feeling more comfortable because a museum director has threatened to take *The Hay Wain* off the wall but all those moves keep the fires of the culture wars burning.

For all that bigotry can be heard at village pubs, up and down the country, there is a sense in which rural Britain is also a very welcoming place. I'll always remember sitting in the *Shooting Times* magazine offices, when the phone went on a Friday morning. Ed, my deputy editor, answered it. It was one of the guys on the shoot he was driving down to Cornwall to write about the next day. It was a working man's shoot, where a team effort, throughout the year, resulted in a dozen or so birds a day when the season rolled round. They just wanted to say that one of their members, a local farmer, always puts a dress on at the end of the day during tea and they didn't want him to be treated any differently. He was one of the boys, nail polish and all. That is the odd thing; the countryside – if you are the odd one out – can be more welcoming than the city often is. In the city people can simply look the other way.

In villages and the deep countryside, however, people will welcome you into the fold only if you stick it out for some time. The countryside is not, if your face doesn't fit, welcoming from the off. Only 3 per cent of people in the countryside are black and outsiders are visible. It is also, undeniably, a place where unspeakable things are said that go completely unchallenged. 'What's the best way to keep trespassers off your land?' a farmer once asked me, as though it was the best joke around, 'Put a sign up saying Black rapist on the loose.'

It was depressing but pretty fair I think to hear Fiona Williams say resignedly that people are tribal. Elderly people in their old village didn't like the old folks from the village next door. It would be naive, she thinks, to suppose that rural England will totally change and become a sort of utopia but she does hope that Black faces in the countryside, appearing on our televisions and on social media, will change things. The media has created a sense that black people are dangerous but it also has the power to create a narrative that fly fishing and having picnics is something that people from ethnic minorities do too. One obvious fly in the ointment is that programmes made, by the BBC for example, about the countryside, often feel pretty detached, no matter what ethnicity the presenter is. There's a reason that farmers call *Countryfile* 'Townyfile'. Sending a man from Lagos to Dorchester in a brand new pair of wellingtons and lending him one of Chris Packham's many bucket hats, is hardly going to make the guy seem part of it all. What we need is to see black and minority ethnic people really *living* the countryside, running sheepdogs, working in conservation, and out on the hill, with a rifle, managing deer.

It is also important to recognise in the context of rural Britain there is no one 'black experience'. Ezekiel's understanding of the countryside, a place that is either 'sweet' or shot through by county lines, is clearly very different to Dan's and Dan's, in turn, is different to Fiona's. They are all real and they all matter but there is class difference and a generational difference as well as all those many other differences that make people who they are. It is reductive, clearly, to group people together but it does make it easier to generalise and generalising allows campaigns, in the early stages, to gather momentum. 'The land was stolen from us by them', 'take back the commons', 'the countryside is racist'. But increasingly, it feels like generalising has led to the current access campaign running aground – politicians want to support popular causes but ultimately they are inclined to be wary when something seems to be little more than noise. To listen to individuals and to think about their struggles, is how we actually understand and when we understand we can move forwards meaningfully.

*

Heat rises off the tarmac and on a lane running down to the river, horse shit dries in the sun. Appleby is usually a quiet town of around 7,000 people, but every summer, tens of thousands of Travellers and Romani Gypsies descend. They come from all over England as well as Scotland, Wales and Ireland. They come in caravans and bow tops, horse boxes and trucks pulling sulkies, and they come in Porsches and Range Rovers. They trade, they drink, they sometimes fight, and they trot bareback through the streets. Fearing trouble, almost all of the pubs in the town close, and an old lady, sitting out on her front steps, next to a sign that reads 'No tethering horses here', tells me that half the residents leave.

At the bottom of Long Marton Road, a boy lies next to the pavement and a crowd of children are gathered round. His head rests on a mess of blonde hair and a woman crouches beside him, running her fingers over his face. The police are pulled up, blocking all passing traffic and one of them tells anybody who asks, no matter what it is they ask, that 'there's been a very nasty incident'. The police officer seems incapable of saying anything else but two young women sitting on a bench, who look like they might be twins, tell me the boy jumped from a moving horse box.

Down by the river Eden, a large crowd is drinking in the mid-afternoon sun and I make almost no progress at all before falling in behind a man who is holding a pony on a lead rein with a foal at its feet. 'Mind your backs', he calls, as he pushes through. The foal can't be more than three months old, and is walking loose behind its mother, through the plastic cups and polystyrene chip trays, perfectly content as though they are the only two creatures in the world. Next to me, a child is trying to get through on the pavement. 'Mummy', he says, looking up at the lady whose hand he's holding. 'Mummy, they keep shoving me.' The lady yanks the boy towards her. 'If they're shoving you, son, you shove them back.'

On the pink sandstone bridge everybody is standing shoulder to shoulder and it's only when two girls drop out, both of them in one-piece lime green jumpsuits, that I find a gap to fill. The river beneath us, which is down on its bones in the sun, is full of horses. Children and teenagers, most of them barefoot, ride them out into the only deep pool next to the far bank, then they turn and scrabble back up onto the shingle. At the side, a little girl and her father are washing a bay pony. He lifts her and she runs her soapy hands over the creature's back, then when he puts her down, she turns and calls towards the bank.

Her mother gets up off the grass and walks down to them with a plastic bucket. Crouching down next to the child, the man fills it, then they pour it over the animal's back, washing off the suds.

A lady standing next to me with dark eye make-up and deep wrinkles across her forehead looks at my notebook and asks if I live local. 'We come from down that way', she says, when I tell her I drove up from London. 'We come from Kent, so we come right through London on our way here.' The lady tells me she's been coming to Appleby every year since 1983. 'I was just a girl then. I should say that'd be before you were born.' Her husband glances at me, then starts looking through his wallet. There is a wad of notes and a learner driving licence with his picture on it. 'There are places to stop', she tells me, when I ask about their journey down, 'but in years past you could just go on the side of the road where you liked, but it's not getting any easier. The councils don't like it.' The lady tells me that part of it is about feeling welcome when you stop off on the way to Appleby and people don't feel welcome anymore. That morning a group of Travellers had woken up at a service station with their caravans spray painted: 'Gypsy', 'No parking', 'Fuck off'.

Although they might not say it themselves, Appleby is special because it's a chance for Romani and Traveller people to simply be. They don't, at Appleby, as is the case in so many villages during the rest of the year, have to walk through the street with all eyes on them and they won't be moved on. Appleby is a radical protest which sees them make part of England their own. For a week in July it becomes their country and their home.

Down below us a boy of maybe 14 or 15 has gone right to the other side on a coloured cob and he's struggling to get it back round. The piebald horse beneath him is kicking as it struggles to swim and water is bubbling up around its nose. On the bank, a man in a white vest, who is holding a can of beer, shouts down at him – 'Let go, lad. Let the horse go.' The boy tumbles off the back of the animal and it surfaces, reins floating around its withers.

On the hill that runs up to the flashing lane, children are running back and forth, asking men on horses if they'll let them climb up. 'Me and the wee fella', a boy who must be about eight, shouts up to a man on a cob. The wee fella, who seems to be a chubby ginger boy, is toddling behind. 'Your father wouldn't allow it', the man shouts down. There is a sense at Appleby that most of the people know most of the people there, and some families have been coming, down the generations, for hundreds of years.

Under the bridge, a tall man in rigger boots and with a cap pulled down low is selling his paintings – all acrylics on paper, spread out across the pavement. 'Twenty quid for the small one', he tells me as I look over them, but he says if it's too much he's got ones that are even smaller still in his bag. As I look over them he tells me he's Irish, then asks where I've come from. 'London', I reply, 'but I used to live just over the border. Not too far.' He nods in acknowledgement, tells me he knows the county well, and asks where I lived. I start to locate it. 'By Dunscore', 'near Moniaive', 'near Thornhill', but he shakes his head – he knows 'that country' well, he insists, but not those places.

There is a painting of a family in a bow top heading up underneath the bridge. Beside them a horse has broken free from its sulky and is rearing up on the road. Two men stand in front, one of them is waving his arms, and the other is trying to bring it under control by grabbing at its harness. 'A great deal of work went into that', he tells me, 'a great deal of work to get the angle of that bridge right.' We call it forty and he shakes my hand then I head up the road.

It is coming up to four o'clock and the sun feels as though it's the hottest it's been all year but the pavements are still busy with horses. Just before the hill where everyone is camped out,

I stop outside a white marquee full of statues and pictures. There is Joseph and baby Jesus, Mary and baby Jesus, just baby Jesus by himself, Jesus the man, and a statuette of Padre Pio, a twentieth-century mystic and stigmatist who some claim inflicted his wounds himself and then kept them weeping by dousing them in acid. In the middle of the marquee, there is a young priest who looks like he's blowing up in the sun and a group of middle-aged ladies are gathered round him.

I stand in the shade of the trees for a moment, next to a sign that reads all welcome for 'conforations' and 'bapitisms'. In front of the tent, two boys pass, no older than five, topless and sunburnt, in a sulky pulled by a small pony. They sit next to each other, their faces turned inwards, deep in conversation. Just as they draw level with the statues, they smile as though they've decided where it is they must go next and what it is they must do, and the little boy on the left brings his reins down across the animal's rump. The pony picks its feet up and breaks into a trot.

One of the ladies, who has big beehive hair, asks if I'll come to mass the following day: 'Two o'clock out in the field there.' I tell I can't and she asks why not and I tell her I can't because I've got to go to Yorkshire to see somebody about people trespassing in a little wood. 'That's no good', she replies, 'you've got to go to mass, son.'

I tell the ladies I'm a writer and I was wondering if it's harder now to park up when they're travelling around. The lady with the beehive hair looks at me. 'Have you a card?', she asks. I tell her I don't and I'm not sure what it would say on it. 'Writer', she replies. She tells me to show her my painting and when I unroll it she looks at it for some time. 'That is lovely', she says turning to the lady next to her. All the ladies nod in agreement. 'He is a good painter, that fella.' The lady looks at me again and then says that the trouble with travelling is 'it's all laws now. It's a hundred times harder, a hundred times harder.' One of the younger women agrees – 'Much harder now, son. It's just all laws now. They don't let you stay there for long now. They put down injunctions on the land straight away. They take your cars and your caravans.' Then she folds her arms, says 'God bless you, son' then she turns away.

On the road south through Cumbria all along the verges there are laminated signs reading 'No stopping', and 'No horses'. Most people going to the fair will probably already be there but at Coupland Beck there's a green bow top, pulled by two big horses, trotting north. Sitting up at the front, there is a bare-chested man holding the reins and next to him, a small girl, probably three or four years old in a pink princess dress, leans against him and sleeps.

*

A farmer once said to me that there are two sorts of people, those who hate Travellers and those who've never had anything to do with them. I'm not sure what had actually happened to the guy, but from stealing GPS units on tractors to driving off from rural petrol stations without paying for their fuel, they get blamed for a lot. It was even put round, after that tree was felled at Sycamore Gap in Northumberland, that 'pikeys' had done it.* After all, despoiling England is said to be their thing.

Hardly a month seems to go by without a news story breaking about Travellers or Romani Gypsies not being served at pubs and whenever they are in the area, farmers' WhatsApp groups start pinging: lock up your barns and shut your gates. Internet forums – since the dawn of internet forums – have hosted long threads from rural and suburban ladies who worry about their horses being stolen. The story always seems to go that Travellers

---

* This word is both highly pejorative and much-used in rural communities. It possibly derives from a 'pike' meaning a highway.

plait a horse's mane to mark it out as one that they will later come back to steal. 'Nonsense', someone invariably replies, to which another person will respond saying that it's absolutely true and it happened to their friend or a friend of a friend or someone in Ireland they met once.

The curious thing about anti-Traveller sentiment in rural places is that it's generally considered to be entirely acceptable. People I know who would preach inclusivity and love about a black guy moving into a new barn conversion or a nice gay couple who have moved into the village to run a hotel, will openly tell you about the trouble caused by 'pikeys'. The criticism, including leaving dead dogs on the side of the road, or being involved in modern slavery, is okay, they'll tell you, because it's what they do. 'They're wronguns.'

Terry Doe was just seven years old when his dad and his uncles started taking him out in the cab of their lorry to read road signs. 'These were grown men with families', he says, slouching forwards in his big leather chair and scratching the back of his head, 'but they couldn't read.'

Terry's dad, he tells me fondly, loved being thrown out of school. 'He wanted to be wild.' His generation didn't, Terry thinks, feel even remotely deprived without an education and school for Romani children like Terry's parents was hard in the 1940s. It was believed, Terry explains, that educating Romani and Traveller children alongside the rest of the population simply didn't work. The assumption was that children like Terry's parents would be so slow to learn that it would hold 'settled' children back. 'Full on fucking apartheid', he says, just as his son appears at the door of the wooden hut, bringing us coffee. 'There were separate start and finish times. Romani kids weren't allowed on school outings and they couldn't even hang their coats on the same hooks.'

By the time it was Terry's turn, much to his dad's frustration, his mum insisted that they have another look and they turned up at the same school they'd been to. They realised, he tells me, that things had evolved and Terry was taught to read and write in the very classrooms where his parents had been segregated. 'Going to school properly', Terry says, gulping at his coffee, 'was one of the great changes for my lot.'

When Terry was born, his parents lived in a static, on a patch of ground near Epsom. His father was born in a mobile caravan and spent most of his childhood sleeping between the wheels, and his grandfather was born in a horse drawn bow top.

Unlike previous generations, Terry has never spent his summers on the road and his parents were the last generation to travel from farm to farm as well as going on traditional Romani pilgrimages, to places like Kent, in search of work. What they'd do, Terry explains, is knock on a farmer's door and say that they saw he had some fruit to pick or some hedges that needed gapping up, and they'd ask about parking up for a couple of months to do the work. Terry tells me that the ladies I met at Appleby, the ones who told me it's all laws now, were probably referring to the end of that way of life, where a handshake and a nod meant you'd be earning a bit of money for a while and would have somewhere to stay. 'That doesn't happen anymore. The farmer won't say, "Right, give yourselves a week or two weeks", or "Stay here all the time you're working then you got to go." Now you pitch up and the next morning the police appear and you're evicted.' Terry also thinks that farmers and landowners have worked out that if they put equipment across gateways or bolt things shut, knowing they'll be smashed open, they can turn a case of trespass into aggravated trespass, meaning it becomes a criminal offence rather than just a civil one.

When Terry was four and was still living in that static, he poached his first rabbit: 'Took a pheasant when I wanted to, took a duck when I wanted. Paid no dues', but his world was about to change. Three years later they got told they were going to be moved into a council house. The farmer's land they were on was to be turned into a 475-acre reservoir where water would be drawn from the Thames and improved before being pumped back into London. 'I guess', he says, 'they were like what are we going to do with all these Gypsy people?' Up until that point his life had been pretty simple, 'Just a strip of land, about forty yards wide and two hundred yards long and there were twenty-five families on that.' The only amenity they had for the first few years of his life was a standing water pipe that Terry and his cousins would go to every day with milk churns on an old pram frame. He sits back and tells me that the pipe was quite low down so you had to tilt the churns at a tricky angle to fill them and as soon as you did, the missiles would start flying. Children from the tied farm workers' cottages would be raining down on them with stones. He lifts his left hand and draws an imaginary piece of elastic back with his right. 'I can see myself doing it now. At the foot of every decent tap there'd be washed out pebbles and I'd scoop them up then be walking backwards returning fire with my catapult as the other kids pushed the pram away. I was only this big.' He holds his right hand out flat, about three feet off the ground, looking at the space in front of him as though he's looking at Terry the little boy.

When they were put into that council house, Terry and his sister spent 'a week solid' running up and down the stairs, flicking the light switches on and off, and playing with the taps. 'Loved that house', he tells me, 'I absolutely loved it.' His mother and his aunt, like all Romani women apparently, went through the whole house polishing everything up and Terry and his sister would slide across the tiles in their socks. 'These faux marble things.'

It's all too easy, Terry thinks, to romanticise the itinerant lives that his father and grandfather led but when he was a bit older and he started asking them about it, he found that there wasn't much nostalgia. His father recalls a childhood of 'freezing half to death in the winter and roasting alive in the summer and it was running with lice'. Terry's father remembers that as a boy, he slept underneath the caravan because there was no room for him inside and he would wake with frost in his hair and the rats. He didn't much mind apparently because as a young boy, Terry's father would hunt the rats with a stick or just draw straw around his head but that life becomes harder as you get older.

Terry gestures to a picture, by the stove, of an old Romani couple standing side by side, his granny and grandpa. The old lady is smiling open-mouthed and the man next to her, white moustache and a blue cap with a matching jacket, stares at the camera as though facing down the photographer. His granny, Terry tells me, feared getting old in the wagons. Terry nods. 'Her fear was based on staying alive. Basically it was about staying alive and my dad, he said to me, when I was older, They feared something their people had always done.

There is a woody smell of incense in the hut, a shotgun fixed to the wall above the door, and a Romani flag pinned up on the ceiling. 'That's not a wagon wheel', Terry says, seeing me look at it. 'That is a sixteen-spoke *dharmachakra*, a spiritual symbol, and that's us you see. That's my lot. The blue is the sky and the green is the land.'

When they still lived in that caravan, his dad, he thinks, knew fine well that he spent his days out in the field with his catapult, or his air rifle or some rabbit snare he'd fashioned. But if he was caught 'by the local bobby', because he'd broken a fence or crashed through some barbed wire, it wasn't the local bobby he had to worry about. His concerns were about what his father would do when he got home. Just like using a knife and an axe, Terry had been shown how to move across ground undetected and to get caught was a failure that brought shame on the family.

There was also a risk that the farmer whose land they stayed on, Mr Wiggins, would throw them out. 'There was no tenancy agreement. No three months' grace. If you lived on land owned by the person you worked for and you were caught poaching you'd get kicked out. You'd lose everything.' But in spite of the risk, if you pulled it off it was worth it. 'It was . . .' he speaks slowly, as though grappling with exactly what it was, 'It was the measure of a man when I was growing up. No one gave a shit about football. But if you could bring home a couple of rabbits or a pheasant or a duck, or some pigeons. Now your dad's approving, you see, now you're growing.' He breaks off to drink the last of his coffee then takes his cap off and lays it on his knee. 'And of course if you had a good running dog. My lot, we love that sport.'

The issue with hare coursing, Terry believes, doesn't actually have anything to do with coursing itself. 'It's what comes with it with Romanis.' You can, he thinks, have 20 people visit a bit of land and course it hard but if they do it right, you'd never know they were there. Where it goes wrong is that you get the odd person who tears across the wheat in their truck or pops back later to steal fuel and, he adds, there's the potential for violence. 'All that stuff that should never go with it.' How it tends to go, he reckons, is that you'll just get one who decides he doesn't give a shit. 'Had a bit of a bad time with the Old Bill last week or somebody turned his granny out of her home or something and he goes spinning it up.' There are plenty of hare coursers who criticise those who cause damage or commit other crimes when they're there but Terry thinks it's complicated. Lots of Romani people 'feel they don't belong, so they don't act as though they belong and because of that they don't belong'. But, he adds, there are 'scumbags' in every community – when a non-Romani does something they shouldn't it's just about them, the individual, whereas all his life Terry believes that when one of his people does something wrong, every one of them is condemned.

Beyond the hut, in the garden, the wind seems to be changing and the cockerel on the weather vane is moving from side to side beneath the grey sky. On the table on Terry's left there are two little polar bears and he reaches out and picks them up. His headmaster, he says, as he holds them out to show me, was a real visionary. He realised that not every child was a genius but that it was important to make everyone feel included. 'You know Noah's Ark', he asks. 'Yeah', I reply, 'with the animals?' He nods. 'My headmaster would put the really good kids together with the not so good ones and the really good ones would build the boat and the not so good ones would make the thatched roof. But they'd have both built the ark, you see?' He looks at the bears then looks at me, then tells me that his headmaster made the horse. He points over to a little table where the carved horse is standing. It must have been at least fifty years ago but he talks about school as though it was just last month.

Terry is a big man. He has large hands, a square jaw and his biceps almost completely fill out the sleeves of his cream Hawaiian shirt. He tells me he's never been a fighter, not really, but over the years he's ended up in the odd scrape and he's defended himself. There was one night, at the pub, a long time ago when someone spat at him and called him 'the P-word.' He lowers his voice. 'I can't even say it.' His father, when he returned home, reckoned he'd played it wrong. He should have, his dad felt, hit the guy a few more times. Should have really showed him but his mother disagreed. 'He thinks you're an ignorant savage', she told him, 'and all you've done is prove him right.' His mother told Terry that what he should have done is said to the guy in the pub that he deserved a slap but he wasn't going to give him one. In a way, Terry thinks that Romanis are the last group that it's acceptable to be racist towards, but he is quick to add that 'just like in any ethnic minority, there are racists among the Romanis'. You'll often, he says, hear a Romani saying 'this or that', and he always, he tells me, takes them up on it. 'We hate the P-word. So do Pakistanis. They don't like that other P-word either.' You can't, Terry believes, separate these things out. He picks his cap up off his knee and places it on the back of his head, with the peak at an angle, 'If you think racism is alright when you do it, then when your kid or your grandson gets called a Pikey, you got to accept it because you've helped build that.' Rain starts to fall on the windows of the hut and I remember that my little dog is waiting for me in the car.

'Do you think', I ask, 'when Gypsy children go around' – Terry seems to sense that I don't feel entirely comfortable asking the question and he cuts over me to say that I can ask him whatever I like. 'Do you think', I continue, 'that they feel out of place in the countryside? You've been in the countryside for as long as almost anyone, in one way or another, but do you think you get looked at as different?' Terry nods. 'Of course we do. We're feared. Nobody is advertising for Gypsies to move in next to them. A hundred per cent and they play on it some-times. They don't mind being feared. You can't know it until you lived it.' Terry shakes his head blankly when I ask him about the land access meetings in London being held in soli-darity with the GRT community and he asks what they mean by solidarity.* GRT is not, he says, an acronym his lot would recognise: 'We're Romani.' He wonders, too, how much well-meaning outsiders can know about a community that often knows very little about itself. 'My lot don't really know about how we came from east to west because where would they have found it out? They don't teach our history in schools.' There are stories that Terry remembers being told as a little boy but it was more about how they'd been persecuted and the injustices they'd faced than about where they came from. 'You got to

---

* GRT is an acronym I first heard at a London Right to Roam meeting – it groups together Romani Gypsies, like Terry, and Irish Travellers.

remember we were illegal at one stage. Henry the Eighth made us illegal. Not to kill us was punishable by death.' He thinks that a sense of being separate and distinct and a refusal to sell out or to comply is what's got them through but he also thinks that it maybe held some of his family back too. When he was a boy a lot of those stories felt, he recalls, as though he was being told, 'This is what's been done to us. Get 'em for us, get 'em back for what they've done.'

I stand to go and Terry looks along his bookshelf, telling me I can take whatever I like. There are books on mythology and the Romani language and books on hunting and fishing. At the end of the shelf there is a well-worn copy of a book called *Gypsy Feast*: *Recipes and culinary traditions of the Romany people*. I take it down and Terry tells me I'm very welcome to it and we walk out into the garden. 'Messy', he says. The lawn is perfect and every rose and every trinket, the statue of a cat and the fancy bird house, are immaculate.

As we duck underneath the laundry, I ask Terry if he thinks the culture will change over the next fifty years. 'I can't see anybody in two generations' time still travelling. I just can't', he replies. 'That lifestyle will be whittled away ever more.' Currently, the most successful Romani people Terry knows buy land. What they do, he explains, is buy a patch, build a ranch-style house, and put a bow top or a couple of bow tops out the back. 'That's what the rich folks do.' But it's apparently not as easy as all that. Even when they've got the money they often have to send a surrogate purchaser because if the seller knows they're Romani, they won't go through with it.

At the gate, he says goodbye then tells me that whatever happens they'll still be around. They'll still be around because being Romani isn't a lifestyle. It's not just about being on the road. 'It's a blood thing. It's in the blood and that can't be lost.'

*

There is, in Britain, often a lot of absolutism when 'settled people' talk about the Travelling community. When George Monbiot writes about them, they are simply an abused minority, anti-Traveller sentiment being an acceptable form of racism, and I've heard it said a number of times at Right to Roam meetings that the reason most landowners don't like access stems from their hatred of 'the GRT community'. I'm not sure that George Monbiot or those young guys at Right to Roam have really spent much time with Travellers but it's undeniable, as Terry recognised, that they often bend and break various laws.

One evening in August, when the nights were starting to draw in, I met with some Travellers on a bridge in Norfolk who were going to poach the river beneath. They pulled up in a car, jumped a wall, and were happily spinning through a reedy pool. They seemed to recognise that we weren't meant to be there 'but the young fellas', they told me, by way of justification, 'wanted to go fishing'. It's hard to explain but they were only breaking laws that you or I might subscribe to. They never signed up to them, their moral and ethical framework is different, and the wish of the wee fella, they seemed sure, should always trump any sort of legislation cooked up by settled folk. I showed them some pictures of big fish that had been caught in other rivers across the county and they told me they would go and try there too. Any sort of permit or permission was not something that seemed to trouble them at all.

It is clearly wrong to suggest they're all criminals but it seems potentially problematic too, almost an act of erasure, to suppose that it's been entirely misunderstood and they just want to live their lives on the right side of the law. They are and have been, since time began, abused, persecuted, and killed, and they have been left ducking and diving in a world that's getting harder and harder for them to survive in. But there's a sense too that some of them want to plant their flag outside the system and frankly, who wouldn't. When I was a little boy, I also liked to fish where I shouldn't have been fishing. Who wouldn't like to live, as Terry put it, a life of paying no dues.

That evening on the bridge was kind of endearing but it would have been different, I suppose, if they'd been poaching with firearms rather than fishing rods and it would be wrong to deny the lived experience of a Yorkshire gamekeeper I met who after being pulled from his bed in the night was badly beaten by Travellers. What would also clearly be wrong, though, would be to accept in any way, as I've often heard it said, that all Travellers are criminals. They are, Romanis and Travellers, people with rich cultures and a very admirable sense of community. I often think about Terry telling me that when he was a little boy, he would go to other children's houses and they wouldn't feed him because he was 'only a pikey', but when other children came to his house, his parents would give that child what little food they had because that is what Gypsies do.

If we managed to get to a place where the rural community accept that many Travellers are kind people and great country folk (a priest I met recently is often asked to bless their fishing rods) and where well-meaning but naive activists recognise that there are problems, it would be easier, I think, to protect a culture that needs protecting. 'Well behaved Travellers welcome in this village' and at this pub might not sound particularly radical but it would be much better than pubs pulling the shutters down and farmers locking their gates when the first caravan appears over the horizon. Like so many things, when a village has trouble with Travellers, the response shouldn't be 'You're all racist' but 'What have you done to make things better?' It's wholly illegal of course but when I met a gamekeeper in Bedfordshire who's had various scraps with Travellers over the years, including shots being exchanged, he told me the only way he made real progress was when he let one group of them course hares on his ground and they in turn kept other boys off. In a roundabout way, I guess you could call it community engagement and you could certainly file it under access.

His feeling, after decades of interacting with Travellers, is that you have to admire them. 'It's really weird', he messaged me, when I was on my way to Appleby. 'I have so much respect for them but so little time! I have been hounded by them for years and they've cost me thousands. They've even rammed my dad on a quad bike, pushing him over the handlebars with his two hip replacements. They are total cunts! But I have time for the fuckers. Give them my best.'

*

The spring of 2024 was cold and windy but when the weather eventually improved, I drove to Northumberland to go beach-netting for sea trout with John Dixon and Edward Dawson.* John is in his late eighties and Edward is 71. My friend, Katrina Porteous, a poet and historian, has lived on the Northumberland coast for most of her life and has written extensively about the decline of inshore sea fishing. When John and Edward pack up, it will be the end of netting for sea trout in Beadnell Bay but not so long ago it provided a reasonable living for six families.

Edward was the only person on the harbour wall when I got down there just after 6 a.m. and we stood there, in silence, while we watched the net for any signs of fish. He had already, he told me, had one that morning. About an hour later, when the first of the dog walkers started to appear on the beach, putting the terns up which had returned to the sand to feed their young, we went out along the line of buoys to have a look at the net. For the first forty yards or so there were only 'flatties' in the net and Edward pulled them up before throwing them out to our left but further along, only three feet or so below

---

* Netting for sea trout has been severely restricted but it is still legal and John and Edward net under licence.

the surface, a sea trout was caught by its gills. He pulled it out, hooking his finger through its mouth, then dropped it into a blue crate with a quietly satisfied expression.

Edward, it seemed, was not a particularly loquacious man but he told me that he was actually from Craster and in the old days, he'd never have been welcome in Beadnell but all that has changed now. The old families are gone and there's not enough fish to bother fighting over. I told Edward I didn't know that much about fish but he seemed reassured to hear that I'd been wildfowling recently with some old boys on the Humber.

We pulled another sea trout out of the net and then returned to the harbour where a number of old fishermen had cycled down, not so much to chat, but just to stand there next to each other, while looking out to sea. Edward, after some time, turned to the others and said, as though it was significant, 'He's a shooter.' He said it as though it had only one 'o', to rhyme with 'otter'. They all turned to look at me as though it seemed pretty unlikely and one of them, pointing out to sea, asked me what those were, the two birds out towards Dunstanburgh Castle. 'A pair of mallard', I replied, 'but they'd be too far away for me.' They nodded and that was that, for the rest of the morning they spoke to me. We spoke about football and dogs and Billingsgate fish market. It felt, after being able to identify those ducks, that I was seemingly okay. I had become, in some way, not an insider, but a moderately acceptable outsider.

At about ten o'clock, Katrina wandered down from her cottage up the road and we stood and talked about her experience of being a woman walking in the countryside. A lot of her poetry is constructed around oral history. Sometimes, she once told me, whole sections of her poems are simply conversations she's had on fishing boats or with farmers in the hills.

I am often aware that the way I write, is perhaps easier in some ways because I'm male. My process of just going out and doing is possible – so I've been told, anyway – because I'm not vulnerable. But interestingly, Katrina has always, she told me, felt safer in the countryside than the city. She grew up in the era of Reclaim the Night demonstrations, which were held in the wake of the horrific murders carried out by Peter Sutcliffe in the 1970s. The countryside for Katrina is something of an escape, particularly open country. Where she has felt less safe, over the years, is urban edgeland, such as East Durham where social problems spill out. She has sometimes had cause for alarm there in 'the wooded denes that run down to the sea'.

There was, though, she told me one particularly grim incident that happened at dusk one evening when she went to see the Uffington White Horse in Oxfordshire in order to carry out some research for a long poem about ritual and community. When she arrived that evening there was a man in the car park and as she set off up the hill to get to the 3,000-year-old horse, she became aware that he too was coming up the hill, not behind her, but a different way so that he would cross her. When their paths met they stopped and she said hello, hoping it would defuse the situation. She thinks that 'saying hello' often does. He said nothing but she remembers his piercing eyes and she is sure now that it was Christopher Halliwell, the taxi driver who later confessed to killing two women. Just a few days after that incident, Halliwell dumped Sian O'Callaghan's body at the bottom of White Horse Hill. That evening, when Katrina got back down the man was sitting by the entrance to the car park in a taxi with the lights on and the engine running. She is quite sure it was him and she suspects he had been scoping the area to try and work out what could be seen. The taxi, she recalls, had the same markings as the one Halliwell was arrested in and later, after the murders, Katrina was called to the police station to give evidence.

Part of her doesn't want me to write about it because she doesn't want, she explained, to put women off walking and oddly she thinks that some of the sort of work we do is easier for her because some men feel much less threatened by a female writer than a male writer. Talking to poachers, she once said to me, is so much easier if you're a woman.

Katrina once had a conversation with Phoebe Power, a young award-winning poet, when they were writing about former pit villages in East Durham. The land there, Katrina explained, has been brutalised by industry, which has made it gendered. The beaches there, she recalls, were once black with slag. 'Like a patina of masculinity', I suggested. 'That', she said, 'is a good way of putting it.' There is, I think, a degree to which farmed landscapes, particularly arable landscapes, where the machines are big and the land is scarred have something, while more muted, not totally dissimilar. The land, I suppose, has been defiled.

In Katrina's new collection, *Rhizodont*, which was published just after I went to see her, there is a brilliant short poem called 'Tinkers' Fires'. The term tinker, which comes from mending pots and pans and sharpening knives, which Travellers often used to do as a way of earning some money, is a pejorative term now but when Katrina was growing up in the North East it was in common use.

The Travellers would often come through the village and would stay for a short while and when they were gone, Katrina as a little girl would go to where they'd been. She'd rake through the ashes they left behind and would sometimes find trinkets, a belt buckle maybe or some tacks that they had used to shoe horses. But it is a poem about much more than that. It's about engaging and understanding and appreciating. Katrina's work really is all about trying to understand. She is not a fisherman, clearly, but she has spent a lot of time on fishermen's boats and I have listened to old recordings of her, talking to fishermen who are now long dead about their words, about their lives, the biggest fish they caught, and what they call the porpoises. The access she has is really about knowledge.

Access, she explained to me, is multi-layered and there is a degree to which you will feel like an outsider if you don't engage with the countryside and respond to it, if you are just a tourist. I suppose just as I felt like an outsider at Appleby and just as I felt like an outsider and was treated as such until those ducks flew over and I was asked to identify them.

There is clearly racism in the countryside. Fiona Williams is absolutely right that the media has a great responsibility to reframe the culture of rural Britain. The other side of that, though, is that Britain owes it to everyone to give them the knowledge to understand the countryside and to understand its history and how its culture was constructed and continues to be shaped. To have knowledge is to have power and to have some understanding is to belong. The countryside owes it to outsiders to welcome them by giving them that knowledge in a way that makes people, all people, think yes, it's a place for me too. I get it, and in some way, part of it is mine.

10

Looking Forward

For you and me and the animals, we need to rethink our relationship with nature and make it central to society

In the summer of 2024, I got a call from a friend in the South West of Scotland who was having some trouble with roe deer eating his young trees. A small population is very welcome, he explained, but the deer numbers were at a level where any young oak and birch saplings didn't stand a chance. Did I, he wondered, want to head north with my rifle and a few other guys to see if we could get on top of them? Renwicks, the local butcher, would take the carcasses and it would be fun anyway, he said, to catch up.

A couple of days after the trip, John posted a picture on the WhatsApp group he'd set up for the weekend. A group of Scouts, who'd been camping on his land down by the river, had written to thank Amir. Amir, an Iranian guy who was one of our group, had wandered down to see them with a roebuck carcass on the Friday evening. He thought they might like to learn how to skin, butcher, and cook the animal. 'It was great', the card read. 'We all enjoyed it and were fascinated by it.'

That evening, I was scrolling through Instagram, feeling pretty wiped after three 4 a.m. starts on the hill, when I was hit with a video of a young guy, with a big bushy moustache, playing the accordion in short lime green shorts. It was, the caption beneath read, a video for 'the Song of Trespass'. If you told me the whole thing was a Country Landowners' Association plant, I'd believe you. Seamas, as I later learned he's called, hits every number on the land access bingo card: 'The land of these islands is vast' – not really true; 'Will you give us our land back?' – just as soon as you can tell me who took it from you and when; 'If you look at the history, it once was our right' – whose history, and what was?; 'The rich folk and Tories have robbed us our home' – I'm not even clear what he means by this and I suspect he isn't either. Of course, finally, inevitably – when a load of Morris dancers and girls in jerkins have joined in to wander along with Seamas – there's 'One day they'll listen and tear down the wall. They'll open the country and share it with all.'

The comments beneath are as positive as the large crowd of campaigners at the end of the video is white. 'Yessss to the message', 'Utterly brilliant', 'Gorgeous and thank you.' There is one dissenting voice, a gardener called Nina who writes 'I don't think the land has ever belonged to everyone. It's always belonged to individuals.' The Right to Roam campaign has replied to Nina but only to recommend their own book *Wild Service*. Doubtless, the woman needs to be educated.

The song itself is actually kind of catchy but to be straight, it's total bollocks: are these walls that must be torn down in the room with us now, Seamas? And for all their ills, 'the Tories' delivered on access in a multitude of ways. A senior Defra official, speaking to me off the record, highlighted the implementation of the Marine and Coastal Access Act. They also, he noted, created the Coast to Coast path,* from the Irish

---

* It's not accurate to say the Conservatives created it – what they did do was make it an official national trail after years of lobbying by the Wainwright Society, named after Alfred Wainwright who 'created it'.

Sea to Robin Hood's Bay in North Yorkshire. They gave further funding to the National Trails network, such as the Cotswolds Way and the Ridgeway, and they developed the concept of 'Social Prescribing'.* We can bash them for all sorts of reasons but in a nuts and bolts way, they really did their bit in terms of giving people access to more acres. Interestingly, my source said he always wanted to increase access around major cities but there were insufficient funds so the Coastal Path was prioritised.

Seamas's 'carry on' is the antithesis of Amir – who, as an Iranian, would have stood out at that 'give us our land back' hootenanny – taking the roebuck along to those Scouts. What Amir did promoted engagement, understanding, and hopefully inspired passion in some of those young people, passion to learn more. What Seamas is up to, born out of mistruths and ahistorical fantasies, is a grenade messily under-armed over the top in the culture wars. I would go so far as to say that a lot of the notes that the current land access campaign hit, harms the very cause these people believe they are fighting for, and as somebody who would genuinely like people to feel more connected with nature, it pains me.

It pains me because I want more for those Scouts. I don't just want them to have the opportunity to skin deer and cook a de-boned haunch over a fire. I want them to have the opportunity, if they're keen, to manage deer, to camp, to be involved in conservation, to coppice, to create ponds, to keep bees, to restore chalk streams, and to understand why it all matters. What that requires is education, collaboration, and structures that facilitate engagement. Telling those kids that if they work at it, they could one day be involved in a local deer management group is empowering. Telling them that my friend John is a wanker and lying to them about the commons doesn't get

---

* The system whereby people are prescribed exercise or activities in the countryside instead of being prescribed drugs or other medical interventions.

anybody anywhere. It might sell books, it might shift merchandise, and it might do good numbers on social media, but anybody who really believes in access and would like people in Britain to have a more positive connection to the land, has a duty to call out those who sow seeds of division.

On Winter Hill, with Emily, standing on those gritstone slabs while listening to her talking about her grandad, I felt acutely that land matters. I realised that she and the hill are one or that the hill is in some way part of her and standing at Stanley Duncan's grave, outside Hull, I understood that the marsh for Paul and Dave is a sacred place. We cannot be our whole selves without access. There are some specific instances where it needs to be preserved and fought for but in the main, access is possible. We don't lack for access. What we lack is the ability to engage and to learn, to eat and to conserve, which relies on a collaborative approach. We need to work with farmers and landowners rather than using access as a stick to beat them with.

What I found on England's great estates was heartening. It's a seductive lie to claim that the public is locked out of such places but at the same time, we do have a suite of landowners in this country who are totally useless. There are, it will reassure some to hear, a cabal of people who have, due to not really needing to do anything, become pusillanimous and detached. There is something about not having to answer to anybody that can make a person hopeless. 'What that cunt needs', a sharp Yorkshire gamekeeper once said to me, of one such person, 'is a paper round – would do the boy a lot of good.' Most of the useless ones, the sort of people who don't engage with the public, shoot pheasants on Mondays, never evolve and innovate, have little time for tenant farmers, and don't find useful ways to share what they've got, simply run out of road. Landed estates are businesses and businesses that are run poorly and myopically eventually go pop. It doesn't matter how many crests you stick up on the wall or whether you've got ancestral portraits in your

morning room – capitalism and policy affords nobody perman-
ence. Anybody who has read David Cannadine's *The Decline
and Fall of the British Aristocracy* knows that in the early twentieth century, due to the agricultural depression and the 'People's
Budget', the fortunes of the once very fortunate changed rapidly.*

As Richard Benyon put it, a landowner can't pit themselves
against a local community anymore. Those who do will find life
hard and landowners who find life hard for too long, by one
means or another, lose what they've got. But that isn't a good
thing. If a 10,000-acre estate becomes four 2,500-acre farms, or
even forty 250-acre farms (a prospect that would make some
very horny indeed) all because the owner of that 10,000-acre
estate was too stupid or idle to run the whole thing properly,
access is almost bound to get worse. As I learned in the context
of Ireland, the smaller the holding, the poorer the access. Very
often landowners make that reductive quip, 'But they wouldn't
like me to wander across their garden', to which campaigners
reply, 'Yeah, but my garden isn't thousands of acres', and the
answer must surely be: 'Yes, so you're suggesting that those with a
little obviously can't make room, whereas those with a lot can and
should.' Such campaigners are correct but, if big holdings are
places that can provide what activists are after, it doesn't then
follow to bash them. Unless it's not actually about access.

You have to imagine that part of the inspiration for the land
access campaign is the very real feeling that we are disconnected
from nature. The symptoms are plain to see but the cause is
not that we are being kept off the land by dark powerful forces.
The problem is quite clearly a lack of opportunities to engage
and a lack of encouragement.

* David Cannadine writes that of 500 landowning families studied in 1880,
who owned over 10,000 acres, fewer than 250 owned any land at all a century
on and only 150 of those families still occupied their houses. Most of them
had either changed hands or had been demolished.

We all like to be able to blame something for a problem and in this instance that something has become farmers and landowners. It's their fault, the narrative runs, that children can't identify crucian carp and that most adults don't know an alder from an oak. It's even their fault, I've heard, that people smash up camping spots – landowners have prevented them from learning to love the natural world. The trouble, though, is that it's not true. It's simply a concocted reason for a much more complicated problem. Landowners and farmers aren't the cause but they could be part of the solution. If only the message was to ask your local landowner what more they can do for the community and what more they can do to facilitate education and engagement, rather than suggesting our ecological ignorance and indifference is a situation of their making. To move forwards we need all stakeholders to be involved. We cannot strongarm our way towards something better without them.

So what can be done to try and ensure that all landowners do more to promote engagement? We need radical policies that target education and inspire understanding. If you own a hectare of water meadow in England, you are eligible for a pretty chunky government payment of £676 for managing that meadow for breeding waders. If you have a hundred-acre meadow you're looking at a nice £27,000 payment and you can still cut the silage and sell that too. It's a tidy sum. Essentially, there are people out there creaming off more than the average British salary just for having a bit of water meadow. Clearly, it isn't possible to have lapwings, which are down almost 90 per cent in England and Wales or curlew, which are essentially extinct in some counties, breeding on those meadows while you have lads with French bulldogs spilling across them. It is, though, money from those bulldog owners' pockets that is funding grant payments. Surely it follows that grant money for conservation should only be payable if the landowner or farmer facilitates a certain number of educational visits each year. Why not say that for every £20,000 of payment for conservation measures, such as maintaining grassland for waders or creating ponds, the recipient must host two educational visits a year with an additional visit required for every £20k of grant money a year thereafter?

There are grants that exist already, available to those whose land is in a stewardship scheme, for hosting educational visits but the amount of money, just £363 per visit, is relatively modest. In the context of tens of thousands of pounds being available for planting up wildflower meadows, or for those previously mentioned wetland grants, a few hundred quid isn't particularly attractive, so why not tie up education and conservation, by making those large payments dependent on access visits.*

Some will no doubt suggest that this is a bit of a burden but stakeholder engagement and education is essential if we are going to learn to care for the countryside and everything that relies on it. It's essential too if we are going to understand each other: farmers and consumers, dog walkers and conservationists. There are already, from the Angus Glens all the way to Suffolk, land managers I know personally who take delight in sharing their passion for the natural world and their knowledge with young people. We only have to think of Lewis Winks of Right to Roam suggesting that field margins should be opened up for the public to wander through to realise that even among those who are ostensibly clued up on conservation, a great deal of real understanding is dangerously lacking. Jon Moses later said to me that as time went by, Winks became a little embarrassed by his suggestion on field margins – fair enough, but he should have accepted that his *boo-boo* made it clear he still has a lot

---

* In January 2025, the Labour Government announced that 10 per cent of farmland must be given up to be restored for nature. The opportunity, if this happens, for public engagement is immense.

of learning to do. But it cuts both ways. If, rather than letting people picnic among nesting endangered grey partridges, a farmer took a school group, or even Lewis Winks, to quietly see those grey partridges, nesting in long grass beneath a thick hedge, we'd be in a better place. We would be further down the road to creating a culture of respect and care.

In a sense, the way the current access movement, with all of its hostility, has flourished, is down to a lack of knowledge. It has taken root in the cracks. The idea of young activists going off to Arundel (see chapter 4) to 'bear witness to the ecological destruction' there is ridiculous and as my Right to Roam insider admitted, they got the wrong place, a place that has been targeted by Right to Roam for some time but they only went there, blindly and naively, because our education system and our whole culture of nature engagement has let us all down. Even from a distance, with just a scintilla of understanding, it's clear to see that Arundel isn't the one (it would be like going to Crufts to bear witness to the lack of dogs) but these young people have been left in the dark. They literally haven't been given the ecological nous to smell the bullshit.

At the time of writing, landowners, farmers, and rural workers are up in arms about Labour's Autumn Budget and the resultant tax implications. Until 2026, landowners, as has been the case for decades, will be able to pass their acres on IHT free, but after that they will pay inheritance tax on assets over a million pounds, at a rate of 20 per cent as opposed to the standard rate of 40 per cent. Labour has claimed this will impact a very small number of farmers but the Treasury's figures (the Government's finance ministry) seem to be, according to critics, at odds with Defra's figures (the ministry responsible for farming). Common sense suggests that a farm big enough to be viable in Britain will be worth well over a million pounds. For instance, the smallest East Anglian farmer I know is sitting on an asset of about £2.6 million (but nonetheless has to drive a digger on the side to make ends meet). He is very rich on paper and relatively hard-up in practice. Frankly, it was a happy budget for wealthy retirees with a few paddocks and four sheep, who like to play at farming, while it was a sorry day for those who feed the nation. While people slog it out over the details, many of which aren't yet known, there are some clear truths to reckon with.

There are, it's absolutely the case, landowners who own land not because they are interested custodians but simply because of the tax benefits. This has contributed to the value of land soaring to artificial heights. It should be recognised that there was 100 per cent inheritance tax relief on land that was farmed by the owner and 50 per cent on land that was rented out but this was open to abuse, with some claiming 'active farmer' status, when in reality they were anything but. I have met landowners who seem to spend a lot of time with clever people in offices ensuring they are doing the right things to retain active farmers status, and very little time actually farming. Much more rigour should have been applied. We need to be able to tell the difference between a person who spends their days in the City and goes to a farm meeting once a month from a person who gets down and dirty with the carrots.

But, overnight, we have gone from a situation where people were able to take the piss and vast wealth was easily passed down tax free to a situation where some farmers are literally killing themselves because of the stress – hang yourself in the barn now and get ahead of the tax changes, rather than be hit with an unpayable bill in five years' time. The whole thing is extraordinary and admittedly, some of the hysteria is probably unwarranted. That said, the Government is believed to be speaking to Defra to try and get a better handle on what their changes really mean for rural Britain. You sort of hope they might have tried to understand the implications before they cooked up the budget rather than looking at the numbers afterwards. According to the Government only 500 farms will be affected and according to farming groups it will be 70,000. Either way, it didn't help matters when Labour insider, John McTernan, who was Political Secretary to Tony Blair, suggested we should do to farmers what Thatcher did to miners. At the time of writing, farmers in their droves are heading to London to protest outside Parliament.

Surely, there could have been another way? The real bogeyman for Labour is apparently those who buy land simply to pass on wealth, tax free, but that wealth is only realised when you sell up. If you could pass a landholding on without IHT but if you sold it, some way down the line, the full 40 per cent becomes payable, farming could continue while those interested in dodging tax would have to look elsewhere.

The situation we're in, where land values are artificially high, benefits nobody with ethical intentions. Small farmers can't grow their businesses, would-be farmers can't get a look in, and conservationists struggle to expand the areas they're working over. A reduction in the value of land would be a great thing. But the system needs to ensure that agriculture remains viable. That said, any estate or farm that benefits from relief of any sort, should be required to commit to educational visits and engagement opportunities for local people. Sure, farmers feed us, which does seem to get overlooked, but if we aren't benefiting from things like flusher public services because of a landowner taking advantage of tax relief (20 per cent is still half what the man in the street pays on his assets), I absolutely want to come and pick apples or fish with my children or collect magic mushrooms to alleviate my depression (legal issues notwithstanding). Not in a sort of tedious, 'Fuck you. I'm going to smash up your crow traps for a TikTok' sort of way but in more of a 'Do you have any giant puffballs I could pick?' kind of vein, and 'Let me know where I can camp without disturbing your livestock.'

Part of the reason we're in this mess, according to many farmers, is because the countryside hasn't explained itself to the rest of the nation. If you farm beef or sheep in the uplands, you could very easily own five or six million pounds worth of land but your annual return, not unlike my digger-driving friend in East Anglia, could be less than 1 per cent.* Sure, you can plan for tax but equally, a young farmer is 21 per cent more likely to die than those working in other professions. An inheritance tax bill of 20 per cent, because your dad had a quad bike roll across his chest or because he shot himself in the face due to loneliness, would potentially mean selling some of the farm and the next generation then makes even less. I can't imagine that in the current climate, many farmers are thinking about public access and promoting engagement. Their thoughts are understandably elsewhere. And yet, opportunities for engagement are needed more than ever.

I wonder too if one consequence of the Autumn Budget, among some landowners and farmers, might be a reduction in generosity and the spirit of custodianship. Farmers who are farming the hell out of their land in order to meet tax bills are hardly going to be thinking about wildlife and the community. Do we want farmers to be generous custodians or ruthlessly commercial business owners, running hard to stay ahead of HMRC at any environmental and social cost?

It was great that those Scouts got to see a deer be skinned and butchered but I want more for them. We should all want more for them. For some years, the indefatigable Mary Colwell, a campaigner from Bristol, has been working tirelessly to get a natural history GCSE onto the curriculum and for a while it looked as though it was about to happen. Amusingly, as it hurtled towards succeeding, all sorts of people jumped on board. Success, as they say, has many fathers. And then in early December 2024 the initiative appeared to be put on hold. Quite

---

* For a comparison, investing in bonds generally yields around 4 or 5 per cent. In short, farming is not a high-return investment.

why wasn't exactly clear but it was reported that Labour felt it was 'a Tory initiative'. I can't help but wonder what Seamas, of the moustache and the lime green shorts, would have to say about it all (I thought the Tories were the bad guys?) but frankly anybody involved in politicising Mary's GCSE should be deeply ashamed of themselves. Putting children in touch with nature matters so much more than any sort of points scoring. It would have been a fine thing but even then, it's just a start. I was disappointed recently, while talking to a friend who heads up the English department at Harwich High School, as well as being an apple farmer down on the Stour, where old Essex looks to Europe, that there is very little on the English Literature A-level course that focuses on rural culture. Children 'in English lit today', he told me, are more likely to learn about 'the lives of American labourers in the 1930s than people in rural Britain'. He did say that Wordsworth, Seamus Heaney, and Ted Hughes are never far away but the emphasis, he added, is on 'nature' rather than 'rural culture or contemporary rural life'. There is a dire need for more. Nature and exploring rural life should run right through humanities syllabuses. Get nature out of the science block and into the English classroom to show people not just what it is but why it matters, culturally and spiritually. Teach George Ewart Evans, John Clare, Mary Leapor, Walter Murray's *Copsford*, and teach the great contemporary poets on rural Britain like Katrina Porteous, who writes on poaching, kittiwakes, and foot and mouth, and teach Matt Howard, who writes about bird migration and the violence of the natural world and whose poem on a stag being shot – 'he's such a poor old boy, mother' – stays with me.* They should be asking children about how deer hunting is depicted in poetry down the ages, is it barbaric, is it necessary? We should be telling them

* Matt Howard. 'The Stag at the Gate.' *Broadlands*, Bloodaxe Books, 2024, p. 34.

that yes we do have Lennie's 'alfalfa' in this country too. We call it 'lucerne'. It has purple flowers, and woodpigeons eat it. Or rather than teaching children John Steinbeck's *Of Mice and Men*, for GCSE English, what about teaching them Melissa Harrison's *All Among the Barley*, a haunting evocation of a lost way of life in rural England?

Whether it's in the English department, the History department, or even in Geography classes, the rural and agricultural past should never be far away. Nobody should get to adulthood in this country without understanding the making of our English countryside. I once said to Guy Shrubsole that we shouldn't be inaccurate about what the commons are. 'It's complicated', he said, evasively. And he's right. Except his campaign has misrepresented the commons at almost every turn and has sought to render enclosure as being a simple theft. That is dangerous. Ignorance leaves young people susceptible to political exploitation such as being sent down to Sussex, with their ukuleles, on a wild goose chase.

The obvious role to be added to the Government's line-up is a junior minister for nature engagement. There is the secretary of state for the environment and the secretary of state for education but neither is focused on furthering a proper and rigorous understanding of the natural world. There are great things going on here and there but it needs somebody with a budget as well as with focus and experience to realise opportunities across British society, from nursery-school children foraging, to young people gaining hedge laying skills, to ex-prisoners getting jobs in the conservation sector. We are at a precipitous moment when so much of our wildlife is hurtling towards extinction and fostering opportunities for people to understand that and help reverse it is the most obvious way to see off impending disaster. We ought to strive for a Britain where every young person can tell you about the turtledove and the nightingale and why they are all but gone. Give a child access to arable fields, so what; get them to gap up some hedges and hear a nightingale sing and you may well light a fire within them.

In Britain, lots of us know that we need more young people who can manage woodland, restore wetland, and lay hedges, but we don't have enough young people with those skills. Again, the education system is how we change that. I recently sat across from an editor in a publishing house who was sifting through over a thousand applicants for an editorial assistant role, the lowest rung of the publishing house ladder. How many of those young people would have welcomed the opportunity to learn crosscutting and tree felling, how many of them would have welcomed the opportunity to learn how to use a billhook? The conservation industry is in much better health than the publishing industry. In a world where it's possible to make the best part of £30,000 from managing a meadow for waders, there are salaries to be had in overseeing that management and making it happen but we simply don't have enough people who are able to do these things. Our workforce is out of kilter and through centring engagement with the countryside, we can start to put that right. It's not about being able to wander across every part of the Holkham Estate. It's about children at Alderman Peel, the school down the road, feeling aggrieved that there is just one pair of turtledoves on that whole estate. That is their cultural inheritance and it's being squandered while activists are distracted by pheasant shooting.

Lining up all sorts of grants but not actually having the workforce to do the heavy lifting is mad. Some of the grant money available should be reallocated for training practical conservationists. If you're running a farm cluster, such as the 6,000-hectare Mid-Suffolk Cluster (which is a grouping of farms that promotes landscape scale conservation), it would make total sense to have at least one trainee who is funded through government grant money. Britain is awash with ecologists who tell me they find it very difficult to get jobs – so why not fund a post-undergrad qualification, which would train them to carry out practical conservation work, as well as their assessments, at a local agricultural college. There is something like 500 kilometres of hedgerow on the Mid-Suffolk cluster, all of which should be under management and that management can currently be paid for with grant money, so why not rework the system so that grant money gets split (half of it could go to the landowners and half it of it could pay for a trainee conservationist's education). I would go further and suggest that any landholding above 3,000 acres in England should have a trainee conservationist.

Richard Negus, a hedge layer and conservationist in Suffolk, said to me recently that the most important day in his calendar is when the Suffolk Agricultural Society hosts 85 different schools for a rural learning day. They are bussed to the Suffolk Show Ground where they meet people like Richard, a man who grows willow to make cricket bats, as well as shepherds and turkey farmers. The RSPB goes along too, as well as the cutely-named Operation Turtle Dove. The list goes on and on. Richard explained that he could be out there earning money but showing those kids how the countryside works and explaining to them that it's all interconnected is more important. Back when the Right to Roam campaign was conceived, Richard invited Guy Shrubsole (through a young journalist) to see his work. The young journalist was told that under no circumstances did Guy want to be put in touch. He could do, he wrote, without the 'education'.

There are other agricultural societies who do the same thing, and of course there are people like Richard Benyon hosting similar days, but there should be such an event every year in every county. That should be on the to-do list of this junior minister for countryside engagement. Last year, a group of children asked Richard Negus if skunks live in hedges, in England, and he was reminded how much work there is to be done.

If Britain was a country where people were given the opportunity to engage and to learn we wouldn't be in such mess. Division feeds into our misunderstanding of rural England, which in turn inspires more division. In the summer of 2024, Mark Cocker, the veteran nature writer who famously swung for Robert Macfarlane, over Macfarlane fiddling with pretty words while Rome burned, wrote a Country Diary for the *Guardian* about coming across a pheasant pen. There are, it's absolutely true, too many pheasants released in places and those releases cause environmental harm but Cocker noted that apparently pheasants aren't even eaten, 'certainly not by those who shoot them'. The piece made a very positive splash but it was flat out wrong – what does Cocker think game dealers are for and why do those who shoot get given a brace of birds to take home? Has he been to a rural butcher? One has to assume that Cocker wasn't being deliberately misleading. He presumably just doesn't know much about a tremendously widespread use of the countryside. I guess he is a nature guy, rather than a countryside guy. I wrote to Patrick Barkham, the *Guardian*'s environment editor, to say that we really must try to get these things right and maybe a correction should be considered. For some weeks I heard nothing and then he eventually did get back to me to say that Cocker's stuff is usually 'fantastic' but admitted that this time round he had been 'vague'. At the time of writing, the piece is still up there, in all its misleading 'vagueness'. One sloppy inaccuracy in a still widely-read newspaper has consequences. If we want to halt the decline of biodiversity we need people, like conservationists and gamekeepers and those who hunt, to work together and misrepresenting rural reality makes that hard. If Cocker doesn't know and Barkham doesn't really seem to care (or care enough to have a correction made anyway), we've got a serious problem on our hands and everybody involved, from farmers to landowners to conservationists has to focus on putting things right.

Part of the problem is that every time a newspaper gets it wrong or every time some campaigner smashes a trap up or tweets pictures of a merry trespass or when Bloomsbury publishes an egregiously inaccurate nature book, it destroys trust. Richard Negus said to me recently, quite apologetically, that he would no longer ask anybody involved in the access campaign to come and see his hedgelaying. He's done with them. He is solely focused now on the next generation and those who are honestly interested and genuinely want to engage. Trust is destroyed overnight and it takes decades to rebuild it but we don't have decades. We need to start now. We need people who know and care and have the time and the means to get on the front foot and drive reconnection and inspiration. We need to call out the bullshitters to bring about culture change, rather than stoking a culture war.

There are, in Britain, vast swathes of publicly-owned land as well as land owned by charities but what you can do there is quite limited. That relationship should be radically rethought. When I was sitting in the sauna, in that forest in Finland, with those old guys, I asked one of them who owned the land where he gathered his firewood. The old guy, who had been telling me about his grandson's love of fishing, looked at me quizzically as though he hadn't really ever thought about it before and then said that he really didn't know. They fished there, they gathered berries there, they collected firewood there, and they hunted moose there and then divided the meat among themselves. As for who owned it, he couldn't say. It would, in Britain, be transformative, I believe, if we could foster a relationship not unlike that on public land or go even further: the public on public land should feel that they own it. The Forestry Commission, for example, owns some 2.2 million hectares. A lot of their land is commercial forestry, which although not of much environmental benefit, is highly profitable. Surely every forest should have some sort of Forest Scouts on it for local young people. They could pick mushrooms, fish, collect berries, and cook in the woods. Equally, every forest with a deer population in it, which needs to be managed, could facilitate a community deer management group. Some of those commercial forestry profits could even pay for people's deerstalking qualifications and for a larder to be set up for the deer to be processed. How about a community venison stew night? The possibilities are endless. I continually hear about how expensive logs are for the sort of wood burners people have in rural areas. Why can't each Forestry Commission woodland have an area of hardwoods, which is coppiced by local people on rotation to burn in their wood burners? At £100 for a bag of logs, at the time of writing, I'm sure you'd get takers. Forestry should be about more than walking your dog. We should even engage the public on limiting access to certain areas of forestry when there is a valid conservation concern.

It would be churlish to suggest that the land access campaign is in some way malicious but it has been co-opted by the self-interested and it has, very regrettably, set the access cause or maybe the engagement cause back quite some way. It certainly wasn't a win to have Daniel Zeichner calling up rural groups on the afternoon of Caroline Lucas's debate in Parliament to poo-poo a possible 'Right to Roam', and it surely follows that the fight for access, more widely, has suffered as a result. It's hard to get political momentum going and it feels like that was the moment to get something sensible and useful under Zeichner's nose rather than something that he apparently rejected as being a nebulous and misguided red herring, something political rather than practical.

Even if Daniel Zeichner had been won over and the countryside had been thrown open, it wouldn't remedy woes around understanding, passion, and respect. If the Holkham Estate was suddenly forced to open 50 per cent of the land rather than allowing people to access a considerable 20 per cent of it, it would change almost nothing. Except for being a bit of a disaster for wildlife and a concern for farmers.

Some months ago, Right to Roam, in a moment of muted humility, posted on social media to say that they needed money for a final push. They aren't planning, they told their followers, to be around forever. They just want to get this Right to Roam Act through and then that'll be them done. Like buses, I guess there'll be another cause along shortly, more rabbles to rouse, more woodcuts to be made, and other Darwalls to rally against. But the problems would still exist. It's not as though, in Scotland, just because of the Land Reform Act, children across the central belt care deeply about capercaillie or even know what they are. It's not as though curlew in Stirlingshire are bouncing back or fly camping doesn't happen on Loch Lomondside.

I was standing last week at a South London café behind a drunk who was arguing with the manager about wanting to unplug the till, 'just for ten minutes', so he could charge his phone. As I stood there, I noticed on the door frame a leaflet about a community garden summer club, off the Old Kent Road for 9 to 16-year-olds. 'Do you have an interest in the natural environment and being creative with food?' it read. Pictured at the top were three small smiling children and next to them were four young women holding chickens. The words 'Food growing and cooking' ran beneath the picture in bold blue lettering. I took a picture of it and sent it to Alexander Darwall. 'Don't you think this is pretty cool?', I wrote. 'You should do something like this for kids on Dartmoor.'

ACKNOWLEDGEMENTS

Thank you to Emily Oldfield, Leonard Baker, Snowy Parker, Ezekiel, Justin, George Fleming, Andy Bloomfield, the boys on Lewis, Richard and Louise, Richard Benyon, the many naturists, Andy down in the West Country, the Kennel Huntsman, Dom Buscall, Jeremy Squirrel, Flavian Obiero, Fiona Williams, Nick Mayhew-Smith, Terry Doe, Nicola Williamson, and everybody else who I met along the way. Your stories mean a great deal to me and without you, books like this wouldn't be possible.

Many thanks also to my publisher Myles Archibald and my agent Katie Fulford, and to all of you who read *Uncommon Ground* in its infancy and suggested edits: Sachin Kureishi, Jan-Peter Westad, and particularly to John Mitchinson and Katrina Porteous.

INDEX